ESTABLISHING PARENT INVOLVEMENT IN FOSTER CARE AGENCIES

ESTABLISHING PARENT INVOLVEMENT IN FOSTER CARE AGENCIES

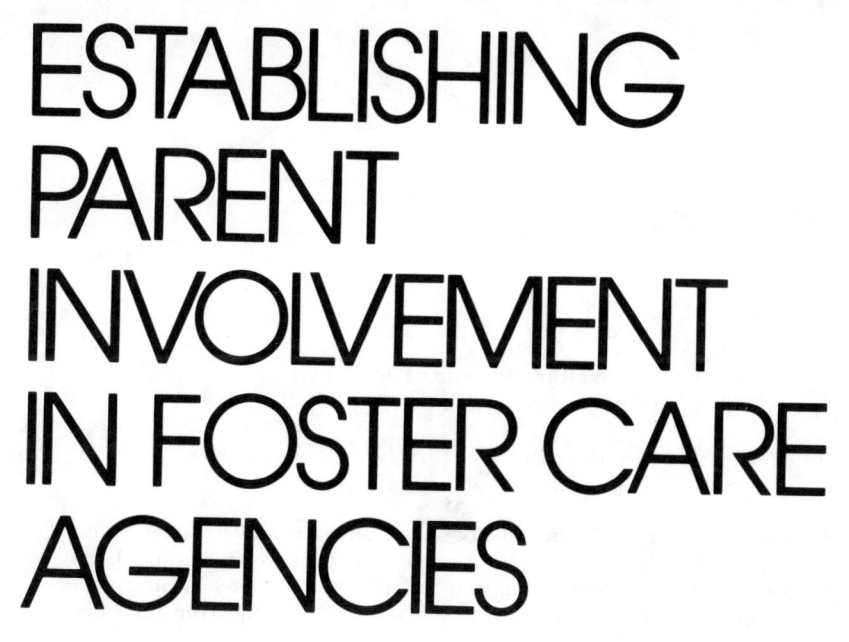

EDITORS
KAREN BLUMENTHAL
ANITA WEINBERG

CHILD WELFARE LEAGUE OF AMERICA, INC.
NEW YORK, NY

Child Welfare League of America
67 Irving Place, New York, NY 10003

Copyright © 1984 by the Child Welfare League of America, Inc.

ALL RIGHTS RESERVED. Neither this book nor any part may be reproduced or transmitted in any form or by any means, electronic or mechanical, including photocopying, microfilming, and recording, or by any information storage and retrieval system, without permission in writing from the publisher.

Current printing (last digit)
10 9 8 7 6 5 4 3 2 1

cover design by Paul Agule

Printed in the United States of America

Library of Congress Cataloging in Publication Data
Main entry under title:
Establishing parent involvement in foster care agencies.

  Bibliography: p.
  1. Foster home care—United States—Addresses, essays, lectures. 2. Parenting, Part-time—United States—Addresses, essays, lectures. 3. Parent and child—United States—Addresses, essays, lectures. I. Blumenthal, Karen L. II. Weinberg, Anita
HV881.E87 1984   362.7'33'0973   84-7647
ISBN 0-87868-214-7

CONTENTS

FIGURES VII

TABLES IX

FOREWORD XI

ACKNOWLEDGEMENTS XIII

INTRODUCTION XV

Chapter 1—**INVOLVING PARENTS: A RATIONALE**
  Karen Blumenthal 1

Chapter 2—**INVOLVING PARENTS: ADMINISTRATIVE RESPONSIBILITY**
  Karen Blumenthal and Anita Weinberg 17

Introduction to Chapters 3 and 4 72

Chapter 3—**CASE MANAGEMENT**
  Victor Pike 74

Chapter 4—**INTERAGENCY COOPERATION AND COORDINATION**
  Karen Schimke 97

Introduction to Chapters 5 and 6   115

Chapter 5—SUPERVISION
Peg Hess   117

Chapter 6—TRAINING
Carla Overberger   146

APPENDIX A—Examples of Agency Policies, Procedures, Forms, and Training Relevant to Parent Involvement (by State)   164

APPENDIX B—Sample Service Plans, Written Agreements, Behavioral Contracts, and Visiting Contracts   202

APPENDIX C—Interagency Agreement Between Lower East Side Family Union and Henry Street Settlement   217

APPENDIX D—

1. Age-Appropriate Activities for Parent-Child Visits   220
2. Levels of Involvement Between Parents and Foster Families   224

APPENDIX E—Attitude Survey   227

APPENDIX F—Annotated Bibliography   232

ABOUT THE EDITORS   249

CONTRIBUTORS   250

FIGURES

FIGURE 1.0—Examples of Parents' Rights and Responsibilities   8

FIGURE 2.0—Reflecting the Importance of Parent Involvement in Agency Manuals   21

FIGURE 2.1—Strengths of Parents   27

FIGURE 2.2—Group Orientation for Parents of Children in Foster Care: An Innovative Program in Tennessee   30

FIGURE 2.3—Parent Handbooks   31

FIGURE 2.4—Assessing Foster Parent Interest, Willingness, and Capacity to Be Involved in Parent-Child Contacts   38

FIGURE 2.5—Promoting Parent-Foster Parent Relationships   40

FIGURE 2.6—Working with Parents in the Residence: Two Examples   41

FIGURE 2.7—An Evaluation of Parent Aide Programs   45

FIGURE 2.8—The Use of Volunteers in the Temporary Foster Care (TFC) Program in Michigan   46

FIGURE 2.9—The Parent-Preschool Education, Empathy, Rapport and Support (PEERS) Program   47

FIGURE 2.10—The Family Living Center   48

FIGURE 2.11—Parent Groups at the Children's Village   49

FIGURE 3.0—One View of Case Management   76

FIGURE 3.1—Criteria for Selection of Objectives   78

FIGURE 3.2—Objectives that Relate to Parent Involvement   79

FIGURE 3.3—Maintaining Contact with Service Providers   80

FIGURE 3.4—Using Evaluation   82

FIGURE 3.5—Documenting the Service Program   83

FIGURE 3.6—The Importance of Organizational Competence   86

FIGURE 3.7—The Importance of Relationship Skills   87

FIGURE 3.8—The Importance of the Parent-Worker Relationship   89

FIGURE 4.0—The Influence of Cultural Diversity on Service Needs   101

FIGURE 4.1—Underutilized Resources for Families   102

FIGURE 4.2—Developing Linkages Between Public Child Welfare Agencies and Responsive Organizations   103

FIGURE 4.3—Extent of Interagency Service Agreements   107

FIGURE 4.4—Inventory of Information to Include in Program Resource File   108

FIGURE 4.5—Program Resource File: 3×5 Card Format   109

FIGURE 4.6—Example of How Resource Inventories Can Fail   112

FIGURE 5.0—Relative Utility of Supervisory Methods in Accomplishing Supervisory Functions Related to Implementation of Total Parent Involvement   139

FIGURE 6.0—Conveying Knowledge   149

FIGURE 6.1—Acquiring Skills   150

FIGURE 6.2—Gaining Commitment to Training   153

FIGURE 6.3—Training for Foster Care Teamwork   156

TABLES

TABLE 1—Parent Involvement—Preplacement   57

TABLE 2—Parent Involvement—Placement   61

TABLE 3—Parent Involvement—Postplacement   69

FOREWORD

Separating children from their parents is a painful action for all who are involved: biological parents, children, foster parents, child care workers, court personnel. As a child care professional, I know that separation (even when necessary) causes children and parents grief and despair.

All of us who have been involved when children are removed from a home have witnessed how youngsters cling even to abusing parents. We have seen children run away from adequate foster homes to inadequate parental homes. Clearly, here is evidence of a need to retain ties between parent and child when the actual parenting role must be taken on by someone outside of the family.

Research confirms the importance of parental involvement with children who cannot live at home. Studies of children placed in foster homes and institutions have found that those who remain in contact with biological families have better self-images and are more likely to return home than those whose contact is severed.

This book focuses on the important issue of parent involvement, which we see as critical to meeting the best interests of children involved in the child welfare system. We are aware that this is not easy to accomplish. Encouraging and arranging visits between parent and child are complex and time-consuming activities—especially when the visits are more than token meetings in the offices of the child-placing agency. Nor is dealing with parents a simple matter, for when one opens the door to involvement one also admits another party to the decision-making process. Let's face it. It is easier to leave decisions to the agency and, perhaps, to the foster parents.

It is also wrong.

It encourages parents to avoid their responsibility to their children, and we must not do that. We need to set appropriate standards for parenting and help those adults who need to learn how to meet those standards. Skills can only be taught in a climate of expectation, supported by the actual and continuing involvement of parent with child.

We are mindful, too, that this involvement can place an added burden on foster parents. We believe they can, and must, be helped to understand the philosophy behind involving parents and the importance of their role as foster parents.

This book presents the important issues surrounding this essential service and provides directions for agencies to take. We ask that you read and consider this subject that is so important for children and their families.

Elizabeth S. Cole
Director
Permanent Families for Children
Child Welfare League of America

ACKNOWLEDGMENTS

This publication is the culmination of the efforts of many individuals, and we are extremely grateful to each of them:

- Elizabeth Cole, Director of the Permanent Families for Children unit of the Child Welfare League of America, for her consistent support, wisdom, insights, and advice.

- Cheryl Atkinson, our administrative assistant, for her unstinting, untiring, and unselfish commitment to our work. Without her outstanding administrative and secretarial support, this volume would not have been completed.

- Our contributors, Peg Hess, Carla Overberger, Victor Pike, and Karen Schimke, for their excellent work, responsiveness to our suggestions, and patience.

- The Edna McConnell Clark Foundation, for its financial support of this effort and its steadfast commitment to children and families.

- The innumerable individuals working for agencies and programs committed to parent involvement, who responded to our call for program descriptions, consulted with us, and sent us invaluable resource material.

- Anthony Maluccio and Paula Sinanoglu, whose pioneering efforts in the area of working with parents of children in foster care inspired and directed us, and who permitted us to adapt some of their materials for this volume.

- The agency administrators, publishers, and copyright holders, who gave us permission to reprint their materials.

- Claire Berman, Carol Smith, Barbara Schwimmer, and David Fleischmann, for their review of chapter drafts and helpful criticism and suggestions.

- The members of the Advisory Board of Permanent Families for Children and the staff of the Child Welfare League of America, who provided guidance, suggestions, and encouragement.

- Carl Schoenberg, Senior Editor, Child Welfare League of America, who critically reviewed each chapter and offered many helpful suggestions.

- Suzanne Hauenstein, Denise Byron-Cox, Maureen Sullivan, Karen Beers, and Erica Mason, who assisted Cheryl Atkinson in the typing of this volume.
- Our families, Mark Miller, and David, Michael, and Jill Blumenthal for their love, support, and patience during a period when there were many demands on our time.

Karen Blumenthal
Anita Weinberg

INTRODUCTION

When children enter foster care, their parents lose the opportunity to behave as parents. Although parents do retain some legal rights, many are not allowed and others are not encouraged to make daily decisions and participate in such ordinary family activities concerning their children as deciding what the children will eat, what time they must return home after school, or what clothes their children will wear.

Moreover, parents often do not receive the services they need to resolve problems that lead to placement, services, such as parent education, homemaker help, housing and financial assistance, counseling, and vocational training and placement.

Most importantly, parents have not always been included in planning for how permanence for their children should be achieved. They have often been excluded from assessing and evaluating initial placement plans, developing and signing written service agreements, or participating in case reviews.

Yet, without returning these critical responsibilities to parents or providing them with needed services, it is neither possible to determine whether parents will be able to resume parenting their children nor to prepare children and families for reunion. The foster care agency holds the power to share the authority for decision making with parents by involving them in the foster care service and can enhance parents' competence by ensuring that parents receive appropriate services.

The purpose of this volume is twofold: (1) to clarify the meaning and importance of parent involvement and (2) to assist agency staff members in their efforts to increase parents' involvement in their work. Many of the efforts described in this book have been carried out with considerable success in particular localities.

The subject of this volume has special import for administrative staff in public and voluntary agencies at both state and local levels. Total support by the administration is the key element in making parent involvement a critical component of foster care service. The development of policy and the program and role changes essential in a foster care system that involves parents depend on the commitment of its leaders.

Some new policies and practices can require substantial changes within an agency. Not all changes will be effective, and some may carry risk. Including parents in services and activities is not always the "safe" approach to accomplishing permanence. In the long run, however, it is the only way that appropriate permanent plans can be identified and pursued. Administrators must be willing to experiment, take risks, and anticipate failures even after some of these changes are made. And they must encourage their staff to do the same, and support staff members in the efforts they undertake.

Chapter 1 defines parent involvement and explains why it is essential to foster care. Chapter 2 identifies what needs to be done by administrators if parents are to be involved in the service, including examination of administrative and program efforts and policies necessary to facilitate and ensure parent involvement; reexamination of the roles of participants in foster care services; and discussion of underutilized or unavailable resources important to parents of children in care.

Once the agency is philosophically and programmatically prepared, these efforts can be taken to include parents. They are discussed in chapters 3 through 6.

Chapter 3 defines case management and explains its relationship to parent involvement. It examines the process of case management and the responsibilities of a case manager.

Chapter 4 is concerned with interagency cooperation and coordination. It considers why agencies must share resources in order to work effectively with families. It also describes the process of developing, using, and maintaining interagency relationships.

Supervision issues are considered in chapter 5; specifically, why the supervisor has to focus on and facilitate parent involvement and the responsibilities of the supervisor that are critical for ensuring that parents are involved in services and activities.

Chapter 6 discusses the importance of training in facilitating and encouraging involvement. It examines what training can accomplish, who should be trained, and potential training resources. The appendices offer sample policy and training excerpts, recording forms, and an annotated bibliography.

All those concerned with the preparation of this volume were sensitive to the limited financial resources of most public and voluntary agencies. Although some of the proposals would require increased budgets, many illustrate new ways of using already existing resources. Nevertheless, hard choices may have to be made. Most agencies will not be able to provide the range of services they would like, and cannot make, at one time, all the changes discussed here. They will have to decide which of the services and programs they can provide and at what point.

Several methods were used to gather current relevant information about parent involvement. We reviewed the literature and contacted some of the authors to explore their comments further.[1] Announcements about this project were placed in several journals and newsletters, eliciting information about "programs that emphasize close and continual involvement of parents whose children are in foster care."[2] Responses to the announcements were followed up either through written correspondence or telephone interviews. Finally, discussions were held with individuals (referred by experts in the field) who are involved in innovative permanency planning efforts and/or parenting programs.

Although the information received was not systematically evaluated, the overall picture that emerged is encouraging. A great deal of activity involving parents is taking place, and there is a pervasive feeling that this involvement is having a positive impact on overall services to families and their children. Examples, some of which are described in this volume, from a wide range of agencies—public and voluntary, large and small—in a variety of settings, show that barriers can be overcome and changes made in policies and practices.

Two omissions merit explanation. There is little direct discussion of placement prevention and the different kinds of preventive services. This does not reflect a lack of commitment on our part to prevention. The first goal of any permanency planning program must be to keep families together whenever possible. The omission, however, is a reflection of the project mandate to focus on issues germane to children already in out-of-home care. (It should be noted, however, that preventive services are often the same as those needed for reunification.)

Detailed "how-to" materials for direct service workers were also omitted because excellent materials on practice elements for working with parents of children in care already exist (e.g., engagement of parents, assessment of family situation, development of written plans and agreements, service intervention, and service monitoring). (See appendices A, B, and F.)

Although this volume focuses on parent involvement in foster care service, there are limits to what can be done with and for families within the context of foster care. Foster care is only one form of help that many families need. An adequate family income program, equal education opportunities for all children, meaningful employment opportunities for all who are able to work, universally available health and medical care, and an extensive housing program are vital to the well-being of all families. Without them, foster care services can accomplish only so much. These critical needs will not be met within the foreseeable future. Therefore, we must do the best we can with what is available. Within the context of foster care and the pursuit of permanent homes for children, parent involvement does produce positive results for families.[3]

Finally, a few words about the terminology used in this volume. *Parent* is used without the modifiers that often precede the term in the child welfare literature, that is, *biological, bio, natural, own*, or *birth*. Although *parent* usually refers to the child's biological parent(s), it also includes any individual who in the past has been the primary caretaker for the child. *Agency* refers to public and voluntary child welfare agencies. *Foster care, placement*, and *care* are used interchangeably. These terms may apply to foster family homes, group homes and residences, institutions, and/or residential treatment centers. *Foster care worker, caseworker*, and *worker* are also used interchangeably. In some agencies, still other titles, such as *permanency planning worker, family worker*, or *protective services worker* may be used to refer to those who work with children and/or parents.

NOTES

1. "Social Work with Parents of Children in Foster Care: A Bibliography," by Anthony Maluccio and Paula Sinanoglu, *Child Welfare* LX (May 1981): 273-303 was an excellent resource.
2. This excerpt appeared in *Child Welfare* LX (January 1981): 57. Announcements were also placed in *Case Record, Perspectives*, and *Highlights*.
3. See notes 28-32, chapter 1.

1

INVOLVING PARENTS: A RATIONALE

Karen Blumenthal

A voluntary child care agency *expects* parents of children in foster homes to participate in making day-by-day decisions about their children's education, meals, clothing, toys, and schedules. *Purpose:* to underscore the fact that parents have judgment and are still important to their children, and to help parents learn how to make these decisions.

The department of social services in a midwestern state uses teams in its foster care service to do planning, intervention, and evaluation; parents are considered to be *core* members of the teams. *Purpose:* to give parents an opportunity to make important contributions to the helping effort.

A voluntary child welfare agency in a northeastern state *urges* foster parents to serve as role models for parents through the teaching of child management techniques. *Purpose:* to develop and strengthen the child-management skills of parents.

A special program for parents and their preschool children sponsored by a county department of social services in a southern state uses volunteers to run support groups, teach classes on parenting, and provide transportation. *Purpose:* to enhance parents' overall competence by improving parenting skills and self-esteem.

A large metropolitan public child welfare department operates a Parents' Rights Unit, which provides a unique forum for the resolution of grievances brought by parents of children in care. *Purpose:* to ensure that parents' rights and responsibilities are properly exercised.

A voluntary residential treatment center in a midwestern state conducts regularly scheduled group meetings of its parents. *Purpose:* to develop an informal support network that reduces parents' feelings of powerlessness and isolation.

2 ESTABLISHING PARENT INVOLVEMENT IN FOSTER CARE AGENCIES

Several voluntary agencies provide rooms within their residential centers for parents to live in while they visit with their children for a weekend. *Purpose:* to maintain and improve parent-child relationships and promote family cohesiveness.

These examples illustrate several ways in which parents can be involved in foster care services. A few show how parent-child contact can be facilitated; others indicate how parents' planning and decision making can be continued or resumed.

By involving parents in different ways, child welfare agencies are able to

- maintain and improve parent-child relationships and promote family cohesiveness and a sense of identification
- enhance parents' overall competence by improving their skills and self-esteem
- ensure that parents exercise their rights and responsibilities
- facilitate family reunion as soon as possible
- identify appropriate alternative permanent plans when needed

When parents are not involved, children are far more likely to remain in foster care for prolonged periods of time.[1]

This chapter looks at parent involvement and addresses why it has not been emphasized in the past and reasons why it must now be considered an essential component of work with families of children in foster care. It includes a working definition of parent involvement and concludes with an explanation of why child welfare agencies need to operate under a presumption of total parent involvement.

DEFINITION OF PARENT INVOLVEMENT

Parent involvement means the inclusion and/or participation of mothers and fathers in activities, tasks, services, and decision making throughout the time the family is involved with the foster care process. Parents must interact with children, foster parents, caseworkers, child care staff, other professionals, paraprofessionals, and/or informal helpers.

By "inclusion and/or participation of," the importance of the parents' presence and active role is recognized. The concept of active role is critical. Parents are not to be merely talked to, taught, or planned for, but rather are to be significant contributors who are expected and encouraged to share their ideas, reactions, and feelings. For example:

- the parent's point of view about an available community service program is to be solicited actively by the caseworker

- service agreements are to be written *with* the parents, not for them
- foster parents are to make shared decisions with parents and their children about clothing, educational supplies, schedules, and discipline
- parents are to be encouraged to speak out at case conferences and reviews

That parents are involved in "activities, tasks, services, and decision making" conveys the range of ways in which they can participate in the placement process. During the preplacement period (or shortly after the child is placed), the parents and caseworker, in consultation with foster parents, child care workers, and other service providers, discuss the possible ways to be involved and decide on the nature of the involvement: when it will take place; who else will be involved; and what it should accomplish. Possible "activities" and "tasks" include

- making a preplacement visit to a foster or group home
- formulating a written agreement with the caseworker, and with their children, when appropriate
- physically caring for their children during visits in the foster home
- making a family scrapbook or tree with their children
- accompanying their children to medical and dental appointments
- participating in school conferences
- reviewing and, if necessary, modifying the agreement on a planned basis with the worker
- participating on an agency committee composed of parents
- attending agency functions for parents and their children

"Services" can be any professional, paraprofessional, or informal assistance provided to families that is intended to have a positive impact on the problems that resulted in placement. Assistance may be provided directly by the caseworker, other staff members at the agency, professional or paraprofessional staff members from other community agencies, and "natural" helpers in the community. Services include individual, marital, and family counseling, homemaker help, parent education classes, psychological evaluation and treatment, vocational counseling and training, financial assistance, medical services, housing assistance, child care, and self-help groups.

Parent involvement must take place "throughout the foster care process" because there is an appropriate, participatory role that parents need to play during the preplacement, placement, and postplacement periods. For example, during preplacement the parents are involved with the worker in assessing the family situation and alternative placement possibilities, selecting a suitable placement resource, and formulating a service plan. During placement, parents and their children see one another frequently and engage in a variety of activities appropriate to the age and maturity of each child.[2] Also during placement, parents and their caseworker meet regularly, parents and foster parents (or child care staff) are in frequent contact, and parents work with other service providers.[3] Finally, during the postplacement period, the caseworker provides aftercare services to parents and children on a planned basis.[4]

Parents "must interact with children, foster parents, caseworkers, child care staff, other professionals, paraprofessionals, and informal helpers." This is much more than contact with children during visits or contact with caseworkers during meetings. For example:

- parents should share important information about children's daily activities with foster parents or child care staff
- parents can participate in special events sponsored by agencies, such as parents' night, parties, trips, and camping weekends
- parents can receive help with household tasks, such as meal planning, budgeting, and assisting with child care needs, from homemakers and parent aides
- parents can help establish a working committee of parents concerned with practices and policies that affect them and their children

In summary, parent involvement should occur in many different ways with several individuals throughout the foster care process.

WHY PARENT INVOLVEMENT HAS NOT BEEN EMPHASIZED IN THE PAST

> A review of the literature [also] elicits humility in the face of the multiplicity and complexity of factors involved in working with parents.[5]

Although parent involvement is one aspect of good practice and enables the agency to achieve many of its goals for parents and children, parents have not received the attention they deserve. Parents have not been engaged at the start of their contact with agencies, nor have they been made equal partners in the task of improving their family life or environments. Too often, they were completely displaced in their children's lives by agency staff and foster parents. They received almost no attention from caseworkers.[6] They were discouraged, and sometimes prohibited, from seeing their children.[7] They were given virtually no information about their children's foster parents and, as a result, had no contact with them.[8] It should not be surprising that many parents became hostile, suspicious, and apathetic.[9]

The many factors that have been identified to explain why parent involvement in foster care has been so limited can be grouped under four broad categories: parents' circumstances, constraints related to the caseworker, constraints related to the agency, and insufficient services.

Parents' Circumstances

Some parents are completely unavailable, and therefore considered impossible to involve in any meaningful way. Parents whose children were removed by the court are involuntary clients; they may well be less interested in working with the service providers. Other child care responsibilities, employment hours, financial limitations, and distance from the agency office or foster placement may reduce participation of parents in service contacts. Problems, such as the parents' failure to keep or be on time for appointments, inability to discuss personal problems, and failure to show concern for their children, may adversely affect the establishment of a continuing service relationship[10] and the effectiveness of parent-child contacts. Many parents have multiple difficulties that cannot be resolved by foster care services alone, difficulties such as insufficient income, inadequate education, unemployment or sporadic work histories, substandard housing, drug and alcohol abuse, physical and mental illness, family violence, and isolation.[11]

Constraints Related to the Caseworker

Excessively large caseloads and numerous and demanding daily responsibilities place severe restrictions on the time that is available for workers to interact with parents.[12] For the reasons identified under "parents' circumstances," workers often have attitudes toward parents that are not conducive to working effectively with them. Because of inappropriate hiring and inadequate training, some workers do not have sufficient knowledge and skills needed to work with parents.[13]

Constraints Because of the Agency

Agency policies, procedures, and training often fail to acknowledge and emphasize the importance of work with parents and to facilitate it.[14] For example, many workers have been provided with almost no direction about how to coordinate provision of services to parents;

how to facilitate, supervise, and evaluate parent-child visits; and how to encourage a relationship between parents and foster parents.[15]

Insufficient Services

The services needed by parents are sometimes unavailable from the agency or other community resources, or are inaccessible.[16] For example, there may be no parent education program, or a substance abuse program that does exist may be inaccessible to a parent because it is not located near public transportation.

These factors impose realistic barriers to parent involvement. Overcoming them requires major changes in foster care practice and policy.

WHY PARENT INVOLVEMENT IS ESSENTIAL

> Although it may be overstating the case to refer to parents as our best-kept secret weapon, their potential as a helping resource has only barely begun to be explored.[17]

Ample justification exists for making parent involvement a high priority in any foster care program. Values and assumptions that derive from the literature on child development and family relationships highlight the significance of parents, even when separated from their children. In addition, rights and responsibilities retained by parents who have children placed in foster care allow for a substantial parental role.

It is also important to consider that parents' competence can only be enhanced by involving them in specific activities and providing them with services. This argument is supported by recent developments in child welfare research and demonstration projects. Finally, policy, regulation, and legislation are beginning to require parent involvement.

Values and Assumptions

Children are entitled to the nurturing environment of a stable, continuing *legal* family that gives support, love, and permanent commitment. They have a basic human need to have someone who wants them and can care for them, someone with whom a deep and stable attachment can be formed.[18] Indeed, children need stable, continuous, and caring relationships for normal character and identity development.[19]

A child's family has a primary, pervasive, and long-lasting influence on the child. Even when parents are overwhelmed by problems, unable to provide adequate care, and need to have their children placed apart from them in foster care, physical separation alone does not interrupt the powerful parent-child bond.

Therefore, preservation and enhancement of the parent-child relationship is one of the most critical tasks facing foster care agencies. Services must be based upon the presumption that the child's own family can best meet the child's developmental needs.[20]

Rights and Responsibilities

When children are placed in foster care, either voluntarily or by court order, their parents retain specific rights and are expected to carry out specified responsibilities vis-á-vis their children.[21] Pike reminds us, however, that "very few *legal* rights exist for the parent whose child is in court custody." [22] Instead, most of these rights derive from three sources:

- *administrative rules* promulgated and enforced by state agencies and departments
- *agency* policy developed by administrative staff in local public and voluntary agencies, carried out by caseworkers and supervisors
- *professional ethics, values, and convictions* that guide agency practice[23]

As a result, states vary as to the "rights" retained by parents. Specific rights can be denied by court order depending on the case. Agency staff members can jeopardize rights in many different ways, and parents often have little recourse.

Nevertheless, agency policies are beginning to spell out the rights and responsibilities of parents of foster children[24] (see fig. 1.0), helping to define how parents must be involved in the foster care service. Staff at all levels, from caseworkers who help formulate visiting plans with parents to administrators who develop agency policy concerning parents, have significant roles to play in protecting rights and encouraging the carrying out of responsibilities.[25]

Recent Developments in Child Welfare Practice and Research

A majority of children enter care because of the problems their parents face.[26] These children are unlikely to leave foster care unless the problems that precipitated placement are changed. Some-

FIGURE 1.0
Examples of Parents' Rights and Responsibilities*

Rights:

To be consulted during the preplacement period about the choice for the specific foster care placement and to participate in preplacement visits.

To participate in planning for their children, to help formulate the specific content of the service plan, and to participate in the review of the plan.

To receive services, in accordance with the plan, that assist them in overcoming the conditions that led to removal of their children.

To visit and communicate with their children in accordance with the service plan.

To be consulted about and have the final say in decisions concerning major medical services, education, marriage, or enlisting in the armed services.

To meet the individuals, such as foster parents, child care workers or houseparents, who directly care for their children.

To receive reports from the caseworker on their children's health and development, progress in school, and behavior.

Responsibilities:

To help prepare their children for the foster care placement.

To work with the caseworker in setting up the service plan, deciding what they must do while their children are in care and what will be best for their children's future.

To work toward solving the problems that prevent their children from returning home.

To visit their children at a time and place agreed upon with the caseworker.

To discuss their children's care and progress with the caseworker.

To inform the caseworker about major changes, such as change of

*Selected from policy manuals and parents' handbooks of several state agencies.

address, telephone number, job, income, marriage, or other living arrangements.

To keep appointments with the caseworker and other service providers.

To contribute toward the cost of their children's care, if they are able to do so.

---

times, parents and children are not getting along. It must also be noted that many parents with children in care have little control over their own and their children's lives. What control they do have is threatened when they must conform to the agency's requirements.[27] To have an impact on these problems, parents' effectiveness must be enhanced. It is not possible to enhance parents' competence without involving them in specific activities and providing them with services. When parents are given the opportunity to learn to improve their behavior, practice what they have learned, and take charge whenever possible, they become more effective in the parenting role.

Four studies—the Columbia University longitudinal study of foster care in New York City,[28] the Oregon Project,[29] the Alameda Project,[30] and the New York State Preventive Services Demonstration Project[31]—underscore the importance of parent involvement in achieving a permanent home for every child in foster care. In each study, some form of parent involvement was linked to the stable, nurturing, and time-limited stay of children in foster care.

With technical assistance from the staff at the Regional Research Institute in Portland, Oregon, many states replicated the Oregon Project by using similar casework techniques. In the majority of cases, the states discovered that more children were moved into permanent placements—either return home or adoption—when there was conscientious work done with parents.[32] It has become clear that successful permanency planning requires parent involvement.

Parents must be involved in many different ways in the foster care service.[33] They must be viewed as responsible adults who are capable of, and interested in, making important decisions about their children and their futures. This view is consistent with the social work value of self-determination. It is only after diligent and appropriate reunification efforts with the parents have been made within a defined time limit and have proved unsuccessful that consideration can be given to alternative ways of providing continuity of care and permanence for children.

Policy, Regulation, and Legislation

As a result of a growing awareness of these values and assumptions and rights and responsibilities, as well as recent findings from research and practice, many states are developing and implementing policies, regulations, and guidelines that specifically address issues related to parent involvement.[34] These issues include:

- parent involvement in the development of case plans
- use of written service agreements or contracts with parents
- parent-child visiting and other contacts
- parent participation in case conferences and informal and formal case reviews
- parent-caseworker contacts

State legislation is also beginning to address many of the issues listed above.[35] Moreover, several state statutes dealing with termination of parental rights have been modified and improved to require "diligent efforts" with parents by child welfare agencies.[36] Without proof that the agency has made diligent efforts to involve and work with parents, courts are unlikely to terminate parental rights. To secure permanent homes for children, therefore, efforts to involve parents during the foster care placement must be made and documented.

The most far-reaching legislative change has been at the federal level. Largely because of the successes mentioned earlier, Congress overwhelmingly passed the Adoption Assistance and Child Welfare Act of 1980 (Public Law 96-272), the first national effort to promote parent involvement in order to provide permanence for children. This landmark legislation acknowledges the need to involve families in their children's placement process from the start. States will not be eligible to receive their full share of child welfare services funding allotments (Title IV-B) until they put into effect a case review system and a service program "designed to help children return to families from which they have been removed or be placed for adoption or legal guardianship."[37] The case review system must assure that "each child has a case plan designed to achieve placement in the least restrictive (most family-like) setting available and in close proximity to the parents' home, consistent with the best interest and special needs of the child."[38] Although the legislation does not say how the states should carry out these requirements, the intent concerning parent involvement is clear.

In summary, parent involvement must become a prominent aspect of every foster care program. Although the importance of keeping parents connected to their children in care was supported in the past by professional values and principles of good practice, standards alone were not sufficient to promote extensive parent involvement.

Today, legislation, regulations, and policy are beginning to mandate parent involvement. Child welfare agencies, both public and voluntary, will have to comply or be prepared to face sanctions.

PRESUMPTION OF TOTAL PARENT INVOLVEMENT

> Nationwide there is no overall, comprehensive and integrated strategy for working with parents as an essential component in dealing with the problems of "foster care drift" and "children in limbo".... [However] there is a general recognition of the importance of the parents to the child in care, reflecting an emerging "focus on the family."[39]

Because of the critical importance of parent involvement in the foster care process, agencies must operate under a *presumption of total parent involvement*. The presumption applies equally to families whose children are placed in foster homes, group homes, or other residential facilities. This presumption is needed to counteract the tendency of many agencies to develop restrictive policies that affect *all* parents and children, although the policies often originate as a response to a small minority of difficult cases or problems.[40] For example, policies may require casework supervision of all parent-child visits because some parents have on occasion harmed children during unsupervised visits. Or policies may prohibit caseworkers from giving parents the addresses of foster parents because some parents have at times harassed foster parents or attempted to kidnap their own children.

Under a presumption of total parent involvement, the norm is for parents to participate in a range of activities, tasks, and services with their children, the caseworker, the foster parents or child care staff, and other appropriate service providers throughout the foster care process. To put this presumption into effect, agencies will have to develop written guidelines describing parent involvement in detail, as well as the circumstances under which it is to be restricted. In those cases in which the guidelines do not allow for involvement of the parents in a particular activity, with a particular person, and/or at a specific time, an appeals process must be available to parents who disagree with the imposed restriction.[41]

The implementation of a presumption of total parent involvement will increase the likelihood that agencies can provide permanence to foster children in the most desirable way: return to their own parents.[42] But sometimes children cannot return home. If, after careful planning and diligent efforts on the part of the agency to promote parent involvement, the parents repeatedly fail to demonstrate their ability to make a home for the child, the decision must be made that the child cannot go home. Then, a decision must be made about an alternative way of providing a permanent home, such as placement with relatives on an adoptive, guardianship, or long-term planned basis, adoption by nonrelatives, or permanent foster care.

A presumption of total parent involvement permits parent participation in the process of determining the best alternative permanency planning option, assuming that the parent is available and willing to participate. Unless parental rights are already terminated, parents are entitled to participate in this planning process. There are parents who, though unable to care for their children themselves, do have significant ties to them and are capable of assisting in the process of choosing the best future living situation for them.

Once the alternative permanent plan is implemented, the presumption of total parent involvement no longer applies. In some situations, continued parent involvement will be detrimental to the child and must end. If the ties between a child and his or her parents are strong and long-standing, however, it may be appropriate to try to maintain these ties through some form of parent involvement. This would have to be agreed to by the parents, the child, and the new primary care person(s). Even when parental rights have been voluntarily relinquished or involuntarily terminated, there may be merit to allowing planned contact between parent and child.[43]

NOTES

1. This conclusion is drawn in several reports of permanency planning demonstration projects. See Annotated Bibliography (appendix F). It was further supported during the telephone survey conducted for the project (see Introduction).
2. See appendix D for a list of age-appropriate activities.
3. For a description of what can take place during these interactions, see table 2 on p. 59. See also Child Welfare League of America, *Standards for Foster Family Service*, rev. ed. (New York, NY: Child Welfare League of America, 1975), 30-34.
4. See table 2 on pg. 61. See also Child Welfare League of America, *Standards for Foster Family Service*, ibid., 34-35; American Public Welfare Association, *Standards for Foster Family Services Systems for Public Agencies*, rev. ed. DHEW Publication No. (OHDS) 79-30231 (Washington, DC; U.S. Department of Health, Education and Welfare, January 1979), 43-44.
5. Paula Sinanoglu, "Working with Parents: Selected Issues and Trends as Reflected in the Literature," in *The Challenge of Partnership: Working with Parents of Children in Foster Care*, edited by Anthony Maluccio and Paula Sinanoglu (New York, NY: Child Welfare League of America, 1981), 5.

6. See Theodore Stein, Eileen Gambrill, and Kermit Wiltse, *Children in Foster Homes: Achieving Continuity of Care* (New York, NY: Praeger Publishers, 1978), 13; Henry Maas and Richard Engler, *Children in Need of Parents* (New York, NY; Columbia University Press, 1959), 390-391; Alan Gruber, *Foster Home Care in Massachusetts* (Boston, MA: Governor's Commission on Adoption and Foster Care, 1973), 50; Deborah Shapiro, *Agencies and Foster Children* (New York, NY; Columbia University Press, 1976), 195.
7. See Jane Knitzer, Mary Lee Allen, and Brenda McGowan, *Children Without Homes: An Examination of Public Responsibility to Children in Out-of-Home Care* (Washington, DC: Children's Defense Fund, 1978), 22-24; Special Services for Children, *Policy Statement on Parental Visiting*, mimeo. (New York, NY: New York City, Human Resources Administration, September 1975).
8. See Patricia Ryan, Emily Jean McFadden, and Bruce L. Warren, "Foster Families: A Resource for Helping Parents," in *The Challenge of Partnership*, Maluccio and Sinanoglu, op. cit. 189-191; James R. Seaberg, "Foster Parents as Aides to Parents," in *The Challenge of Partnership*, Maluccio and Sinanoglu, op. cit. 209-211.
9. Shirley Jenkins and Elaine Norman, *Filial Deprivation and Foster Care* (New York, NY: Columbia University Press, 1972).
10. See David Fanshel, *Computerized Information on Child Welfare: The Availability and Capacities of Parents and Children in Foster Care for Service Involvement* (New York, NY: Columbia University School of Social Work, November 1978); Karen Blumenthal, "Worker-Biological Parent Contact in Foster Care: A Discussion Paper," draft 1, mimeo. (New York, NY: Child Welfare League of America, August 1980).
11. See Esther Dean Callard and Patricia Morin, *PACT—Parents and Children Together: An Alternative to Foster Care* (Detroit, MI: Wayne State University, 1979), 13; Jenkins and Norman, op. cit. 2, 19-20; Charles Horejsi, *Foster Family Care: A Handbook for Social Workers* (Missoula, MT: University of Montana, 1978), 72.
12. See Arthur Emlen et al., *Overcoming Barriers to Planning for Children in Foster Care*, DHHS Publication No. (OHDS) 80-30138 (Washington, DC: U.S. Department of Health and Human Services, 1978) 30; Helen Stone, "An Orientation to Foster Care Theory and Values: An Introduction," in *Foster Care in Question*, edited by Helen Stone (New York, NY: Child Welfare League of America), 6.
13. See Eileen Gambrill and Kermit Wiltse, "Foster Care: Plans and Actualities," *Public Welfare* 32 (Spring 1974): 15; Robert Mnookin, "Child Custody Adjudication: Judicial Function in the Face of Indeterminancy," *Law and Contemporary Problems* 39 (Summer 1975): 226-293.
14. Stein, Gambrill, and Wiltse, op. cit., 17.
15. This, however, is changing. See appendices A, B, and F.
16. See Jessica Pers, *Government as Parent: Administering Foster Care in California* (Berkeley, CA: Institute of Governmental Studies, University of California, 1976); Norman Herstein, "The Image and Reality of Foster Care Practice," in Stone, op. cit., 174.

17. James K. Whittaker, "Family Involvement in Residential Treatment: A Support System for Parents," in *The Challenge of Partnership*, Maluccio and Sinanoglu, op. cit., 83.
18. John Bowlby, *Attachment and Loss*, vol. 1 (New York, NY: Basic Books, 1969); Selma Fraiberg, *Every Child's Birthright: In Defense of Mothering* (New York, NY: Basic Books, 1977).
19. John Bowlby, *Maternal Care and Maternal Health* (Geneva, Switzerland: World Health Organization, 1952); Erik Eriksen, "Identity and the Life Cycle," *Psychological Issues*, monograph 1 (New York, NY: International Universities Press, 1959); Peg Hess, "Parent-Child Attachment Concept: Crucial for Permanency Planning," *Social Casework* (January 1982): 46–53.
20. This presumption may not apply in all situations, especially as concerns children who have been in care since they were infants, had no contact with their parents, and formed strong attachments to their foster parents.
21. Child Welfare League of America, op. cit., 20–25; American Public Welfare Association, op. cit., 26–27.
22. Victor Pike, "Parental Legal Rights," mimeo. draft, 1981, 7. Some state legislation, however, is beginning to address issues that give a few legal rights to parents.
23. Pike, ibid.
24. See, for example, South Carolina Department of Social Services, *Policy and Procedure Manual*, vol. VII-A, "Manual of Children and Family Services," chap. 08, "Permanency Planning," 1980, 9, .08.12.20; Kentucky Department of Human Resources, *Foster Care Policy Manual*, P65.080, 1978.
25. Rights and responsibilities must be carefully discussed with parents during intake so that parents know what is expected of them from the outset. Parents should understand that if they do not carry out their responsibilities, they may endanger or lose their rights. A description of rights and responsibilities should be included in written material that is routinely given to parents. Throughout the placement, a range of parent involvement activities must be encouraged and facilitated by staff members so that parents are enabled to exercise rights and carry out responsibilities. Moreover, a grievance mechanism must be put in place to provide protection to parents whose rights are endangered by staff members who disregard those rights.
26. Gruber, op. cit.; David Fanshel and Eugene Shinn, *Children in Foster Care—A Longitudinal Investigation* (New York, NY: Columbia University Press, 1978); Child Welfare League of America, op. cit., 3–4.
27. Elizabeth Davoren, "Services to Multi-Problem Families," in *Child Abuse and Neglect—3rd National Conference, April 1977* (Washington, DC: U.S. Printing Office, 1978), 111–113.
28. This 5-year (1965–1970) longitudinal study of foster care in New York City, conducted at the Columbia University School of Social Work, consisted of three substudies: the children, the biological families, and the foster care agencies. For reports of these substudies, see Fanshel and Shinn, op. cit.; Shapiro, op. cit.; Jenkins and Norman, op. cit.; Shirley

CHAPTER 1: A RATIONALE 15

      Jenkins and Elaine Norman, *Beyond Placement: Mothers View Foster Care* (New York, NY: Columbia University Press, 1975).
29. The Freeing Children for Permanent Placement Project, a 3-year demonstration in Oregon funded in 1973 by the Children's Bureau, used aggressive planning and casework techniques to achieve permanent homes for foster children. The project was successful, and the federal government funded replications in other parts of the country, as well as a technical assistance project by the Regional Research Institute in Portland, Oregon. See Victor Pike, "Permanent Planning for Foster Children: The Oregon Project," *Children Today* 5 (November-December 1976): 22–25; Arthur Emlen et al., *Overcoming Barriers to Planning for Children in Foster Care*, op. cit.; Arthur Emlen et al., *The Oregon Project County by County: Outcomes of Permanency Planning for Children in Foster Care* (Portland, OR: Regional Research Institute, 1978); Janet Lahti et al., *Follow-up Study of the Oregon Project* (Portland, OR: Regional Research Institute, 1978).
30. The Alameda Project, begun in 1974, was a cooperative endeavor of the Children's Home Society of Oakland, California, and the Alameda County Department of Social Services. Its three objectives were to increase continuity of care for children in out-of-home placement, to compare the effectiveness of a systematic case management procedure with the methods typically employed by child welfare workers, and to test the feasibility of having one worker provide concentrated services to parents while another worker served the child and foster parents. See Theodore Stein and Eileen Gambrill, "Facilitating Decision Making in Foster Care: The Alameda Project," *Social Service Review* 51 (September 1977): 502–513; Theodore Stein, Eileen Gambrill, and Kermit Wiltse, *Children in Foster Homes—Achieving Continuity of Care*, op. cit.; Theodore Stein, Eileen Gambrill, and Kermit Wiltse, "Contracts and Outcome in Foster Care," *Social Work* (March 1977): 148–149.
31. The New York State Preventive Services Demonstration Project, created by an act of the New York State Legislature in 1973, was designed to test the feasibility of preserving family units by providing services to eliminate the need for foster care and to prevent its recurrence. The demonstration involved nine child welfare agencies and was administered by the New York State Department of Social Services. See Mary Ann Jones et al., *A Second Chance for Families: Evaluation of a Program to Reduce Foster Care* (New York, NY: Child Welfare League of America, 1976); Mary Ann Jones, "Reducing Foster Care Through Services to Families," *Children Today* 5 (November-December 1976): 6–10.
32. Susan Whitelaw Downs et al., *Foster Care Reform in the 70's: Final Report of the Permanency Planning Dissemination Project* (Portland, OR: Regional Research Institute for Human Services, 1981).
33. For example, they must be given as much responsibility as they can handle for the care of their children. Agencies must facilitate parent-child contact and interaction. Parents should be helped to explore all acceptable alternatives to resolving problems and be given an opportunity to choose among the options. Caseworkers must assist the par-

ents in developing a problem-solving support system consisting of a network of community resources. See tables on pp. 57-71 for a complete listing of ways to involve parents.
34. See appendix A for examples of policies.
35. For example, see New York State, "Child Welfare Reform Act," chapters 610 and 611 of the laws of 1979. In 1976, the California State Legislature enacted the Family Protection Act, which implemented a demonstration project in two California counties.
36. Oreg. Rev. Stat. Sec. 419.523(2) (e) (1981); Wisconsin Stat. Ann. Sec. 48.415(2) (1918); New York State Social Services Law Sec. 384(b) (7) (f).
37. Public Law 96-272, "Adoption Assistance and Child Welfare Act of 1980," Sec. 427(a) (2) (C).
38. Ibid., Sec. 475(5) (A).
39. Sinanoglu, op. cit. 17.
40. See Special Services for Children, op. cit. for a further discussion and additional examples.
41. The first step of this process would be a conference involving the caseworker, the supervisor, and the parents. The agenda at the meeting would include discussing the relevant guidelines, making a decision about the restriction that is agreed to by all participants, and documenting in the case record why parent involvement is being restricted. If parents disagree with the decision, they must be able to appeal it, either through the agency's internal grievance mechanism, the state's grievance process, or the court. Any decision to restrict involvement must be reviewed frequently, as there could be changes in the case situation that might affect the restriction. For a description of a service grievance procedure, see American Public Welfare Association, op. cit., 9.
42. In numerous publications, this is identified as the highest priority permanency planning outcome. See, for example, Victor Pike et al., *Permanent Planning for Children in Foster Care: A Handbook for Social Workers*, DHEW Publication No. (OHDS) 78-30124 (Washington, DC: U.S. Department of Health, Education and Welfare, Children's Bureau, 1977); Martha Jones and John Biesecker, *Trainer's Manual for Goal Planning and Permanency Planning in Children and Youth Services* (Millersville, PA: Training Resources in Permanent Planning Project, Millersville State College, 1979); Forrest A. Mercer et al., *Case Management in Social Services: Foster Care* (Richmond, VA: Virginia Department of Welfare, Division of Social Services, n.d.).
43. See Arthur Sorosky, Annette Baran, and Reuben Pannor, *The Adoption Triangle: The Effects of the Sealed Record on Adoptees, Birth Parents, and Adoptive Parents* (New York, NY: Anchor Press, 1978); Annette Baran, Reuben Pannor, and Arthur Sorosky, "Open Adoption," *Social Work* 21 (March 1976): 97-100; Joan Laird, "An Ecological Approach to Child Welfare: Issues of Family Identity and Continuity," in *Social Work Practice: People and Environments*, edited by Carel Germain (New York, NY: Columbia University Press, 1979), 200-204.

2
INVOLVING PARENTS: ADMINISTRATIVE RESPONSIBILITY

Karen Blumenthal
Anita Weinberg

Promoting parent involvement throughout the foster care process is a challenge because, for reasons described in chapter 1, the current foster care system has rarely effectively involved parents. This, however, is changing. Several states and localities have reexamined their foster care systems and have developed new policies and practices that require and facilitate parent involvement. Administrative preparation, however, must precede agency staff involvement of parents in foster care services.

First and foremost, administrators* in state departments and local public and voluntary agencies must demonstrate their commitment to the belief that parent involvement in foster care programs is essential. This belief is put into practice by

- reflecting it within the objectives and goals of the agency
- incorporating it into the written policies, procedures, and forms that make up agency manuals
- recruiting and hiring new staff members committed to practice that involves parents, and training existing staff members in this practice
- supporting staff members who are prepared to take responsible risks, try new techniques, and carry out new roles

*The words *administrator* and *administrative staff* are used interchangeably. The responsibilities described in this chapter may be carried out by different individuals on the administrative staff.

- implementing an incentive structure for staff members at all levels in recognition of the fact that parent involvement can be time consuming and stressful
- making budgetary allocations for resources and programs that involve parent participation
- advocating for families in the community, the courts, and the legislature
- establishing an advisory group composed of parents and staff members interested in policy and program issues concerning parent involvement

The administrative staff also must reexamine the roles and responsibilities of individuals in the foster care system—parents, workers, supervisors, children, foster parents, child care workers,* and adoptive parents. This reexamination of roles can identify strengths, skills, and experiences possessed by these individuals that can be used more fully to rebuild families.

Finally, administrators must make decisions about which needed resources and programs will be available through their agency and which will be provided through other community agencies. These resources include day care, homemaker programs, housing assistance, parent aide and volunteer programs, parent education programs, groups for parents, drug and alcohol abuse programs, and employment counseling. Which services an agency decides to provide depends on the agency's goals, priorities, and available funds, and on the availability and accessibility of already established programs.

Administrators may be reluctant to undertake the efforts described in this chapter. They may worry that making changes in order to work intensively with parents requires resources of time, services, and money that do not exist. They may be even more reluctant when funding for child welfare and other social services is in jeopardy. These efforts, however, are not only necessary to make continuous parent involvement possible, but to enable the agency to use existing resources effectively and efficiently.

Several innovative projects are discussed in this chapter. Many of the activities, tasks, services, and programs needed to involve parents, however, are traditional, rather than new or innovative. Major policy changes and substantial resources may not be necessary to facilitate all of these interactions.

The contents of this chapter are divided under three major headings: administrative commitment, reexamination of roles, and resources for parents.

---

*Child care workers are those persons who provide a major portion of the round-the-clock care, supervision, and resources for children and youths in residential group care.

Three tables, included at the end of this chapter, identify the activities, tasks, programs, and services—the traditional and the innovative—in which parents should be involved during the preplacement, placement, and postplacement periods. These tables can be used as a checklist by agencies to promote parent involvement throughout the foster care process.

ADMINISTRATIVE COMMITMENT

The agency administrator is in a position to establish a working environment that promotes parent involvement. Staff members who understand why parent involvement is essential and are prepared to work under a presumption of total parent involvement (see pp. 11-12) are thwarted unless they have administrative support for their efforts. Without this commitment, there can be no consistent approach within an agency to working with parents of children in foster care. Even though some caseworkers may experiment with new methods, or a small number of supervisors may focus on work with families, or a handful of foster parents may become directly involved with parents, the impact will be limited without administrative support.

Administrators must believe that parent involvement is an essential component of a foster care service. This belief can guide the actions administrators must take to eliminate existing barriers to parent involvement and to create a climate that facilitates it.

Agency Objectives and Goals

Because an agency's mission and ideology are established through its objectives and goals, administrators must first examine objectives and goals for how they reflect the agency's recognition of the importance of parents to children, commitment to the preservation and reestablishment of families, and support of parent involvement and services to parents as a means of achieving stability and continuity of parental care for children.

Written Policies, Procedures, and Forms

The written policies, procedures, and forms contained in agency manuals must reflect the agency's objectives and goals.[1] Policies spell out why parent involvement is essential and how it affects the daily work of the staff at all levels. Procedures provide guidance to the staff concerning how to initiate, facilitate, and assess parent involvement.

Forms enable the staff to collect essential information about parents and their participation in the foster care program and to monitor the agency's activities in facilitating parent involvement and in working to reestablish families.

Suggestions from staff members at all levels, as the materials are developed and revised, will assure that the materials are realistic. Once developed, the materials should be accessible to all staff members. Staff meetings, memoranda, and other means of communication, such as the director's report in the agency's newsletter, can be used to discuss and clarify policy and procedural issues that are controversial. (See fig. 2.0.)

Staff Commitment

Next, administrators must try to ensure staff commitment to parent involvement. Written policies and procedures are necessary first steps, but cannot alone effectively change staff attitudes and behaviors toward parents. Existing staff members need training regarding the importance of parent involvement, and new staff members who share this perspective should be recruited and hired.

Administrators should assess the attitudes of current staff members toward parent involvement and determine the extent and strength of their commitment to this idea.[3] A variety of approaches can be used to effect attitudinal changes, including informal staff meetings, in-house training, and conferences or workshops outside the agency.

Administrators can exercise greater control over the hiring of new staff members and the recruitment of new foster parents than they can in reeducating current staff members. They can and should develop job descriptions that include responsibility for facilitating parent involvement. This is important because negative attitudes act as a strong barrier to reunion with parents. In fact, training can better address a lack of relevant experiences and underdeveloped skills for working with parents than it can deal with basic attitudinal barriers.

Administrative Support to Staff

When administrators are confident that staff members will work under a presumption of total parent involvement, they must be willing and ready to support those who take responsible risks and experiment with new methods and techniques. These activities may be criticized. The administrator should be prepared to face this criticism and support the staff members who have taken this risk.

FIGURE 2.0
Reflecting the Importance of Parent Involvement in Agency Manuals

Agency manuals can encourage maximum parent participation in the foster care service by including:
1. discussion of
   - why parents are important to children
   - the concepts of case manager, teamwork, shared decision making, and changing roles
   - how to prevent parents from becoming "lost" once their children are placed
   - ways to overcome parents' inability to participate because of access problems (possible efforts would include use of evening and weekend hours, case aides and/or volunteers to provide transportation and/or child care, home visits, and reimbursement for travel expenses)

2. statements addressing the importance of
   - placing children as close as possible to their home communities
   - using relatives for placement
   - placing siblings together

3. list of parents' rights and responsibilities

4. sections on
   - voluntary placements: when appropriate, use of voluntary placement agreements, time limits, right of return
   - preplacement preparation of families, including visit to foster home
   - initial and continuing planning conferences involving all team members (including parents and foster parents) with a description of their responsibilities
   - service plans and written agreements, including a description of the parents' responsibility to prepare, monitor, and modify them
   - parent-child visiting; discussing issues of frequency, length, location, participants, supervision, limitations, and termination.
   - foster parents, including recruiting with message concerning the importance of parents, sharing relevant information concerning parents, degrees of foster parent involvement with parents
   - ongoing services to parents, whether provided by the worker or by other community resources
   - case review, including the role of parents in internal and external review
   - an appeal or grievance mechanism that can be used by parents experiencing problems with the agency

- returning children home: guidelines for making and implementing this decision
- aftercare services to parents

5. discussion of parents' role when the plan is not to return children home[2]

Some agencies have received negative publicity because of their inactivity in moving children out of foster care. To move children out of care and into permanent situations, however, agencies must involve parents in their programs, with attendant possibilities of new criticism and publicity. Some agencies that have initiated parent involvement in their services have had negative experiences. When there is more parent-child interaction, there may be more risk to the child of physical or emotional harm. Cases that are especially horrifying may receive widespread media attention and generate lawsuits against the agency or a particular worker. In addition, the agency may also be confronted with service delivery problems. For example, experienced foster families may decide not to continue fostering if the parents' behavior toward the foster family or the child is disruptive and abusive.

However, parent involvement should not be curtailed because severe problems sometimes occur as a result of parent-child interactions. Some perspective is needed. In fact, the number of headline-catching horror stories is small when compared with the majority of situations in which maintenance of the relationship between parent and child has been beneficial.

Actions can be taken to reduce possible risks resulting from more parent-child contact. Training for workers is the most important way (see chap. 6). Because intensive parent involvement cannot happen all at once, workers must learn to identify the circumstances under which parents and children can be together and how to facilitate the interaction.

Even when workers have undergone training, administrators cannot allow an individual worker to carry all the responsibility for significant decisions. Administrative staff must review significant situations with the worker and arrive at an agreement on the best way to deal with them. Other agency resources, such as legal services and community education, may be helpful to the worker. Staff members who feel secure that the agency will defend them if difficulties arise from increased parent involvement are more likely to continue to take responsible risks.

Incentives for Staff

Administrators also can help ensure staff commitment to parent involvement by establishing incentives for staff members that acknowledge in a variety of ways conscientious and effective work.[4] For example, administrators can award recognition or titles for a particularly good effort or accomplishment, provide greater opportunities for staff members to participate in special agency projects, and reduce the number of working days per year by special leaves, "sanctioned mental health days," and attendance at conferences.[5] Administrators should be careful to assure that strong disincentives do not exist. For example, currently some states or counties are cutting staff as workers reduce their caseloads through improved practice. It is ironic but true that good practice sometimes can lead to the loss of a job. Instead, reduced caseload size could be a positive incentive. Efforts to involve parents often result in intense stress for staff at all levels. Even the most capable and conscientious workers will burn out unless the stress can be mitigated by rewards—concrete and otherwise.[6]

Budget Allocations

Administrators make critical program decisions when they allocate funds. To eliminate existing barriers to parent involvement and create a climate that facilitates interaction, there is a need for

- training in issues related to parent involvement
- special agency programs and projects involving parents, for example, a parent education program, an orientation to the foster care system for parents with children entering care, a parent aide program, a parents' ombudsman, and a parent support group
- ways to overcome access barriers that make parents unavailable for involvement, for example, reimbursing travel expenses, establishing evening and weekend hours, using case aides or volunteers to provide transportation and child care, and facilitating visits in parents' homes by workers
- sufficient staff so that workloads are kept at reasonable levels
- attractive, readable materials for parents about foster care and the role of parents, for example, handbooks and newsletters

Limited budgets may not allow funding all of these efforts. Administrators must then decide which will bring about the changes most needed at their agencies and how they can get the greatest benefit from the money they do have.

Advocacy

Administrators will have to look beyond their own agencies to overcome existing barriers to parent involvement; for example, by influencing the legislative, budgetary, and policy-making processes at all government levels to promote adequate child welfare services and to make fundamental changes in behalf of families.

Many of the problems that cause children to enter foster care are outside of the child welfare service system. Therefore, the administrators' role extends to advocacy for other human services, such as income maintenance, health, housing, education, and employment. It is also important to educate the community about the needs of families, and to gain its support for service programs.[7] These services rarely are given high priority. If child welfare administrators fail to defend their clients' rights to service, it is unlikely that these programs will be sufficiently funded.

Advisory Group

The administrator committed to parent involvement should take a critical view of current policies and practices, welcome suggestions for their modification, and accept proposals for new programs and policies. An advisory group established by the administrator and consisting of parents, foster parents, agency staff members, and community advocates interested in policy, program, and practice issues in parent involvement can provide this evaluation. The group can help the administrator explore new ideas for programs and services, write or review written materials, develop job descriptions, and prepare training exercises. An advisory group familiar with agency practice is also in a position to help administrators advocate within the community for services for families, for sufficient funding levels for programs, and for important legislation, as well as to support the agency when confronted with controversial issues.[8]

In conclusion, the actions so far described require substantial administrative time and attention. Administrators who undertake them may feel overwhelmed. Some of the written materials already exist, however, and some of the program and staffing needs already have been considered and implemented. Therefore, the effort required may not be as great as it appears. Public and voluntary agencies that have taken these steps are excited by the results. They have found that requiring, encouraging, and facilitating parent involvement enable the agency to provide permanent homes for many more children.

REEXAMINATION OF ROLES

Parent involvement is not possible until the agency's objectives and goals are clarified, its written policies and other materials developed, and its services determined based upon need and budget allocations. But effective implementation depends upon staff at all levels. Supervisors, caseworkers, foster parents, and child care workers have roles and responsibilities in foster care service. The administrator is responsible for determining which individuals must assume which roles and responsibilities in order to maximize parent involvement and desirable outcomes.

Reexamination of roles is critical in the development of more effective ways to assist parents, although resultant redefinition of roles may require major changes throughout the agency structure. The role changes described below enable parents, caseworkers, supervisors, children, foster parents, child care workers, and adoptive parents to become "partners in a shared undertaking, with common goals and mutually supportive and complementary roles."[9] These new role definitions use most fully the strengths, skills, and experiences of the participants in the foster care system.

Administrative decisions concerning roles and responsibilities should be based on a careful analysis of the tasks that must be accomplished, and the roles that parents, staff, children, and adoptive parents can assume. Examined here are these potential roles, and explanation is given about how the individuals who assume them will help make parent involvement a reality in their agencies.

Parents

The effects of having a child placed in foster care are profound. Parents must cope with the stressful circumstances that resulted in placement, the feelings associated with the loss of a child, the isolation and rejection from neighbors and relatives in the community, and the messages of parental failure communicated to them in their experiences with social agencies, courts and legal systems, and foster families and residential facilities.[10]

Parents who have children placed in foster care are "in-between" parents.[11] They are no longer called "parents." Instead they are referred to as "birth parents," "natural parents," or "biological parents," and are legally assigned new role expectations and are subject to sanctions that limit their authority. The new position, therefore, is neither that of parent nor of nonparent, but somewhere in between.

Because there has been virtually no recognition of, or orientation to and preparation for, this new role of "in-between" parent, role discontinuity accompanies the abrupt change in parental status, increasing the confusion, anxiety, and stress already felt by parents.

In the past, if parents were assigned any role, it was that of "client." They were viewed as the target of treatment; that is, they had to change dramatically before their children could be returned to them. The current emphasis on permanency planning and greater parent involvement, however, requires that parents be viewed in a different light and carry out many additional roles. This view holds that parents are the most important persons in their children's lives. Children continue to love and need their parents despite the difficult times they may have shared. No matter how sad or guilty or confused parents may feel, it is critical that they stay involved with their children during placement and show their concern and interest in their children's welfare. The parent must understand that the worker will make every effort to facilitate this contact and involvement. (See discussion in chap. 1).

It is important, however, that the agency view parents as potentially responsible adults with many strengths and capacities, including:

- motivation for change
- intelligence
- love for their children
- concern about their children's well-being and development
- strong parent-child attachment
- access to a natural support system
- desire to have children return home
- adequate living quarters, good hygiene, adequate food supply, and planful budgeting of money[12]

Some parents will not have any of these strengths and should not be long-term resources for their children. The presumption for child welfare workers, however, must be that parents do have strengths. Workers must demonstrate a belief in these strengths and a commitment to reinforce them so that children can return home. (See fig. 2.1.)

In contrast to past practice when parents either were ignored or viewed only as "clients," there are several roles parents can assume that enable them to be involved in foster care service. These roles include the following.

Parent[14]

Every day, parents make decisions for, or with, their children. Although most of these are routine decisions, they are significant in

FIGURE 2.1
Strengths of Parents

According to a recently published report of a Preventive Service Demonstration Project carried out in the borough of the Bronx in New York City on the matter of "strengths":

> Despite the serious problems in functioning, most of the "experimental clients" had strengths on which we could build to enable them to overcome at least some of their problems in functioning and help them try new approaches to long-standing problems.
>
> The major motivating factor was the clients' concern for their children's well-being and desire to keep the children with them. Over a period of time, most of our clients were slowly able to change their parenting style and to utilize services more effectively to meet their own and their children's needs.
>
> Project staff found they were able to see improvement in over 80% of the mothers who had the problem, in areas which were directly related to child care such as physical care of children (83%), supervision, guidance and training of children (81%), household management (81%), use of community resources (81%), a decline in the physical abuse of the children (83%).[13]

---

the life of a child. They include decisions about eating, dressing, playing, schedules, and education. Parents also have opportunities to be involved with their children in many activities, such as shopping trips, sports events, school programs, doctor's appointments, and haircuts.

When their children are in foster care, parents lose the opportunity to make these day-by-day decisions and to participate in activities concerning their children. It does not have to be that way. Parents can often continue to fulfill some parental roles and responsibilities. Special emphasis should be given to having parents make or participate in making some of these decisions. Parents can have shared or even exclusive responsibility in many activities. It is important that parents feel that these responsibilities are manageable and that they have a specific emotional importance in the parent-child relationship.[15] It is also important to clarify with foster parents and child care workers why parenting should be shared and why total substitute parenting is inappropriate.

Parent involvement in decisions and activities concerning the child is beneficial because it

- maintains the parent-child relationship
- enhances the parents' self-esteem
- gives the parents more information about the child
- allows the foster parents to model appropriate behavior
- eases eventual reunion
- helps the parents to use or connect with resources
- helps the parents to grow in understanding of the child's needs and appropriate expectations and management of the child

Allowing parents to carry out the parental role demonstrates to them the agency's belief in their importance to their children.

Team Member

Foster care teams (see chap. 3, pp. 89–92) are working units responsible for ensuring that children are provided with stable, permanent environments. Teams are composed of individuals significantly involved in the service plan for the child and family. They are characterized by shared purpose, clear communication, coordinated efforts, individual accountability, joint decision making, and mutual support. Team members work together to

- assess the problems that resulted in foster care and the strengths that could be used to facilitate return home
- make decisions about the provision of agency services, the use of other community resources, the day-to-day care of children, parent-child visits, and parent–foster parent involvement
- formulate written agreements that reflect those decisions
- evaluate progress toward achieving goals

Because parents' input into these tasks is essential, they must always be members of the foster care team.

Teacher

Parents possess a vast amount of information about their children that would be useful to the caseworkers, foster parents, child care workers, or other individuals working with, and responsible for, their children. Therefore, parents should be allowed to teach them about their children: their schedules, food preferences, behaviors, and interests. This communicates to parents that their knowledge and opinions are important and that others can learn from them.

Parents also should be encouraged to give workers, supervisors, foster parents, and other interested parties their view of the foster care service. This can occur during training, at conferences and special meetings, and during recruitment.

Informed Party

During the preplacement phase, parents need to understand

- the purposes of foster care
- the processes that occur during foster care
- the services provided by the agency
- the agency's expectations for parent participation
- the legal rights and legal status of parents and children[16]

Ways to provide this information include:

- worker-parent review of information presented to parents during initial contacts with the agency
- group meetings for parents conducted by the agency and other parents
- handbooks for parents on foster care
- joint foster parent–parent meetings[17]

Once the parent is informed, expectations for parent participation can be greater. (See figs. 2.2 and 2.3.)

Advocate for Change

Groups of parents can work to effect changes in agency, state, and national foster care policy and practice.[20] This role requires a degree of sophistication and savvy, as well as the support of professionals, and therefore is not one that is likely to be assumed by a large number of parents.

Resources for Other Parents

Parents who take an active role throughout the foster care process are often in a position to assist other parents of children in care. For example, they might

- participate in orientation programs for new parents
- help develop written material for new parents
- help prepare a parents' newsletter[21]
- provide a support network for new parents

To sum it up: It is no longer acceptable to "forget" parents who have children placed in foster care or even to limit their role to that of "client." Parents have a right to understand what additional roles are available to them and to be encouraged to decide which ones they can fulfill. Not all parents will be able to assume all roles. In today's

FIGURE 2.2
Group Orientation for Parents of Children in Foster Care
An Innovative Program in Tennessee

The Tennessee Department of Human Services pioneered an innovative program for informing parents about foster care. This 6-week group orientation series for parents with children in care provides information, education, and support to parents during the initial phase of the child's placement and engages parents in decision making about the child's future. The program was designed by a team of public agency social workers and a consultant from the University of Tennessee School of Social Work. The group approach is efficient, introduces parents to others experiencing comparable situations, and provides a supportive environment. The service does not replace individual/family casework services during the period when parents attend the group; it supplements them.

The focus and major content areas for the group include:

- getting acquainted, introduction to foster care basics
- typical reactions of parents to placement of their children in foster care
- rights and responsibilities of parents whose children are in foster care
- who the foster parents are and what they do
- typical reactions of children to foster placement
- planning visits
- making decisions

The responses of the initial group of parents, the workers involved, and the administration of the public agency were overwhelmingly positive. Of the five families who participated in the first orientation group, two had their children successfully returned to them within the 4-month period following the series. Parents in the other three families felt the group had helped them develop a clear, definite permanent plan. All five families said that the group helped direct energy toward permanency planning and clarified their roles as parents of foster children.

Upon completion of the pilot group, the local administrative staff immediately initiated plans to include all families served by the regional office in the orientation group series whose children had been in foster care for one year or less, and to offer the series regularly. Plans are under way for the group orientation to be piloted in other areas across the state.[18]

FIGURE 2.3
Parent Handbooks

Several public and private agencies have developed handbooks to communicate important information about foster care to parents.[19] Many of these handbooks are modeled after *The Parents' Handbook: A Guide for Parents of Children in Foster Care,* developed by Special Services for Children in New York City. The following table of contents from New York City's handbook indicates the kind of information that often is included.

Section

A. WHAT IS FOSTER CARE?
B. HOW DOES MY CHILD COME INTO FOSTER CARE?
  1. Upon Your Request
  2. By Order of the Family Court
    a. Because of Abuse or Neglect
    b. As a Person in Need of Supervision (PINS)
    c. As a Juvenile Delinquent
  3. In an Emergency
C. HOW SHOULD I WORK WITH MY AGENCY CASEWORKER?
D. HOW DO I PLAN FOR MY CHILD'S FUTURE?
  1. Return Home
  2. Adoption
E. WHAT ARE MY PARENTAL RIGHTS AND RESPONSIBILITIES?
  1. Your Rights
  2. Your Responsibilities
F. WHAT CAN I DO IF I HAVE A COMPLAINT?
  1. Speak to Your Agency Caseworker
  2. The Parents' Rights Unit
  3. Fair Hearings
  4. Court
G. HOW CAN I GET A LAWYER?
H. WHAT COURT ACTIONS CAN TAKE PLACE CONCERNING ME AND MY CHILD?
  1. Court Actions Concerned with the Plan for Your Child
    a. 358-a Proceeding
    b. 392 Review
    c. Extension of Court Placement
  2. Court Actions at Which Your Parental Rights Can Be Ended
    a. Abandonment
    b. Permanent Neglect
    c. Inability to Care

SUMMARY
"REQUEST FOR DISCHARGE OF CHILD FROM FOSTER CARE" FORM

TELEPHONE DIRECTORY

---

foster care service, however, they must be encouraged and helped to carry out the roles of parent, team member, and informed consumer.

Caseworkers

In most child welfare settings, workers often are overwhelmed by the complex and intense demands placed on them as they attempt to work with children and parents. A major problem is that the social worker is often required to be all things to all people: therapist for child and biological parents; consultant or supervisor with foster parents; case manager; advocate; etc. Moreover, these multiple roles have to be carried out in the context of insufficient training, high caseloads and limited resources.[22]

In the past, direct services and support were provided primarily to foster children and foster parents. Workers are now also expected to work with parents. This makes the worker's job that much more time consuming.

There are no easy solutions to this situation. Administrators, however, can carefully examine the worker's many roles and responsibilities to determine what changes will make workers as effective as possible with parents and children. The caseworker should retain those responsibilities for which he or she is best suited, and transfer those that others may be better able to carry out because of knowledge, experience, skill, and available time. For example, foster parents and child care workers have better opportunities to demonstrate child management and care techniques to parents than does a worker;[23] and parent aides or volunteers have more time than workers to transport parents who do not have access to needed services.

The caseworker still must assume a number of responsibilities as a case manager and an enabler. Although a commitment to parent involvement takes up more of the worker's time, the reconceptualization of worker responsibilities frees up some time that would otherwise be devoted to other tasks.[24]

As *case manager*, the worker is

- *coordinator*—bringing together relevant individuals, including the parents, in a team effort to share information, plan, and make and review decisions
- *team member*—participating in the team process
- *resource mobilizer*—identifying appropriate resources and ensuring their availability to parents
- *monitor*—ensuring that critical activities are taking place within reasonable time frames and that progress (or lack of it) is documented
- *advocate*—clarifying the needs of child, parents, and foster parents to one another, to the agency, and to other service providers, and informing all of these of choices, rights, and responsibilities[25]

A fuller discussion of the case management process and the role of the worker as case manager is in chapter 3.

The caseworker must also serve as an *enabler*—providing the parent with support and encouragement. This help must be based on a view of parents as competent human beings capable of being partners in the helping process. As enabler, the caseworker helps parents enhance their functioning and their capacities to cope. For example, during the preplacement period or the early part of placement, workers can assume major responsibility for teaching parents about foster care and preparing them for their new roles. In addition, caseworkers should give recognition and support to parents' improvements or accomplishments, no matter how small, and encourage parents to assume as much responsibility as they can for performing parenting tasks and making decisions.

This does *not* mean that the worker should provide parents with intensive therapeutic counseling (for a discussion of this, see chap. 3, pp. 87 and 92). The parent may not need this help, and even when it is appropriate, the worker always lacks sufficient time and often lacks the necessary skills to provide therapy.

In summary, an emphasis on parent involvement places more restrictions and limitations on a worker's time. Therefore, a reexamination of the roles and responsibilities of the caseworker is necessary. Because foster parents, child care workers, parent aides, and other service providers can offer some of the necessary assistance that foster families, children, and parents need, the workers are freed to devote more time to two crucial responsibilities:

- serving as a case manager—a coordinator of services, a team member, a resource mobilizer, an advocate for service delivery and change, and a monitor to assure that appropriate services are provided

- serving as an enabler—providing guidance, information, and support to the parent

Supervisors

Workers cannot carry out the roles described above without the consistent support of line supervisors. Line supervisors are critical in the task of creating an agency climate in which work with parents is not only encouraged or facilitated, but also made a priority. In chapter 5, the supervisors' role in a foster care service committed to promoting parent involvement is described. The present chapter, however, briefly identifies several of the essential roles supervisors must fulfill if parents are to become more involved in foster care services. These are *teacher, provider of support*, and *monitor*.

As *teacher*, the supervisor helps workers to

- interpret policy, rules, procedures, and statutes germane to parent involvement
- gain information and knowledge about parenting, parent-child relationships, separation, permanency planning, and resources
- understand their attitudes about parents and the way their attitudes affect work with parents
- develop skills needed to work directly with or in behalf of parents
- set priorities for caseloads
- use case recording forms and other kinds of documentation

This teaching role becomes increasingly important as budget cutbacks curtail training programs and the ability of agencies to hire highly skilled workers who command higher salaries.

Good supervisors recognize that workers committed to parent involvement are under multiple sources of stress.[26] As a *provider of support*, therefore, supervisors have to create an environment that prevents, reduces, and/or helps the worker adjust to stress. For example, difficult cases should not be assigned to new workers or workers who are showing signs of burnout; in cases that are particularly stressful to workers, decision making can be shared by supervisors and workers; cases of unusually difficult clients can be shared by workers; and specialization of staff members should be facilitated.[27]

As *monitor*, the supervisor reviews all the cases in his or her workers' caseloads according to selected criteria, and then identifies those cases needing greater supervisory attention. Since accountability has assumed greater importance, the supervisory monitoring process must become an essential part of an information system and a foster care review process.

In summary, the supervisor plays a major part in facilitating parent involvement by ensuring that workers possess knowledge, skills, and attitudes essential to that effort. The performance of the teaching, supporting, and monitoring roles by supervisors will enable workers to help parents.

Children

A hazard in focusing intensively on parent involvement is that too little attention may be paid to the children who are in foster care. Working with parents is only one component of permanency planning; the paramount consideration should always be meeting the needs and protecting the rights of children.[28]

Nationwide, the majority of children in foster care are 10 years of age and older.[29] That factor, combined with a commitment to the process of permanency planning, suggests two important roles for children and adolescents: *informed consumer* and *team member*. In addition, children continue to be members of their own families, even after they are placed in care. As in the case of parents, it is inappropriate to view children only as "clients."

Children often are abruptly and without explanation separated from their families. They may react to this separation by withdrawing, becoming aggressive, or denying the situation.[30] An understanding of what is happening, and why, should alleviate some of the distress felt by children, thereby shortening the time required for a child to adjust to foster care.[31]

First, children in care or coming into care should know about foster care in general. It is important that they understand the role of the various "parents" in their lives, as well as the role of the caseworker and the court.[32]

Second, children should be given information about the foster family or residential setting in which they are, or will be, living. Preplacement visits can help eliminate some of a child's fears of the unknown.[33]

Finally, children must understand, and be encouraged to discuss, the reasons why they cannot currently live with their parents. Most importantly, a child should be told what his or her parents plan to do while the child is in care and what contact will be maintained between them. The importance of parent-child visits and other contacts must be emphasized by the worker. The many different ways in which the parents can be involved in the foster care placement should be described. The child should understand that the parents and foster parents are likely to spend time together, with and without the child.

As a member of the foster care team, the child participates in the development of the case plan. The role of team member is appropriate for any child who is capable of understanding

- his or her responsibilities while in foster care
- what the parents must accomplish to have the child return to them
- the caseworker's job in terms of facilitating this process

A written agreement between the child and the worker can make clear each person's responsibilities. Team responsibility includes involvement in meetings at which progress and problems are discussed and goals and objectives are reevaluated.

Foster children should continue to be considered members of their own families also. Their roles as informed consumer and team member facilitate this. In addition, as family members, they should be included in family activities, such as birthday celebrations and family outings.

In summary, the assumption of the roles of informed consumer and team member by foster children enables them to understand what is happening to them and their families. It is likely to accelerate the process of adjusting to new settings and understanding and coping with strong negative emotions. As a result, the children are more likely to understand why parent involvement is so important and perhaps will work to make the interactions with their parents during placement more gratifying and productive.

Foster Parents

In the past, foster parents were primarily viewed as substitute caretakers for children and "quasi-clients" of foster care agencies.[34] They were strongly discouraged from developing any kind of relationship with parents.[35]

During the last decade, however, the foster parent role has become increasingly ambiguous. Foster parent responsibilities have been viewed as those of client, colleague, nonprofessional volunteer, and supervisee.[36] Role ambiguity combined with several additional factors have led to a reexamination and reconceptualization of the foster parent role.[37]

Foster parents are in a position to play a significant part in maintaining ties between children and their parents, rebuilding the parent-child relationship, and reestablishing the family unit.[38] Moreover, they have an important role in helping parents resolve the problems that led to placement. Thus, foster parents become invaluable resources to agencies *and* parents. And the two most important roles they need to assume are *team member* and *"parallel" parent*.

As team members, foster parents are partners with the worker, parents, child, and other service providers. They must be provided with such essential information as the reasons why the child is placed in care, the goals for the family, and the plan for working with the child and parents. Foster parents are collaborators who participate in the continuing planning and decision-making process. Because they are likely to observe parent-child visits and work directly with parents, they are in a position to make invaluable contributions. In accordance with the case plan, foster parents may be responsible for monitoring and documenting parent-child contacts. Foster parents also may become advocates for parents during case conferences.

The current emphasis on permanency planning has resulted in an increasing number of agencies defining foster parents as team members. For example, many agencies require foster parents to participate in the planning process and to help formulate the parent-child visiting plan.[39] Other agencies convey the expectation that foster parents will play a facilitative role in parent-child visiting. This may involve the foster parents' encouraging frequent and lengthy visits, permitting visiting in their homes, bringing children to their parents' homes and to the agency's office for visits, and complying with agreed-upon visiting schedules.[40] (See fig. 2.4.)

As "parallel parents," foster parents are family aides. They do not assume parenting responsibility; they *share* it. Parents continue to help with the care of their children and to make decisions concerning them. Foster parents serve as

- *supporters*—they listen and encourage; are accepting and respectful
- *teachers*—they discuss with parents what they know about child development, child care, community resources, and agency policies
- *models*—they demonstrate "loving and caring, sharing and giving, structure and limits, discipline, daily problem solving, mutual respect, a value on individual separation and growth, values such as patience, tolerance of difference and fair play, dealing with feelings that are both painful and positive, communication and household management and child management techniques"[42]
- *advocates*—they use their knowledge of community resources, agency policy and practice, and legal processes to assert the needs of parents on behalf of their children[43]

Some foster parents may be interested in assuming additional roles. They may be capable of being *team leaders* responsible for the coordination of services available to foster children and parents. Be-

FIGURE 2.4
Assessing Foster Parent Interest, Willingness, and Capacity to Be Involved in Parent-Child Contacts

Have the foster parents indicated an interest in being involved in parent-child contacts?

Given the foster parents' schedules and responsibilities, what extent of foster parent involvement in parent-child contact is realistic?

Have the foster parents been involved in interpreting visiting constructively to the child?

Have the foster parents demonstrated the ability to observe and evaluate the child's responses to visits and other contacts?

Are the foster parents:

> able to maintain confidentiality about the foster child and birth family?
>
> able to attempt to understand the behavior of the parents?
>
> willing to allow visiting in their home?
>
> able to provide transportation to visits elsewhere?
>
> willing to coordinate parents' visits to the child's school, doctor or other resources?
>
> aware of the impact of parent-child visits [on] other foster children in the home?
>
> willing to meet to review visitation with the parent and worker?
>
> able to discuss their feelings regarding the parents?
>
> willing to allow telephone calls between parents and child?
>
> able to share the child on special days?
>
> aware of [the] child's need for continuing identification with parents?
>
> able to set limits appropriately on their relationship with parents?

What concerns have these foster parents expressed regarding parent-child contacts?

What special skills or capacities have you observed these foster parents to have?[41]

---

yond that, there are foster parents who are able to advocate for all foster children at policy and funding levels.[44] (See fig. 2.5)

To sum up, the assumption by foster parents of new roles in relation to parent involvement has the potential of having profoundly positive effects on the foster care system. Although the foster parents' responsibilities may be more difficult, challenging, and time consuming than in the past, their experiences are also likely to be far more rewarding and satisfying. After all, cooperation between parents and foster parents results in the provision of concrete assistance needed by parents to bring about return home, a more consistent emotional environment for foster children, and a reduction of the demands placed on caseworkers to be all things to all people.

Child Care Workers

> The best measure of a [residential] treatment program lies in the quality, training and commitment of its staff. Effective intervention builds on an institutional team of child care worker, social worker, teacher, consulting psychiatrist and psychologist working closely together. There must not be a fragmented system, where the child belongs to one team member, the family belongs to another, the soul and psyche to the third and the mind to the fourth.[46]

Traditionally, child care workers in residential settings were viewed as primary caretakers for the children in those settings. Their involvement with the parents of the children was limited to visiting day.[47] Parents were not welcome in the residences on a daily basis because they were considered "disruptive," "creators of problems," and "incapable of being helpful."[48]

Increased attention has been directed recently to parent involvement in residential settings.[49] Most of the changes described in the literature occur within the living units of the centers; child care workers must therefore assume a variety of new roles.

In the past, the social worker tended to be the exclusive liaison between the family and the residential setting, informing the child care worker of the family situation and plans, and explaining the child's treatment to the family.[50] Now, in order to carry out newly defined roles, the social worker and the child care worker will be working together, and both will interact directly with parents and

FIGURE 2.5
Promoting Parent–Foster Parent Relationships

In Iron County, Michigan, a local foster parent association promotes parent–foster parent relationships. Parents and other family and community members are invited to attend selected foster parent association meetings that focus on topics such as how parents and foster families can work together, the role of the guardian ad litem, and the process by which children come into care. Opening meetings to participants other than foster parents has proven positive. Foster parents have changed their attitudes about parents and other family members, and the foster family and parent relationship has been more constructive. Since the program began, involvement has risen, including more visiting in the foster home by all family members, and foster parents have devised creative ways of involving family members in activities, such as camping, shopping, parties, and school conferences. "Once the foster parents and parents pass the reluctance point, it snowballs. They think of more and more ways to spend time together," reports the director.[45]

---

children. This change in the type and method of service delivery is both dramatic and fundamental to the approach under discussion. Members of the child care staff do not eliminate the social worker's primary function of family counselor; they support it. By working in a team, social workers and child care workers can accomplish more than either could alone.

The child care workers' roles concerning parents are quite similar to the ones described for the foster parent. They, too, should be "parallel" parents who

- *teach* parents about the child and his or her living environment
- *model* child management and care techniques, attitudes, and appropriate ways to express affection, and the ways child and parents can have fun together
- *support* parents, develop mutual trust, and help them have a positive, nurturing experience
- *facilitate* communication between child and parents
- *advocate* for services needed within the residential setting (See fig. 2.6.)

In summary, the redefinition of the role of the child care worker requires a greater commitment to parent involvement in residential settings. Only when agencies require, or at least allow, parent participation in more than clinical treatment and occasional visiting, will

FIGURE 2.6
Working with Parents in the Residence: Two Examples

The Parsons Child and Family Center in Albany, New York, has adopted a model of family-centered group care in its residential treatment program. The agency has incorporated child care worker-family involvement as a treatment component. Child care staff work with families can be divided into five categories:

1. *Assessment:* Child care workers observe parents' visits to the residence, record these events, and then share their notes with the social worker, thereby playing a crucial role in assessment and treatment planning.

2. *Modeling:* Child care workers model for the parents not only child management skills, parental role expectations, and clear communication, but also ways of enjoying their child.

3. *Direct help to the parents:* Through nurturing, socializing, and increasing trust, the worker is able to help the parents.

4. *Increasing the child care worker's own effectiveness:* Parents provide useful information and demonstrate their own techniques in managing the child, thereby making the workers' job easier.

5. *Aftercare:* Child care workers may make home visits and help in the transition when a child goes home.

At the Infants' Home of Brooklyn Day Treatment Center and Residence, parents participate in planning, evaluation, visiting, counseling, and parent groups. Opportunities to interact with child care staff members are also provided, for example, through the "parents in residence" program. In this program, parents observe child care staff members in situations they had difficulty handling in their own homes—such as mealtime, bedtime, or playtime—helping parents learn better responses to those situations. Another way the residence includes parents is by involving them in a camping weekend with the entire center. Again, through observation and participation, parents learn about structure and limits, as well as how to relax and enjoy their children. Other projects allow parents and child care staff members to work together on task-oriented, time-limited, concrete activities. A few years ago, an adventure playground made from tires was built on the grounds of the facility, and everyone participated in its construction.

Some of these activities are possible because the agency has a multifaceted program and is based in the community where most of the families live.[51]

child care workers be more likely to interact frequently with parents. These interactions will be most helpful to parents, child care workers, and social workers if the child care workers are prepared to be models, providers of support and nurture, enablers, and even advocates.

Adoptive Parents

> For parents who may not have the desire or the psychological resources to raise a child themselves, there is a pressing need for a new kind of adoptive placement in which they can actively participate. In this arrangement, parents who have previously been reluctant to surrender their children for adoption but may not be in a position to raise them can have the security of knowing they have provided their child with opportunities for a healthy, loving environment, *without giving up the possibility of knowing their child's fate and without abandoning the hope of maintaining some ties.* [emphasis added][52]

It may seem inappropriate to include a discussion of adoptive parent roles in a book about involving parents in the foster care system. In the past, most adoptions were of infants, and adoption practice developed on the assumption—supported by the community—that adoption was a closed system, completely excluding the parents.

Today, many children are not infants when they are adopted.[53] They are older foster children with memories of, and ties to, their own parents. Not infrequently, they are being adopted by their foster parents, who have already had contact and involvement with the parents.

For these reasons, some agencies provide for open adoptions.[54] In an open adoption, parent contact continues and is sanctioned by the adoptive parents, agency, parents, and child. The nature and degree of openness varies depending upon the needs and abilities of the child, the adoptive parents, and the parents. The issue of maintaining ties between parents and children after adoption must be explored carefully with the prospective adoptive parents, parents, and children. (A few agencies are experimenting with open adoption for infants.)

In open adoptions, adoptive parents must assume the role of *planner:* along with the parents and child, agreement is reached about the frequency, duration, location, and type of contact. The role of the adoptive parent as planner may be limited, however. While allowing parent-child contacts, the adoptive parents may not themselves be involved with the parents. In these situations, the agency retains responsibility for facilitating parent-child visits.

In other situations, the adoptive parents may assume the role of *facilitator:* the adoptive parents prepare the child for visits, provide transportation if needed, encourage phone calls, and permit the child to spend special days with the parents.

Finally, some adoptive parents will assume the role of *informal helper,* assisting and supporting the parents.

New adoptive parents and foster parents should be informed through training, workshops, conferences, and written material about what open adoption is and why it is an important permanency planning option.[55] They need to learn what roles adoptive parents can play vis à vis parents when an open adoption exists.

Parents, too, should be informed about open adoption. When open adoption is recognized as a legitimate permanency planning option, more parents might be willing to voluntarily relinquish their legal, moral, and nurturing rights to their child, since continuing contact would still be possible.[56]

RESOURCES FOR PARENTS

As the roles of caseworkers, foster parents, child care workers, and parents are redefined, more individuals will serve as essential resources to parents whose children are in foster care. As indicated earlier, these individuals can provide support and information, share parenting tasks, engage in advocacy, and teach and demonstrate parenting skills.

Another group of resources provides forms of assistance that complement and supplement those provided by the individuals cited above. They include parent aide and volunteer programs, parent education programs, groups for parents, and other community services. These resources can be available through child welfare agencies, human services organizations, or independent groups. The types of services these resources can provide usually are given a low priority; are not widespread; and where they do exist, are the most vulnerable to funding cutbacks. But because they are important, they are focused on here.

Although these resources are needed to enhance parents' competence and self-esteem and to improve parent-child relationships, they are not sufficient to meet the complex needs of the many families with tangible problems that require concrete services, such as drug and alcohol abuse programs, employment counseling and training, housing assistance, psychotherapeutic counseling, day care, public health services, homemaker programs, legal services, financial aid programs, and formal educational programs. Because these services usually are available from human service organizations in the community other than child welfare agencies, they are not described here.

Caseworkers should ensure that parents use these resources when they would be beneficial. Administrators can facilitate this process by developing formalized linkages with these programs. (See chap. 4.)

This section describes the first group of resources and discusses their importance. Parents benefit greatly from these programs.[57] They often can be developed by using volunteers and/or paraprofessionals, thereby keeping costs fairly moderate. Where these programs exist, some of the emotional burden felt by caseworkers and foster parents is relieved, and time is freed for them to carry out other important responsibilities. In a foster care service committed to parent involvement, these parent-oriented programs tend to facilitate parent participation.

It is crucial for agencies to make sure that parents have access to these programs. The following descriptions can help administrators decide whether to develop specific programs within their agencies or create ties to programs that exist elsewhere in the community. These decisions should be based on the agency's goals, priorities, and available funds, as well as on the availability and accessibility of already established programs.

Parent Aide and Volunteer Programs

Parent aides are either trained volunteers or trained, paid paraprofessional workers who form one-to-one relationships with parents.[58] Parent aides work with parents to resolve family problems. Parent aides

- establish relationships of trust and friendship with parents by being caring and honest, showing primary concern for the parent, listening and offering encouragement and support, and reaching out to the parent
- help parents become involved in activities designed to reduce isolation and to establish support systems by showing parents how to locate and use appropriate community resources
- encourage school attendance and keeping medical appointments by providing transportation and/or accompanying parents to and from appointments
- engage in enjoyable activities together, such as shopping and picnicking, to reinforce the role of the aide as a noncritical friend
- provide guidance in household tasks, such as meal planning, budgeting, and child care needs
- help parents learn appropriate and consistent child management techniques through modeling and suggestions
- encourage parents to become involved in parent education courses or groups, when appropriate. (See figs. 2.7 and 2.8.)

FIGURE 2.7
An Evaluation of Parent Aide Programs

A descriptive-comparative study, conducted in 1978-1979, to provide detailed information about three parent aide programs in Michigan, suggests that families do change during the period of their involvement with parent aides.
Specifically:

1. Families began spending more time with their children and in activities outside the home.

2. Families shifted from requesting help from formal systems, such as agencies, to requesting help from informal systems, such as friends and neighbors.

3. Families developed new, or strengthened existing, relationships to reduce isolation.

4. Families showed positive change on measures of family functioning, especially parenting skills, family bonding and self-image.

5. The quality of parental functioning improved, especially in the areas of nutrition and health, supervision, control and discipline, and family interaction.[59]

Although volunteer programs can be established formally within agencies,[61] administrators also can encourage workers to use natural helpers in the community in an informal way to assist parents on a one-to-one basis.[62] Informal or natural helpers may be relatives, friends, neighbors, and coworkers. They are usually unpaid; untrained; immediately available; and familiar with the parents and their strengths, weaknesses, and coping abilities.[63] They have fewer time constraints than the caseworker, and share common life experiences with the individuals needing help.

Parent Education Programs

Parent education is aimed at helping parents recognize and use their strengths to better meet their personal needs and increase their awareness of, and ability to meet, the needs of other family members. The education programs offer information about child growth and development, parenting skills, available community services, home-

---

FIGURE 2.8
The Use of Volunteers in the
Temporary Foster Care (TFC) Program in Michigan

The TFC program in Michigan uses volunteers to help the foster care workers provide direct services to the families whose children are in care. A VISTA volunteer who coordinated the volunteer program acquainted herself with community resources and developed job descriptions and a training program for the participants she recruited. Volunteers were used in three ways:

1. clerical aides—performing tasks to free the caseworkers for field work;

2. transporters—taking children or family members to visit doctors or dentists, or to other appointments;

3. home aides—counseling young, retarded, or otherwise needy mothers in child development, parental skills, homemaking and money management, and finding better housing, arranging for training and developing support systems.

The volunteers developed a creative play group. Each week, they transported mothers and their preschool-age children who were in foster care to a central place where the group met (for the first few months, the group was located in a church basement; later, participants met in a playground building). The purposes of this play group were to help mothers learn to enjoy playing with their children, to show them how simple materials could be used for play, to introduce them to other mothers who faced common problems, to promote knowledge of child development, and to use snacks as a springboard for discussion of better nutrition. The group also made several field trips—to a farm, an exhibit of small animals, a beach.[60]

---

making, health care and budgeting, and job training and formulation of career goals. Parent education programs can be conducted at child care agencies by specially trained consultants, or at local community colleges and schools of social work. (See figs. 2.9 and 2.10.)

Groups for Parents

There are two different kinds of parent groups: self-help and parent support. Self-help groups are begun by the parents, while support groups are generally organized under agency auspices.

FIGURE 2.9
The Parent—Preschool Education, Empathy, Rapport and Support (PEERS) Program

The Parent—Preschool Education, Empathy, Rapport and Support (PEERS) Program is a family-centered, volunteer-supported component of the Onslow County Department of Social Services (DDS) in Jacksonville, North Carolina.

Designed primarily for families who are receiving protective and foster care services (although any family under stress may participate), PEERS offers a range of programs aimed at strengthening families. Basic programs include the following:

1. The Parent Readiness Education Project (PREP) addresses issues of particular concern to newly formed families: family planning, budgeting, improving family relationships, and disciplining the young child.

2. Child Care, Homemaking, and Health is directed by a pediatric nurse who is also the agency's Director of Homemaker Services.

3. Community Awareness and Self-Help uses field trips and group discussion to inform and educate parents about locally available resources and self-help options.

The program also runs a preschool, in which children are cared for while parents are learning to understand and rebuild their family.

The Director of the PEERS Program, a paid member of the DDS staff, is assisted by a group of approximately 25 volunteers, 8 of whom are former participants. Many of the volunteers have been recruited from the military community at Camp Lejeune, the nearby Marine Corps base. An administrative assistant's position, rent, and utilities are funded by United Way of Onslow County. Money to run the program, and the Center's furnishings, have been provided by the civic organizations, churches, and chapels of the civilian and military community.[64]

Self-help groups are composed of individuals facing common problems and seeking knowledge and emotional support.[66] They are characterized by small-group interaction; peer helper roles; and the group as a source of acceptance, support, and identity. Many are available in the parents' own neighborhood, which makes the groups accessible and reduces isolation. In these groups, help is personalized; it is given with understanding and feeling; it is generally quick, immediate, and

FIGURE 2.10
The Family Living Center

The Family Living Center in Grand Rapids, Michigan, is a unique parent education program that exclusively involves parents of children in foster care. It is also unusual in that classes are supported totally by educational monies, not by social services funding. Organized in 8- and 16-week sessions, classes are offered in life skills; parenting of infants, preschoolers, school-aged, and teen-age children; single parenting; stepparenting; and family communication. Transportation and child care are available to participating parents. Social service staffs from local public and private agencies use the Family Living Center as a treatment resource for many of their parents. Program evaluations indicate that families have made positive changes through their participation. Although center staff members are not involved in deciding whether children should return home from foster care, they do share information about the educational gains of the parents that may affect decisions. In addition to its educational aspects, the program improves parental self-esteem and reduces isolation through the development of informal support networks.[65]

responsive. There are a great many self-help groups; among the best known are Parents Anonymous, Parents Without Partners, and Alcoholics Anonymous.[67]

Some agencies have established parent support groups. Although they serve educational functions, these groups are primarily intended to be forums for airing complaints, providing support by sharing experiences, resolving problems, and advocating in behalf of group members. In addition, they provide opportunities for socialization and encourage the development of informal helping networks. Professional staff members from child welfare agencies serve as group facilitators. (See fig. 2.11)

Services Available from Community Resources

These resources are difficult to categorize. They exist in every community but are almost always overlooked by child welfare agencies:

- *Large companies* often lend staff or resources. For example, the personnel manager may do group employment counseling, or a company bus may be used for transportation.

FIGURE 2.11
Parent Groups at The Children's Village

   The Children's Village in Dobbs Ferry, New York, a residential treatment center for boys between the ages of 6 and 13½, runs several parent groups. In the Martin Luther King Unit, twice each month a Children's Village bus picks up parents and their preschool children at a central location in New York City and brings them to the Village. While the preschoolers are involved in play experiences with trained personnel, the parents participate in a group session in which the emphasis is on parenting skills. In another unit at the Village, a mothers group has been meeting regularly since 1974. The group's goal is to help mothers identify and modify any factors that could interfere with the satisfactory adjustment of their sons once they are discharged from the Village.[68]

- *Church youth groups* may volunteer recreational or babysitting support as a group project.
- *Home economists* may offer training sessions on inexpensive food preparation and wise budgeting.
- *Nursing schools* may be enlisted to provide infant care seminars.
- A *grocery store manager* or *consumer consultant* may explain the use of food stamps and how to improve shopping skills.[69]

It is the responsibility of administrative-level staff to identify and contact these community resources and request their assistance in providing services to families.

Use of Parents

Finally, it is important to reiterate a point made earlier in this chapter: *parents* can serve as resources for other parents, and should be encouraged to do so by agencies. Parents are the primary resources for other parents in all parent support groups and many parent education programs. Parents who have experienced problems with their own children may effectively assist other parents in handling child-related problems. This success builds their own self-esteem, which in turn enhances their relationships with their own children. In addition, parents can serve on policy committees and agency boards, thereby representing a parent's viewpoint; participate in orientation programs for new parents; develop telephone buddy systems; and prepare newsletters for parents.

NOTES

1. Child Welfare League of America, *Standards for Foster Family Service*, rev. ed. (New York, NY: Child Welfare League of America, 1975), 73-74.
2. For further discussion of program manuals, see American Public Welfare Association, *Standards for Foster Family Service Systems for Public Agencies*, DHEW Publication No. (OHDS) 79-30231 (Washington, DC: U.S. Dept. of Health, Education and Welfare, 1979), 75-76.
3. See Peg Hess, *Working with Birth and Foster Parents: Guide to Planning Parent-Child Visitation* (Office of Continuing Social Work Education, University of Tennessee School of Social Work, 1981). Module 1 focuses on understanding attitudes and their importance. In addition, see appendix E for an example of an attitude survey.
4. See chapter 5 on supervision. Also, see Theodore Stein, Eileen Gambrill, and Kermit Wiltse, *Children in Foster Homes: Achieving Continuity of Care* (New York, NY: Praeger, 1978), 19-20, 127-28; Anthony Maluccio, "Promoting Client and Worker Competence in Child Welfare," in *Social Welfare Forum, 1980* (New York, NY: Columbia University Press, 1980).
5. See Charles Horejsi, Anne Bertsche, and Frank Clark, *Social Work Practice with Parents of Children in Foster Care: A Handbook* (Springfield, IL: Charles C Thomas, 1981), 191-195, for additional examples.
6. For discussion about burnout, see Anne Bertsche, "Worker Burnout in Child Welfare and Its Effect on Biological Parents," in *Parents of Children in Placement: Perspectives and Programs*, edited by Paula Sinanoglu and Anthony Maluccio (New York, NY: Child Welfare League of America, 1981), 445-460; Martha Bramhall and Susan Ezell, "How Burned Out Are You?" "Working Your Way Out of Burnout," and "How Agencies Can Prevent Burnout," a three-part series appearing in *Public Welfare* 39 (Winter 1981, Spring 1981, and Summer 1981).
7. Child Welfare League of America, op. cit., 102-110.
8. For further discussion concerning advisory groups, see American Public Welfare Association, op. cit., 71-72.
9. Anthony Maluccio, "An Ecological Perspective on Practice with Parents of Children in Foster Care," in *The Challenge of Partnership: Working with Parents of Children in Foster Care*, edited by Anthony Maluccio and Paula Sinanoglu (New York, NY: Child Welfare League of America, 1981), 29.
10. Rosemarie Carbino, "Developing a Parent Organization: New Roles for Parents of Children in Substitute Care," Maluccio and Sinanoglu, *The Challenge of Partnership*, op. cit., 183-184.
11. This discussion of "in-between" parents is adapted from Peg Hess and Linda Williams, "Group Orientation for Parents of Children in Foster Family Care," *Child Welfare* LX1 (September/October 1982): 457-458.
12. Additional examples of strengths are identified in Gertrude Halper and Mary Ann Jones, *Serving Families at Risk of Dissolution: Public Preventive Services in New York City* (New York, NY: The City of New York, Human Resources Administration, February 1981), 15-16; Esther Callard and Patricia Morin, eds., *PACT: Parents and Children Together: An Alter-*

CHAPTER 2: ADMINISTRATIVE RESPONSIBILITY 51

native to Foster Care (Detroit, MI: Wayne State University, 1979), 142-144. See appendix A for a list of family strengths from PACT.
13. Halper and Jones, op. cit.
14. Some of the material covered in this subsection is quoted or adapted from Emily Jean McFadden, *Working with Natural Families, Instructor's Manual* (Ypsilanti, MI: Eastern Michigan University, Foster Parent Education Program, 1980), 49-53.
15. Ralph Davidson, "Restoring Children to their Families," in *New Developments in Foster Care and Adoption*, edited by John Triseliotis (London, England: Routledge and Kegan Paul, 1980), 45.
16. Carbino, op. cit., 183. See also American Public Welfare Association, op. cit., 30.
17. Ibid.
18. This discussion is adapted from Hess and Williams, op. cit.
19. Other examples include Barbara Rutter, *A Way of Caring—The Parents' Guide to Foster Family Care* (New York, NY: Child Welfare League of America, 1981); Jewish Child Care Association of New York, "Your Child in Foster Care," *Child Welfare* LV (February 1976): 125-131; Hillside Children's Center, "Parents' Manual," mimeo. (Rochester, NY, n. d.); Jan Baum, "Foster Care Handbook for Natural Parents," mimeo. (Children's Service Society of Wisconsin, May 1, 1977).
20. See Carbino, op. cit., 165-186, for a discussion of parent organizations.
21. The "Natural Parent Newsletter" is an excellent example of this. It can be obtained by writing P.O. Box 5012, Postal Station B, Victoria, British Columbia, V8R 6N3, Canada.
22. Maluccio, "Promoting Client and Worker Competence," op. cit.
23. See Patricia Ryan, Emily McFadden, and Bruce Warren, "Foster Families: A Resource for Helping Parents," in Maluccio and Sinanoglu, *The Challenge of Partnership*, op. cit., 192-194.
24. Ibid., 194.
25. This definition of advocate is provided by Hess, *Working with Birth and Foster Parents*, op. cit., 99.
26. See note 6 for further information about the sources of stress.
27. Horejsi, Bertsche and Clark, op. cit., 191-193.
28. See American Public Welfare Association, op. cit., 25-26, for a list of rights of foster children.
29. See, for example, *Planned Permanency for Children, 1980 Plan: Phase II, Vol. I* (Springfield, IL: Illinois Department of Children and Family Service, 1979), 83-84; Virginia Sibbison and John McGowan, *New York State Children in Foster Care* (Albany, NY: Welfare Research, Inc., 1977), ix, 23; *Your Neighbor's Kids* (Augusta, ME: Governor's Task Force on Foster Care for Children, 1980), 16, 20, 78-81.
30. Rutter, op. cit., 13-16; Peg Hess, "Parent-Child Attachment Concept: Crucial for Permanency Planning," *Social Casework* 63 (January 1982): 46-53; Vera Fahlberg, *Attachment and Separation* (Lansing, MI: Michigan Department of Social Services, 1979).
31. Heather Craig et al., *Team Training; Manual II: A Foster Care Staff Development Curriculum* (Virginia: Department of Welfare, n.d.), 18.

32. Information can be conveyed through the use of individualized conversations with workers, group meetings involving other children, handbooks specially written for foster children, and the Child's Eco Map. See Vera Fahlberg, *Helping Children When They Must Move* (Lansing, MI: Michigan Department of Social Services, 1979), 30-31.
33. Craig et al., op. cit. Other means include: foster family preparation of albums with pictures of their home, family, and pets to be kept at the agency; members of the foster family write letters to the child about to be placed with them.
34. Alfred Kadushin, *Child Welfare Services* (New York, NY: Macmillan, 1980), 394; Charles Horejsi, *Foster Family Care: A Handbook for Social Workers* (Missoula, MT: University of Montana, August 1978), 220-221.
35. Ryan, McFadden, and Warren, op. cit., 191; James Seaberg, "Foster Parents as Aides to Parents," in Maluccio and Sinanoglu, *The Challenge of Partnership*, op. cit., 210-211.
36. Kadushin, op. cit.; Horejsi, op. cit.
37. See, for example, Kadushin, op. cit.; Horejsi, op. cit.; Ryan, McFadden, and Warren, op. cit.; Seaberg, op. cit. For a list of foster parents' rights, see American Public Welfare Association, op. cit., 27-28.
38. Evelyn Felker, "Maintaining Relationships with the Biological Family," in *Raising Other People's Kids: Successful Child-Rearing in the Restructured Family* (Grand Rapids, MI: William B. Eerdmans, 1981), 94-112.
39. Pamela Marr, "Foster Care Teamwork Comes to Kansas," in *Case Record* 5 (January 1981): 1-2; Kenneth Watson, "A Bold, New Model for Foster Family Care," *Public Welfare* 4 (Spring 1982): 14-21. Authors' conversation with Patricia Bannen, director of the Manitowac County Department of Social Services in Wisconsin, and Elaine Rakouskas, director of the Wake County Department of Social Services in North Carolina in 1981, revealed that these counties had implemented such requirements.
40. In fact, both Hess, *Working with Birth and Foster Parents*, op. cit., and Ryan, McFadden, and Warren, op. cit., have described differential levels of involvement between parents and foster families (see appendix D for Hess's description of minimum, moderate, and maximum involvement). They assert that foster parents are capable of different degrees of involvement with parents, and that attempts should be made to match parents who could most benefit from intensive involvement with foster parents who can be "maximally involved" (Hess's term) or are "oriented to biological families" (Ryan, McFadden, and Warren's term).
41. Hess, *Working with Birth and Foster Parents*, op. cit., 112-113.
42. Judith Lee and Danielle Park, *Walk a Mile in My Shoes—A Manual on Biological Parents for Foster Parents*, mimeo. (West Hartford, CT: University of Connecticut School of Social Work, December 1979), 26.
43. These four roles are more fully described in McFadden, op. cit.; Hess, *Working with Birth and Foster Parents*, op. cit.; Linda Davies and David Bland, "The Use of Foster Parents as Role Models for Parents," *Child Welfare* 57 (June 1978): 380-386; Lee and Park, op. cit.
44. *Case Record*, "Foster Parent Education Project Stresses Professional Development," *Case Record* 5 (January 1981), 3.

45. Authors' conversation with Linda Knechtges, director of the Iron County Foster Parent Association in Michigan, 1981.
46. Nadia Finkelstein, "Family-Centered Group Care—The Children's Institution, from a Living Center to a Center for Change," in Maluccio and Sinanoglu, *The Challenge of Partnership*, op. cit., 101.
47. James Whittaker, "Family Involvement in Residential Treatment: A Support System for Parents," in Maluccio and Sinanoglu, *The Challenge of Partnership*, op. cit., 79. Whittaker refers to visiting day as a difficult day.
48. Alan Klein, *The Professional Child Care Worker: A Guide to Skills, Knowledge, Techniques and Attitudes* (New York, NY: Association Press, 1975), 252.
49. See Anthony Maluccio and Paula Sinanoglu, "Social Work with Parents of Children in Foster Care: A Bibliography," *Child Welfare* 60 (May 1981), 296-298.
50. Klein, op. cit., 243.
51. The description of the Parsons Child and Family Center is based upon several articles, including "Permanent Families for Children in Group Care: Parsons Child and Family Center," *Case Record* 5 (Summer 1981): 4; Finkelstein, op. cit.; and Celia Littauer, "Working with Families of Children in Residential Treatment," *Child Welfare* 59 (April 1980): 225-234. The authors visited the Infants' Home of Brooklyn Day Treatment Center and Residence and interviewed the director, Elma Denham, in 1981.
52. Joan Laird, "An Ecological Approach to Child Welfare: Issues of Family Identity and Continuity," in *Social Work Practice: People and Environments*, edited by Carel Germain (New York, NY: Columbia University Press, 1979), 201.
53. William Meezan, *Adoption Services in the States*, DHHS Publication No. (OHDS) 80-30288 (Washington, DC: U.S. Department of Health and Human Services, 1980), 4-7; Ann Shyne and Anita Schroeder, *National Study of Social Services to Children and their Families*, DHEW Publication No. (OHDS) 78-30150 (Rockville, MD: Westat, 1978), 124-134.
54. See Annette Baran, Reuben Pannor, and Arthur Sorosky, "Open Adoption," *Social Work* 21 (March 1976): 97-100; Laird, op. cit., 200-204.
55. See note 53; see also Arthur Sorosky, Annette Baran, and Reuben Pannor, *The Adoption Triangle: The Effects of the Sealed Record on Adoptees, Birth Parents, and Adoptive Parents* (New York, NY: Anchor Press, 1978), 207-214.
56. Ibid., 210-214.
57. See, for example, Mary Andrews and Jane Swanson, *An Evaluation of Parent Aide Programs* (Michigan: Institute for Family and Child Study, Michigan State University, 1979); Callard and Morin, op. cit.; Hess and Williams, op. cit.
58. For a discussion of parent aides, see Andrews and Swanson, op. cit.; Carla Gifford, Felisa Kaplan, and Marsha Salus, *Parent Aides in Child Abuse and Neglect Programs*, DHEW Publication No. (OHDS) 79-30200 (Washington, DC: U.S. Department of Health, Education and Welfare, 1979).
59. Andrews and Swanson, op. cit.

60. Patty Boyd, "They *Can* Go Home Again," *Child Welfare* 58 (November 1979): 611.
61. See American Public Welfare Association, op. cit., 72–74, for a discussion of volunteer programs in foster care agencies.
62. See, for example, Carol Swanson, "Using Natural Helping Networks to Promote Competence," in *Promoting Competence in Clients: A New/Old Approach to Social Work Practice,* edited by Anthony Maluccio (New York, NY: Free Press, 1981), 125–151; Armand Lauffer, *Resources for Child Placement and Other Human Services* (Beverly Hills, CA: Sage Publications, 1979), 109–125; Horejsi, Bertsche, and Clark, op. cit., 139–174; Virginia Withey, Rosalie Anderson, and Michael Lauderdale, "Volunteers as Mentors for Abusing Parents: A Natural Helping Relationship," *Child Welfare* 59 (December 1980); 637–644; Melvin Delgado and Denise Humm-Delgado, "Natural Support Systems: Source of Strength in Hispanic Communities," *Social Work* 27 (January 1982); 83–89.
63. Lowell Jenkins and Alicia Cook, "The Rural Hospice: Integrating Formal and Informal Helping Systems," *Social Work* 26 (September 1981): 416.
64. Adapted from *Case Record,* "Promoting Parental Involvement in Permanency Planning: Resources," *Case Record* 5 (Summer 1981): 2. The authors also discussed this program with its director, Nancy Cowperthwait, in 1981.
65. Based on conversation with Beth Dilley, director of the Family Living Center, in 1981.
66. Horejsi, Bertsche, and Clark, op. cit., 169–174; "Self-Help in America," special issue of *Citizen Participation* (January/February 1982).
67. For descriptions of these programs, see Horejsi, Bertsche, and Clark, ibid.
68. Based on conversations with several staff members in 1981; also see Neil Silver, "Mothers' Group," *Children's Village Bulletin* (June 1976): 14; Wilma David, "Parent Participation in the Treatment Process," *Children's Village Bulletin* (June 1976): 9.
69. These suggestions are adapted from John McGowan and Christine Deyss, *Permanency Planning: A Casework Handbook* (Albany, NY: Welfare Research Inc., March 1979), 58.

TABLES OF PARENT INVOLVEMENT ACTIVITIES, TASKS, SERVICES, AND PROGRAMS

Throughout the first two chapters and in the chapters that follow, programs, services, activities, and tasks relating to parent involvement are identified and/or described. The following tables list the different ways parents can be included throughout the foster care process. A few listings may concern parents but not require their direct participation. Administrators can use these tables to examine how their agencies currently involve parents and to develop new policies and programs.

The first table (table 1), on preplacement, covers the period of time from when the decision is first made to place a child in care through when the child is actually placed. This would mean that the "worker" is likely to be an intake worker or a protective services worker. Many of these activities may not be able to take place until after the child is placed (especially in emergency placements). Table 1 reflects what would be ideal.

The second table (table 2), on placement, covers the period of time from when the child is placed through when a permanent plan for the child is implemented. Several of the activities listed (especially toward the end of the table) could also be included in the postplacement table (table 3) since they can also involve parents whose children have been in foster care.

The third table (table 3) on postplacement, is concerned with those children who return to their own families.

Several items in the tables require differentiation based on whether the child is placed in a foster home or in a residential program, such as a group home or residence, residential treatment center, or institution. The distinction is made when foster parent or child care worker involvement is essential or optional.

The notation "X" on the tables indicates that the involvement of those individuals in the particular activity is essential; an "O" indicates that although the participation of the individual is not essential, serious consideration should be given to whether the individual should be involved. When a staff person must be involved, an "X" is usually placed in the "worker" column. We recognize, however, that some agencies may expect other staff members to carry these responsibilities. Individual agencies will need to decide who has responsibility, given the agency's organization.

Although we have tried to sequence the listings, it was not always possible to do so. Many of these activities, particularly those listed in the placement table (table 2) should occur simultaneously.

These tables do not mention every activity, task, or program that characterizes a foster care service, but concern only those that in-

56 CHAPTER 2: ADMINISTRATIVE RESPONSIBILITY

volve parents in some way. Similar programs may be desirable for children or for foster parents, but including them in these tables would detract from the focus on parent involvement.

The descriptions are extremely brief. Many of these activities, tasks, and programs are more fully discussed in other references (see appendix 00).

TABLE 1: Parent Involvement—Preplacement

Description of Activity, Task, Service, Program	Type of Program[1]	Parents[2]	Workers[3]	Children[4]	Foster Parents	Child Care Staff[5]	Other Agency Staff[6]	Other Community Resources[7]
1. Make decision that child needs to be placed in foster care based on assessment of the family situation, determination of service needs, and evaluation of the alternatives to placement		X	X	X			O	O
2. Discuss foster care service: goals and process		X	X	X				
3. Provide and discuss written material to parents about foster care and their rights, responsibilities, and roles		X	X					
4. Discuss and clarify: • importance and purpose of parent involvement • importance of regular parent-child contacts • importance of regular parent-worker contacts		X	X					

TABLE 1: Parent Involvement—Preplacement *(continued)*

Description of Activity, Task, Service, Program	Type of Program[1]	Parents[2]	Workers[3]	Children[4]	Foster Parents	Child Care Staff[5]	Other Agency Staff[6]	Other Community Resources[7]
• meaning of time to children and why placement needs to be time-limited • parental financial obligation to support								
5. Inform parents of right to appeal and the mechanism available to them		X	X				O	O
6. Identify preferred characteristics of foster care placement		X	X	X				

[1]Type of Program—refers to foster home (FH) or residential program (RP).
[2]Parents—refers to child's birth parent(s); also includes any individual who in the past has been the primary caretaker for the child; how parents are involved will depend on their physical, emotional, and mental condition.
[3]Workers—refers to the worker with some direct responsibility for the family at preplacement—may be referred to as intake, protective service, or foster care worker; continuing worker; permanency planning worker; case manager; generic worker.
[4]Children—level of participation of children will depend on their age and maturity.
[5]Child Care Staff—individuals responsible for round-the-clock care in the living units of residential programs (often referred to as child care workers. houseparents, or counselors).
[6]Other Agency Staff—includes supervisors; executive directors; directors of services, foster care, permanency planning, special programs, etc: licensing workers; mental health staff; teachers; legal staff.
[7]Other Community Resources—representatives of other community agencies or organizations and informal helpers providing services to parents and/or children.

TABLE 1: Parent Involvement—Preplacement (continued)

Description of Activity, Task, Service, Program	Type of Program[1]	Parents[2]	Workers[3]	Children[4]	Foster Parents	Child Care Staff[5]	Other Agency Staff[6]	Other Community Resources[7]
7. Select placement (as close to parents' neighborhood as possible)	FH	X	X	X	X			
	RP	X	X	X		O	X (depending on whether placement is within agency or with other resources)	X (depending on whether placement is within agency or with other resources)
8. Preplacement visit	FH	X	X	X	X			
	RP	X	X	X		X	X (depending on whether placement is within agency or with other resources)	X (depending on whether placement is within agency or with other resources)
9. Help prepare child for placement: • explain why child will not stay in own home • explain what the placement will do for the family • reassure about parental love		X	X	X				

TABLE 1: Parent Involvement—Preplacement *(continued)*

Description of Activity, Task, Service, Program	Type of Program[1]	Parents[2]	Workers[3]	Children[4]	Foster Parents	Child Care Staff[5]	Other Agency Staff[6]	Other Community Resources[7]
• explain importance of parents' visits and other contacts								
10. Share important information about child	FH	X	X		X			
	RP					X	X (depending on whether placement is within agency or with other resources)	X
11. Determine ability, availability, and willingness of community resources to work with parents		O	X					
12. Formulate written service plan, including parent-child visiting plan	FH	X	X	X	X		O	O
	RP					X	O	O
13. Prepare written service agreements or contracts based on service plan	FH	X	X	O	O			
	RP					O	O	
14. Group orientation program for parents of children entering care		X	X		O	O	O	O

TABLE 2: Parent Involvement—Placement

Description of Activity, Task, Service, Program	Type of Program[1]	Parents[2]	Workers[3]	Children[4]	Foster Parents	Child Care Staff[5]	Other Agency Staff[6]	Other Community Resources[7]
1. Use parent-worker conferences to discuss: • child's situation in the foster home or residential program • provide counseling service • provide support, compliments • discuss parent-child visits • consider issues concerning child, such as choice of school, medical needs, camp • modify visiting plan if required, especially increasing frequency and length of visits if child is headed for discharge home • discuss services being provided by other resources		X	X					

TABLE 2: Parent Involvement—Placement (continued)

Description of Activity, Task, Service, Program	Type of Program[1]	Parents[2]	Workers[3]	Children[4]	Foster Parents	Child Care Staff[5]	Other Agency Staff[6]	Other Community Resources[7]
• review progress made toward achieving goals of written service agreement • modify provisions of agreement as needed								
2. Supplement in-person contact between parent and worker with telephone calls, postcards, and brief notes		X	X					
3. Arrange for services to parents and their families, and serve as a liaison, coordinator, and advocate between parents and service providers: • parent education classes • parent support groups and self-help groups • individual, group, family, and marital counseling		X	X					X

TABLE 2: Parent Involvement—Placement *(continued)*

Description of Activity, Task, Service, Program	Type of Program[1]	Parents[2]	Workers[3]	Children[4]	Foster Parents	Child Care Staff[5]	Other Agency Staff[6]	Other Community Resources[7]
• parent aides and volunteers • financial assistance • medical services • legal services • consumer advice • housing assistance • vocational counseling, training, and placement • substance abuse programs • remedial education • respite care • homemaker service • day care • socialization/recreation programs • psychological evaluations • advocacy services • transportation								
4. Use of informal supports (relatives, neighbors, or community people) to help parents		X	O					

TABLE 2: Parent Involvement—Placement *(continued)*

Description of Activity, Task, Service, Program	Type of Program[1]	Parents[2]	Workers[3]	Children[4]	Foster Parents	Child Care Staff[5]	Other Agency Staff[6]	Other Community Resources[7]
5. Use parent-child visits to update child's situation (re. school, friends, and activities); enhance skill development for parenting (e. g., accompany children to medical and dental appointments, bathing, feeding, and dressing); share recreational time with child (go on excursions to parks, zoos, on picnics or shopping)	FH	X	O	X	O			
	RP					O		
6. Supplement parent-child visits with: • letters • cards • notes • videotapes/movies (if appropriate) • photos of the family • homemade birthday and holiday cards and gifts		X		X				

TABLE 2: Parent Involvement—Placement (continued)

Description of Activity, Task, Service, Program	Type of Program[1]	Parents[2]	Workers[3]	Children[4]	Foster Parents	Child Care Staff[5]	Other Agency Staff[6]	Other Community Resources[7]
7. Child's caretaker facilitates parent-child visits by: • cooperating with the visiting plan • explaining importance to child • providing transportation	FH	X		X	X			
	RP					X		
8. Meetings of cottage staff and children at residential centers to discuss and resolve complaints and make cottage rules		O		X		X		
9. Use parent-foster parent/parent-child care worker contact to: • share decisions about child's clothing, toys, diet, schedules, chores, discipline, and religious education • share child's progress directly	FH	X	O	O	X			O
	RP					X		

TABLE 2: Parent Involvement—Placement (*continued*)

Description of Activity, Task, Service, Program	Type of Program[1]	Parents[2]	Workers[3]	Children[4]	Foster Parents	Child Care Staff[5]	Other Agency Staff[6]	Other Community Resources[7]
• serve as role models/teachers • reinforce positive parental behavior by giving genuine praise and compliments and support, and by being understanding • accompany parents to school conferences • refer parents to community resources • accompany parents to parent-ed. classes • include parents in special meals, birthday and holiday celebrations, important occasions, and special outings • assist parents in making family trees, scrapbooks, etc.								
10. Case conferences at regular intervals to evaluate family's situation	FH	X	X	X	X		O	
	RP					X	O	O

TABLE 2: Parent Involvement—Placement (continued)

Description of Activity, Task, Service, Program	Type of Program[1]	Parents[2]	Workers[3]	Children[4]	Foster Parents	Child Care Staff[5]	Other Agency Staff[6]	Other Community Resources[7]
11. Internal review to ensure that case plans have been made and are being implemented	FH	X	X	X	O		O	O
	RP					O		
12. External review (judicial, citizen) at legislated intervals of family's situation and decisions made about permanent plan	FH	X	X	X	O		O	O
	RP					O		
13. Formulate and implement discharge plan when decision is made that the child should return home	FH	X	X	X	X		O	O
	RP				O	X		
14. If decision is reached that child cannot return home, help parents accept and adjust to the idea of alternative permanent plan	FH	X	X					
	RP					O		

TABLE 2: Parent Involvement—Placement (*continued*)

Description of Activity, Task, Service, Program	Type of Program[1]	Parents[2]	Workers[3]	Children[4]	Foster Parents	Child Care Staff[5]	Other Agency Staff[6]	Other Community Resources[7]
15. Discuss and decide on alternative placement plan when return home is not possible	FH	X	X	X	X		O	O
	RP					X		
16. If child continues in placement in accordance with a plan for permanence, determine whether parental contact with child and substitute caretakers should continue	FH	X	X	X	X			
	RP					X		

Programs for Parents:
17. A viable grievance mechanism for parents' complaints
18. Support network for parents with children entering care; parents' committee or organization; parents' newsletter
19. Live-in arrangement for parents at residential settings at specified times to provide additional time for parents to observe child-caring practices
20. Parent Loan Fund to be used for funds for carfare for visits, meetings, and events

Additional Ways of Involving Parents:
21. Special events for parents and children; e.g., Parents' Night, lawn festivals, open houses, and parties
22. Parent involvement in educating and training new workers and new foster parents
23. Parent involvement in helping to recruit new foster parents
24. Parent involvement in making recommendations to policy-makers and legislative committees concerned with foster care

TABLE 3: Parent Involvement—Postplacement

	Description of Activity, Task, Service, Program	Type of Program[1]	Parents[2]	Workers[3]	Children[4]	Foster Parents	Child Care Staff[5]	Other Agency Staff[6]	Other Community Resources[7]
1.	Provide aftercare services for a specified period of time after the child has returned home: • support • assist with adjustment • help resolve problems		X	X	X				
2.	Supplement in-person parent-worker contact with calls		X	X					
3.	Arrange for services to parents and their families and serve as liaison, coordinator, advocate and/or broker between parents and other service providers: • parent education classes • parent support groups and self-help groups • individual, group, family, and marital counseling • parent aides and volunteers		X	X					X

TABLE 3: Parent Involvement—Postplacement *(continued)*

Description of Activity, Task, Service, Program	Type of Program[1]	Parents[2]	Workers[3]	Children[4]	Foster Parents	Child Care Staff[5]	Other Agency Staff[6]	Other Community Resources[7]
• financial assistance • medical services • legal services • consumer advice • housing assistance • vocational counseling, training, and placement • substance abuse programs • remedial education • respite care • homemaker service • day care • socialization/recreation programs • psychological evaluations • advocacy services								
4. Use of informal supports (relatives, neighbors, or community people) to help parents		X	O					X

TABLE 3: Parent Involvement—Postplacement *(continued)*

Description of Activity, Task, Service, Program	Type of Program[1]	Parents[2]	Workers[3]	Children[4]	Foster Parents	Child Care Staff[5]	Other Agency Staff[6]	Other Community Resources[7]
5. Secure information concerning parent progress on a regular basis from service providers, with parental permission		X	X					X
6. If child leaves placement setting but a relationship has developed between parents and child's substitute caretakers, determine if continued contacts between parents, substitute caretakers, and child are viable, and if so, what they should be like	FH	X	X	X	X			
	RP					X		

INTRODUCTION TO CHAPTERS 3 AND 4

As indicated in the previous chapters, the range of services required by parents with children in foster care can place excessive demands on an agency's resources. Yet parents must receive these services to resolve the problems that resulted in placement and to ensure that children can return home to their families or, when that is not possible, to benefit from alternative permanent plans.

Chapters 3 and 4 describe two processes essential to the provision of services to families—case management and interagency coordination. In chapter 3, Victor Pike presents the case management process, which facilitates the coordination of all resources working with, and in behalf of, a family, and enhances, according to specified time frames, decision making, task accomplishment, and services provision. Pike defines and describes the case management process, examines the use of teams in case management, and discusses the characteristics and responsibilities of case managers.

As agencies identify the variety of services needed by families, they often find themselves unable to provide those services directly. While retaining primary responsibility for the child, they refer families to other programs for additional resources or services. Several agencies may simultaneously be responsible for providing services to a child and his or her family. The development of interagency coordination facilitates the case management process.

In chapter 4, Karen Schimke offers a broader picture of management—the coordination of working arrangements among agencies. She describes the administrative process for establishing and strengthening interagency coordination. Some of the case management components discussed in chapter 3 are also important to this process. For example, assessment of the service needs of individual families in case management is similar to the identification of resources needed by the types of clients served by the agency and for the development of interagency coordination. Also, just as worker and parents must formulate a written agreement before services are provided (to specify the objectives, goals, responsibilities, and time frames), linkages among agencies should be formalized through written interagency agreements before clients are referred from one agency to another.

Through case management, a worker can effectively identify and coordinate the resources needed by an individual family in order to achieve permanency for a child. Establishing interagency relationships facilitates the provision of a range of services from a variety of provider agencies. But neither of these processes can be undertaken without administrative action, support, and guidance.

3
CASE MANAGEMENT

Victor Pike

I was talking with a 4-year-old foster child who had come into placement when he was 2. I asked him how old he was and he replied, "Four years old." I asked him how long he had lived with his foster parents, and he said, "Fourteen years."

The child's sense of time should be a compelling force in foster care permanent planning.[1] A middle-aged adult remembers the past 5 years as having slipped by with astounding speed, but 6 months is 25% of a 2-year-old's life time. Each year, thousands of foster children reach chronological maturity while parents "intend" to return and workers "intend" to make a plan for the child.

In social work, we talk of interminable foster care as "keeping children in limbo." In fact, no child actually remains in limbo. As time continues, children absorb their surroundings, emulate those around them, incorporate behavior caused by fear and anxiety, and defend against repeated disruption. These experiences influence their development; the results of their experiences may be modified but never undone.[2]

In the past decade, because of a growing awareness of the negative consequences of unplanned foster care for children and their parents, an understanding of the child's sense of time, and knowledge of the numbers of children who experience unplanned foster care, child welfare professionals realized that major changes within the foster care system were necessary. The primary change, a goal-oriented and time-limited process for achieving permanence for children, has been referred to as *case management*.

Historically, case management carried a negative connotation to many professional social workers.[3] It was considered mechanical, devoid of sensitivity, and lacking in the interpersonal relationship that is the essence of social work practice. Case management has been viewed as a series of tasks requiring little professional skill or training. In fact, however, management of a situation in which family members are separated involves a considerable number of complex and professional skills (fig. 3.0).

Chapter 1 examined the reasons why parent involvement has not occurred and why it is essential in order to move children into permanent homes. Workers must aggressively involve parents to ensure that children can return home to their families or, if that is not possible, to benefit from alternative permanent plans. Case management can ensure that parent involvement occurs, thereby increasing the chances of providing secure and stable environments to children. Essentially, case management is good social work practice. It facilitates the coordination of all resources working with, or in behalf of, a family, and enhances decision making, task accomplishment, and service provision according to specified time frames.[5] In this chapter, the case management process is defined and described, the characteristics and responsibilities of case managers are discussed, and the use of teams in case management is examined.

THE CASE MANAGEMENT PROCESS

Case management is a process of linking, coordinating, and monitoring various segments of a service delivery system to ensure the most comprehensive program for meeting a family's needs.[6] In foster care, this process facilitates the achievement of objectives in a timely fashion that will result in the implementation of the best permanent plan for the child. The case management process involves six components:

1. assessing the family situation by using all available information;
2. developing a service plan that identifies an outcome, objectives, responsibilities, and time frames;
3. involving and coordinating all appropriate agency and community resources in behalf of the family;
4. monitoring the provision of services and the accomplishment of tasks, and evaluating progress or the lack of it in carrying out objectives defined in the service plan;
5. implementing the permanent plan;
6. documenting all activities, tasks, and services concerning the implementation of the permanent plan.

These components are not discrete and orderly; for example, the assessment of information and documentation of interactions occur throughout the entire process.

FIGURE 3.0
One View of Case Management

People ask whether case management is social work or merely paperwork. I say it's one method of social work practice, one that involves working with and through other providers on behalf of a client.[4]

The first part of this chapter briefly describes these components. More detailed information is available in the literature.[7]

Assessment

Assessment has been described as the cornerstone of sound social work practice and is especially important in child welfare situations in which decision making and choosing services have critical consequences.[8] An assessment should produce the information necessary for case planning to occur. It requires the identification of:

- *problems and needs* of the parents and child—the extent, severity, and duration[9]
- *strengths and assets*[10] of the individuals involved that can be used to resolve problems and meet needs
- *available resources*[11]

Case management begins when a case first reaches intake. Except in desertion cases, parents are available, facts are fresh, complacency has not set in, and above all, the relationship between parents and the child has not become jaded by long periods of minimal contact.

Parents are the most critical source of assessment information. What the parents tell, how they say it, how much responsibility they accept for problems, how often they project problems onto others—these are all factors that indicate how working with parents will proceed. Additional information may come from the child depending on his or her age or maturity. The worker should also examine agency records, police and court reports, and other social agency information, and communicate with relatives, friends, teachers, and other individuals familiar to the family.[12]

Development of a Service Plan

When information and an understanding of the family's situation have been gained, service planning can begin. Important and often difficult decisions must be made during the initial service planning that require judgments about future events and taking risks.[13] Although one worker is responsible for ensuring that decisions are made, the decisions should not be made alone. Responsibility for decision making can and should be shared with others who also have knowledge and insight about the case (see subsection on Teams, p. 89). At a minimum, this includes the family members. It is also likely to involve other agency personnel (e.g., supervisors and foster parents) and staff members from other community agencies.

During initial service planning, the following decisions must be made:

- the initial *goal or outcome* of the foster care service—for example, return home or adoption by foster parents[14] (this goal may change over time as new information is acquired)
- the specific *objectives* that must be achieved to attain the outcome—for example, the parents must attend a parenting skills class at the local community center and receive a passing grade (see figs. 3.1 and 3.2)
- the *time frame* for objectives and goal attainment[15]—for example, the parents must attend the parenting skills class twice a week for 8 weeks and receive a passing grade
- the *roles and responsibilities* of agency staff, community resources, parents, and children—for example, the worker is responsible for identifying the parenting skills class and arranging tuition payment, transportation, and child care; the parents are responsible for regularly attending the class, preparing the child for the sitter, and reporting progress to the worker

These decisions about outcome, objectives, time frames, and responsibilities must be incorporated into written documents. Putting decisions into writing offers the following advantages:

1. It facilitates service interactions by clarifying the purposes and conditions of giving and receiving services, delineating roles and tasks, ordering priorities, and allocating time constructively.[17]
2. It establishes expectations that might later be distorted, denied, or confused.[18] It provides a mechanism by which the parents can hold the agency accountable for the provision of services and a document for the agency to use in court (in termination of parental rights proceedings) if the parents have not fulfilled their responsibilities.
3. It provides a baseline for periodically reviewing accomplishments, assessing progress, and examining the conditions of the agreement.[19]

FIGURE 3.1
Criteria for Selection of Objectives

1. *Specific:* Objectives must be stated in specific, not global terms.
    Example: Mrs. Smith will attend a parent education class on adolescents once a week for 10 weeks.
2. *Measurable:* Objectives must be selected so that progress toward attainment can be measured.
3. *Realistic:* Any objective selected must be realistic and attainable for the parents and their current situation.
4. *Understandable:* Objectives must be stated in such a way that they are understandable to everyone involved in the planning process.
5. *Priority:* The selection of an objective must reflect certain priorities. Depending upon the situation, this may mean starting with the objective of alleviating the most serious difficulty, or selecting an area easier to change than the more serious problem.
6. *Cost Benefit:* The selected objective should be worth the efforts of all concerned for the possible benefits to be derived by the family.
7. *Timing:* The objective must be one that can be achieved in the time available.
8. *Consequence:* The anticipated consequences to the parents if objectives are not achieved must be clear.
9. *Acceptable:* The selected objectives must be acceptable to both client and worker.
10. *Resources:* There must be resources available to achieve the agreed-upon objectives.
11. *Flexibility:* Selection of an objective should reflect an awareness of possible changing circumstances. Often circumstances render objectives inappropriate or unattainable.
12. *Barriers:* Barriers to attaining objectives must be identified and decisions made about how they can be overcome.[16]

---

4. It gives the participants a sense of immediate involvement and meaningful participation and signifies their mutual commitment and readiness to assume responsibility.[20]

Service plans,[21] written agreements,[22] and behavioral contracts[23] may be used to document decisions; "visiting contracts" can be used to focus specifically on the crucial issue of parent-child visiting. Sometimes these forms may be used alone, often together (see appendix B for samples of each). Service plans are usually longer and more general, and include assessment information. They usually do not include measurable, time-limited specific objectives. Written agree-

FIGURE 3.2
Objectives that Relate to Parent Involvement:

- increased parent-child communication
- improvement in the management of financial resources in relation to providing for a family's physical and social needs
- development of appropriate expectations for and disciplinary techniques to use with children
- improvement in the family's ability to use community resources to meet needs
- improvement in the safety, organization, and cleanliness of the household
- improvement or resolution of a drinking problem that caused abuse of the child

ments and behavioral contracts are generally more limited in focus and time duration and contain a select group of objectives for parent and service-provider attention. In deciding which format to use, or whether to develop a document that combines particular strengths of the different documents, agencies will have to determine what works best for them.

Initial planning decisions require information that may not be available until assessment is well under way. It is essential, however, that these decisions are made as soon as possible after the child is placed in care.[24] In nonemergency situations, assessment should have occurred before placement; in these cases, initial service planning should be completed within a week of the placement date. In emergency placements, it should still be possible to formulate a service plan within 30 days of placement.[25]

Coordination of Resources

To meet the multiple needs of parents and children, a range of services from a variety of agencies and community resources is needed (see fig. 3.3). Coordinating the activities of all parties involved in a case is essential to effective case management. The goals of coordination are to

- arrange for, and monitor, the delivery of all services deemed essential to accomplish a service plan

FIGURE 3.3
Maintaining Contact with Service Providers

Contact with other providers should be maintained at least monthly and in times of crisis or unusual circumstances, on a weekly basis. Such regular contact will keep the worker informed as to whether, and how, the family is using services. Although relationships and procedures for collaboration with other agencies will have been established at the administrative level, it is up to the worker to establish a working relationship with the agency worker providing services to the client assigned to his or her care. The agency worker should feel that he or she can call the social service worker at any time, that it is not necessary to wait for the regular check-in telephone calls. Another option is to meet with staff from the various agencies that may be involved in a case. Personal contacts are most important in developing and maintaining relationships; many problems can be worked out when all participating agencies meet together to discuss the case.[27]

- provide the services in a timely manner in recognition of the need to arrive at, and accomplish, a permanent plan in the earliest stages of a child's placement
- avoid the duplication of services
- collect, summarize, and report all data regarding progress or failure in attainment of the objectives[26]

Chapter 4 is an examination of the process for establishing interagency coordination and cooperation.

When more than one agency or more than one worker is involved in a decision-making process, the issue of confidentiality must be addressed. There must be written agreement that the treating professional will provide the worker with verbal and written communications concerning the parents' progress in treatment and will participate as a team member. When court hearings are necessary, the professional accepting the referral must be willing to testify. Some social workers fear that this violates the parents' right to confidentiality.[28] Two factors, however, should be considered. First, before treatment and service relationships are established, all parties, including the parents, are advised that "traditional" confidentiality cannot be maintained if achievement of objectives is to be evaluated. Second, in reporting progress or failure, the service provider should not have to divulge the personal communications between the parents and himself or herself.

Monitoring and Evaluation

Monitoring is the continual tracking of the case and evaluation of progress toward the agreed-upon outcomes. Its purpose is to obtain accurate, timely information about the success or failure of service-planning efforts.[29] Monitoring requires workers to obtain information from parents and service providers about the delivery of services and the accomplishment of tasks. It enables workers to answer the questions: Are all needed services being provided to the child and his or her family in accordance with the service plan? Are time frames being adhered to? If the service has been unsuccessful, or if the parents have been unable to accomplish a designated task, the reasons for this must be explored. In this case, the evaluation is likely to lead to a modification of objectives, time frames, and/or responsibilities. Original objectives and time frames may have been unrealistic. Services believed to be available for client use may not have been (see fig. 3.4).

Thus, monitoring and evaluation are ongoing processes for reassessing service needs, service planning, and service delivery. They stimulate goal-oriented decision making about the child's permanent placement. Monitoring can occur during regularly scheduled parent-worker conferences and periodic calls to service providers. Evaluation can take place informally during conferences and calls, but is likely to be a more formalized process occurring at specified intervals during case conferences involving the key parties.[30] Internal case review epitomizes formalized evaluation. Aggressive and persistent case management should result in more "positive" internal and external review findings.

Implementing the Permanent Plan

If an accurate assessment of the family situation has been made, appropriate services have been identified and coordinated, progress or the lack of it toward achievement of objectives has been monitored and evaluated, and modifications in the provisions of the service plan have been made when needed, then the choice of the appropriate permanent placement plan should become clear by the time the child has been in care for 6 months.[32] A final decision, however, regarding return home or an alternative permanent arrangement must be made within 9 months to 1 year. This decision may differ from the goal or outcome identified in the initial service plan. This new goal would be based upon the results of the monitoring and evaluation process.

The implementation of any permanent planning goal or outcome

FIGURE 3.4
Using Evaluation

A word needs to be said about what is to be evaluated. The only parts of the client relationship which can be evaluated are the objectives and steps mutually agreed on by you and your client in the service plan/agreement. These are to be evaluated for the purpose of discerning a future direction to take. The client's personality is not to be evaluated. Neither are facts which occurred prior to the case, creating the problem, etc. Also, the evaluation is to be conducted mutually by you and your client. After all, if your client helped develop his/her objectives and his/her part of an agreement, s/he certainly has a right to the feedback.[31]

---

requires taking many steps and accomplishing many tasks.[33] For example, if the goal is return to parents, the frequency and duration of parent-child visits should be increased. If the goal is adoption, voluntary surrender of parental rights should be discussed with parents and a decision obtained from them within a specified time period. Thus, during implementation, the worker is responsible for coordinating, initiating, sustaining, and monitoring essential activities.

Documentation

Although service plans and written agreements establish the goal, objectives, responsibilities, and time frames, the case record must also include documentation of the service program (see fig. 3.5) and any other information germane to the case situation. There are many reasons why continuing documentation is important. Recording

- establishes a continuing record of family involvement, casework action, and parental behavior that will support a plan to return a child home or be admissable evidence in court if a termination hearing is indicated;
- enables a worker to keep track of the many activities that characterize permanency planning, to recall all essential facts about the case, and to prevent cases from getting lost;
- enables a worker to think clearly about a case and facilitates problem solving and decision making;
- is an important way of communicating significant case information to others. If the worker leaves, recording prevents unnecessary

FIGURE 3.5
Documenting the Service Program

- Detailed and documented description of problems related to placement of the child; current parental problems that may be barriers to a return home
- Substance of plan arrived at between parents and agency to effectuate child's return to parents within a reasonable time, and all dates on which implementation of plan was discussed with parents (e.g., parents to relocate to larger apartment, mother to finish school, father to join Alcoholics Anonymous, etc.)
- Periodic reassessment of parents' progress; reevaluation of service plan at six-month intervals
- Dates and description of any services facilitated by worker to assist parents in achieving planning goal (psychological evaluation; medical care; work, educational, drug/alcohol referral; homemaking or counseling)
- Dates and places of all parent appointments, with worker or other persons, including:
  — Appointments kept by parents (prompt or late arrival by parents, summary of meeting)
  — Appointments canceled (How? Reason given)
  — Appointments not kept (Reason given)
- Dates and places of all scheduled child-parent visits, including:
  — Visits kept by parents (Were parents prompt or late?)
  — Was reunion successful? (If not, why not?)
  — Visits canceled (How? When? Effect on waiting child)
- Dates and descriptions of all parent-child communications (Christmas cards, gifts, etc.)
- Dates and descriptions of any efforts made by worker to locate parents during any period of time when parental whereabouts may have been unknown to agency
- Dates, places, and reasons for any parental hospitalization, incarceration, or institutionalization during period of child's placement
- Dates and copies of letters from agency to parents and of letters from parents to agency
- Dates and content of all telephone communication between agency and parents (Who initiated telephone calls?)
- Dates of all home visits made by worker (scheduled or unscheduled, summaries)
- Any adjustments in the service plan, recorded as they occur[36]

repetition of past events and actions and enables mutually agreed-upon objectives to proceed smoothly without undue hardship on the client. Recording permits supervisory review and assessment of the appropriateness of service plans. It also provides accountability to administrators and clients.[34]

Documentation is most useful when it is accurate and factual, relevant, concise and specific, complete, clear and understandable, and current.[35] Good documentation strengthens each component of the case management process.

Advocacy

Advocacy in behalf of both parents and child is likely to be necessary throughout the case management process because so many individuals are responsible for the outcome of the case. Workers often have to intercede on the parents' behalf to obtain initial commitments from community resources for services to parents and/or to mediate problems that arise during service provision. Furthermore, when the service plan is not being adhered to and the agreed-upon results are not being achieved, the worker must try to overcome the barriers to successful intervention.

Working with other service providers requires the worker to be an advocate in the child's behalf. All service providers must understand the child's sense of time, the effects of foster care limbo, and the need for reasonable speed in achieving the permanent plan.[37] Working with parents cannot be an interminable process; time frames must be adhered to and decisions made about the futures of children.

THE CASE MANAGER

The use of the case management approach in foster care requires that there be an individual who is responsible for ensuring that, in each case, the essential steps in the process are accomplished within specified time limits.[38] This individual is the case manager. The case manager directs the efforts of all the individuals involved in the case. These other individuals actively participate in planning, service provision, evaluation and decision making, as a team (see next section, Teams in Case Management), facilitating the case manager's job. Where teams are not used, the case manager must assume major responsibility for assessment, planning, coordination, monitoring, and evaluation. Although the manager still relies upon other individuals for achievement of objectives and consultation concerning critical decisions, the lack of a formal team structure may diminish their contributions.

The job that must be performed by the case manager is extremely demanding and requires many sophisticated skills. Skills can be categorized into four broad areas: organizational, relationship, analytical, and administrative.[39] Examples of each follow.

Organizational Skills

The case manager must be able to

- link family members to appropriate community resources and ensure that they receive services promptly
- assemble a case management team by identifying those individuals who should be a part of the team and obtaining their commitment to the team effort
- coordinate the activities of the members of the team so that they support one another's efforts in behalf of the family while minimizing duplication of effort
- set priorities for proceeding with the case, guide the decision-making process, bring consensus among a variety of opinions, and identify next steps during team meetings
- monitor any activities impeding case movement and facilitate them if at all possible (see fig. 3.6)

Relationship Skills

The case manager must be able to

- establish a supportive, facilitating, and forthright relationship with parents
- clarify with the parents the agency's expectations and explain to them the consequences of their behavior
- motivate continued parent participation during the time the child is in care
- accept client differences and work with people of different lifestyles
- assist parents in understanding the need to provide a child with a permanent family even if it results in ultimate separation
- be familiar with other staff members in community agencies to facilitate the cooperative nature of the treatment
- infuse case participants with encouragement and a sense of progress when they are discouraged, pessimistic, or apathetic (see fig. 3.7)

FIGURE 3.6
The Importance of Organizational Competence

A particular case seemed at first to concern 6 people: a mother and a father, their 2 children, a third child conceived out of wedlock, and that child's father. The children were in foster care, which involved 4 foster parents. The legal father was referred for alcohol treatment and job training. The mother was enrolled in parent education classes, received homemaker assistance, and was transported to visits by an aide. A psychologist evaluated the two siblings; the half-sibling was examined by a neurologist for motor coordination problems. Because the foster parents of this third child wanted to adopt, they were evaluated at a family clinic. The mother's parents, through their attorney, requested custody of the two older children. Ultimately, 24 people were involved in this case. This number, multiplied by a caseload, emphasizes the need for organizational competence.

Analytical Skills

The case manager must be able to

- identify those family problems and needs that are detrimental to the child and might impede reunification of the family
- identify all existing and potential family strengths
- identify appropriate formal and informal community resources capable of alleviating common parental problems and be committed to work in a team effort
- develop a service plan that considers assessment information and identifies desired outcome, objectives, and responsibilities of all participants, and time frames
- verify the accuracy of information obtained during the early part of placement by seeking additional sources of information
- evaluate the degree to which service provision and task accomplishment are resulting in achievement of specific objectives
- consider diverse opinions from a variety of professional disciplines and weigh them within the context of the child's needs
- determine when consultation from specialists is needed

Administrative Skills

The case manager must be able to

FIGURE 3.7
The Importance of Relationship Skills

In another case, a 5-year-old child had been in foster care for 3 years while his mother moved, visited sporadically, and experimented with drugs. Several workers had verbally admonished her to "shape up" but, eventually, permanent planning staff members apprised her of the prospects of losing the child and, concurrently, negotiated an explicit, written service agreement. Within 6 months, the child was home. In a follow-up interview, the mother commented that the permanent planning worker was the first agency person who (1) warned her that termination of parental rights could result, and (2) gave her specific direction and then support toward the return of her child.

- keep track of a great many activities and tasks identified in the service plan by obtaining information regularly from service providers and parents
- share important information with all team members
- make decisions, either independently or based on group participation
- prepare written service agreements or contracts with parents
- prepare for, call, and conduct team meetings
- maintain records with precise documentation
- use time effectively and efficiently
- ensure that time does not elapse needlessly because of a lack of direction for subsequent case planning
- arrange for consultation if needed, direct the nature of the consultation, and be responsible for obtaining timely reports

The case manager must be knowledgeable about the permanency planning process and committed to the philosophy of permanence for every child. He or she must be decisive, tenacious, goal-oriented, direct, and honest, with a sense of urgency and willingness to take risks. He or she must also be very familiar with the agency's operation, community resources, relevant state and federal laws, and the court process.

The case manager is not the primary treatment person, although, as indicated above, he or she has an important and essential relationship with the parents. One individual's skills cannot cover the spectrum of needs presented in most cases, nor is there sufficient time for one person to provide all the required services.

The case manager may be the protective services worker, the foster care caseworker, the parents' worker, the child's worker, the permanency planning worker, or the supervisor, depending upon the agency in which the case management process is being carried out. The selection is an important one for administrators. In some states, the choice may be simplified because a single worker has responsibility for all aspects of the foster care case.

In other locations, primary case responsibility is shared between a parents' worker (responsible for working with the parents) and a child's or foster care worker (who manages the foster care placement).[40] When there are two workers, the parents' worker is more likely to be the case manager. Because the parents usually require the majority of services when a child enters care, the worker assigned to the parents becomes responsible for ensuring that the parents' needs are met, and therefore is the most appropriate individual to manage the case.

As mentioned above, the relationship that develops between the parents' worker and the parents is a critical one. The case manager, as the parents' worker, helps parents understand that he or she is prepared to support them, locate and obtain the commitment of resources, and do whatever is possible and necessary to help children return home. If it becomes clear, however, that return home will not be possible because the essential changes cannot or will not be made, the parents' worker is obligated to work toward another permanent home for the child.

Although this approach may seem threatening and obstructive to forming a productive relationship between the worker and parents, permanent planning practice has established the viability of this approach.[41] Honesty and forthrightness in advising parents of the reality of their situation—that time is of the essence for their child— enhances the relationship instead of threatening it. Candor eradicates previous uncertainty and mystification. Parents know what is expected of them and what will happen if changes do not occur. When parents observe that the worker directly makes or facilitates efforts to reunite their family it becomes easier for them to consider releasing their child for adoption when essential changes cannot be made (see fig. 3.8).

The fact that confidentiality cannot be assured need not pose real problems. Parents understand that the use of other resources is contingent on the willingness of resource persons to report regular progress or the lack of it. In addition, it is clear that the worker is responsible for sharing important, relevant information with other team members.

In summary, the case manager as parents' worker is responsible for

FIGURE 3.8
The Importance of the Parent-Worker Relationship

I recall a case in which we made referrals and coordinated a treatment program for an alcoholic mother with a child in foster care. After a year of intensive services, throughout which the mother's dependence on alcohol never diminished, the worker, despite clamorous objections from the mother, filed a petition to terminate, causing great trauma for the mother, who then voluntarily turned to the worker for help in accepting the loss of her child. To maintain a productive relationship with the parent during this episode required the utmost sophistication on the part of the worker.

- supporting and encouraging parents and sustaining them during difficult times
- explaining to parents the importance of permanent families for children and the need to develop a plan, make decisions, and resolve problems quickly
- explaining to parents their responsibilities and the case management process, as well as the consequences of not following through with responsibilities
- ensuring that parents are receiving needed and planned services
- discussing the parents' progress with them and with other resources while continually evaluating and documenting their progress

TEAMS IN CASE MANAGEMENT

Traditionally, a social service team is a group of individuals working together under a team leader who is responsible for coordinating their efforts to accomplish the objectives and goals for each case.[42] Each team member brings a particular expertise or competence to bear on the case situation. The team members may share decision-making responsibilities, or each member may be assigned specific cases for which he or she makes the decisions.

A new concept of the team has emerged, however, in conjunction with permanency planning and case management. For each case situation, a *unique* group of individuals works together to ensure that the foster child is provided with a "stable, healthy growth-producing environment" as rapidly as possible.[43] This case management team has taken different forms. In one state, the team always consists of the parents, foster care worker, foster parent, foster child (if appropriate), a representative of the court, and the protective services (family) worker. Other individuals with information necessary to creating a successful placement plan may be included as well.[44] In another state, the team always includes agency social workers and the parents; it may also consist of the child, foster parents, child care workers, relatives, attorneys, and friends.[45] Some team members attend all team meetings; others attend when specifically invited to share information and participate in the decision-making process. The number of agency workers on a team will depend on how the case comes to the attention of the agency initially (e.g., if it came through the protective services unit, the protective services worker will be present) and whether the agency assigns one or more workers to cover each case once the child is in care (i.e., whether a single worker is responsible for the entire foster care case, or case responsibility is divided between a worker assigned to the parents and another assigned to the foster parents and child).[46]

Several purposes and responsibilities of case management teams have been identified. Their major purpose is to ensure that a permanent plan is implemented as quickly as possible for every foster child. To do this, the team is responsible for

- formulating a service plan based on information obtained during assessment
- sharing information about service delivery and task accomplishment
- evaluating the degree to which objectives are achieved
- revising service plans when indicated
- deciding which permanent plan will best meet the needs of the child and parents

Although one worker can carry out these responsibilities, there are many advantages to using teams that include parents, foster parents, child care workers, and children:

1. A greater range of expertise and creative imagination can be brought to bear in considering alternative courses of action and providing services.
2. Individual workers are relieved of the sole, overwhelming responsibility of making critical decisions about the futures of children.
3. Responsible risks are more likely to be undertaken when a number of individuals share responsibility for decisions and their consequences.

4. The likelihood of individual bias, prejudice, values, and judgment error is substantially minimized.
5. Even when case movement is discouragingly slow or other setbacks thwart progress, there will be team members who maintain optimism, dispel apathy, and sustain momentum—that is, there is a greater likelihood of continual mutual moral support.
6. Accountability is enhanced because progress or the lack of movement is visible to several concerned individuals.
7. Knowledge and skills of individual workers can be enhanced by increased exposure to additional experts.
8. Families are more likely to act upon suggestions made when they hear a consistent message from several different individuals.
9. If a worker leaves, the impact on the progress of the case is minimized because other individuals are familiar with the plan.
10. Worker turnover and absenteeism are reduced because morale improves substantially as a result of the team process.[47]

These potential advantages are far more likely to be realized when several basic elements exist. First, team members must share common values and assumptions about the nature of foster care service, permanent planning goals, and the rights and needs of children and parents. Second, individual members must respect each other's skills and knowledge. Third, the roles and responsibilities of each team member must be clearly spelled out and understood by everyone. And finally, the team atmosphere must be conducive to discussion and criticism.

Although there are many advantages to case management teams, they are not a panacea for all problems in foster care. And there are difficulties associated with the use of teams that must be considered and addressed before forming them:

1. Control over the particular composition of a team is limited. Team members may be unable to work together, or there may be individuals with strong personalities who will not consider the opinions of others.
2. There are always logistical problems—time commitments, coordinating of schedules and expenses (e.g., for travel)—that make it difficult for team members to meet.
3. It may be difficult to work efficiently and reach consensus on important questions when so many points of view must be taken into account.
4. Many workers are fearful of having their work examined or questioned by others.
5. Parents may be unable or unwilling to participate in team meetings because they are fearful or hostile.

6. The volume of case detail that must be communicated to all team members can become unmanageable.
7. Elitist attitudes held by different professionals may impede the teamwork process or intimidate the team leader.
8. The family's right to confidentiality cannot be assured during team meetings.[48] (See p. 80.)

Some of these difficulties may arise even after efforts have been made to alleviate them. In that circumstance, problems must be weighed against potential benefits.

SUMMARY

The problem of children in unplanned foster care is both a professional and a community responsibility. A complacent attitude toward parents can no longer be maintained. Sensitive but aggressive case management can provide a means by which foster children can achieve the stability and continuity of permanent placements, and it offers the greatest opportunity for parents to be successful in the parenting role. The case manager is *not* the primary provider of treatment, although he or she needs to have a supportive relationship with parents. With speed and accuracy, the case manager must assess family problems and have a comprehensive knowledge of community treatment resources for referral. He or she must manage a treatment process that often involves significant numbers of community professionals and then synthesize information obtained to eventually, with group help, arrive at the most acceptable plan for parents and child. He or she must ensure that time is not wasted and that records that facilitate permanent plans are kept. Finally, the case manager must put the plan into effect and continue supporting the family to assure the permanency of the plan.

Considering the number of children in foster care; the impact that long-term, unplanned foster care can have on children; and the fact that the technology of permanent planning and case management is proven and accessible; the foster care worker of the 1980s is in one of the most crucial jobs in social welfare. The work is taxing, and the obstacles are formidable, but the results are productive and gratifying. Despite indicators pointing to reduced funding in the coming decade that translates into limits in services and programs, reductions in the number of foster care placements and lengths of stay in care through good case management will allow quality social work to be sustained.

NOTES

1. For a discussion of the child's sense of time, see Joseph Goldstein, Anna Freud, and Albert Solnit, *Beyond the Best Interests of the Child* (New York, NY: The Free Press, 1973).
2. David Fanshel and Eugene Shinn, *Children in Foster Care—A Longitudinal Investigation* (New York, NY: Columbia University Press, 1978); Alfred Kadushin, *Child Welfare Services*, 3rd ed. (New York, NY: Macmillan, 1980); Ner Littner, *Some Traumatic Effects of Separation and Placement* (New York, NY: Child Welfare League of America, 1956).
3. *Practice Digest*, special section on "Case Management," *Practice Digest* 4 (March 1982): 3-17; Bertram Beck, "A Practitioner's View of Management in Social Work," in *Training Social Welfare Managers: Social Work-Business School Cooperation*, edited by George Brager and Megan McLaughlin (New York, NY: Columbia University School of Social Work, September 1978); Kermit Wiltse, "Education and Training for Child Welfare Practice; The Search for a Better Fit," mimeo., University of California at Berkeley, School of Social Welfare, January 1981; Susan J. Wells, "Case Management and Child Welfare," for Region IX Child Welfare Training Center, UCLA School of Social Welfare, September 1980, 8.
4. This statement was made by Sumiko Hennessy, whose doctoral dissertation was on case management. See *Practice Digest*, "Definitions and Precursors," op. cit., 5.
5. Wells, op. cit., 4.
6. Joanne Dormady and Michele Gatens, *Case Management: Issues and Models* (New York, NY: Board of Social Welfare, 1980), i, 5-6, 23-25. There are a variety of definitions for case management. See also "Definitions and Precursors" in *Practice Digest*, op. cit., 5-6; Wells, op. cit., 2.
7. For example, see Sister Mary Paul Janchill, *Guidelines to Decision-Making in Child Welfare: Case Assessment, Service Planning and Appropriateness of Service Selection* (New York, NY: Human Service Workshops, 1981); C. Anne Finley and Deborah Rothe, *The Handbook for Service Plan Development*, Oklahoma Department of Institutions, Social and Rehabilitative Services, n.d.; Eileen Gambrill and Theodore Stein, "Decision Making and Case Management: Achieving Continuity of Care for Children in Out-of-Home Placement," in *The Challenge of Partnership: Working with Parents of Children in Foster Care*, edited by Anthony Maluccio and Paula Sinanoglu (New York, NY: Child Welfare League of America, 1981), 109-134; Victor Pike et al., *Permanent Planning for Children in Foster Care: A Handbook for Social Workers*, DHEW Publication No. (OHDS) 77-30124 (Washington, DC: U.S. Department of Health, Education and Welfare, 1977); Esther Dean Callard and Patricia Morin, eds., *PACT—Parents and Children Together: An Alternative to Foster Care* (Detroit, MI: Department of Family and Consumer Resources, Wayne State University, 1979); Wells, op. cit.; Anne V. Bertsche and Charles R. Horejsi, "Coordination for Client Services," *Social Work* 25 (March 1980): 94-98.

94   ESTABLISHING PARENT INVOLVEMENT IN FOSTER CARE AGENCIES

8. Sister Mary Paul Janchill, ibid., 7.
9. Several conceptual frameworks for problem indentification have been developed. See, for example, Sister Mary Paul Janchill, op. cit.; Gambrill and Stein, op. cit.; Pike et al., op. cit.; Callard and Morin, op. cit. These works include charts, forms, and checklists.
10. For examples of these, see Sister Mary Paul Janchill, op. cit.; Callard and Morin, op. cit.; Finley and Rothe, op. cit.
11. See Sister Mary Paul Janchill, op. cit.; Callard and Morin, op. cit., 51-60.
12. For discussion of methods for obtaining assessment information, see Finley and Rothe, op. cit., 15-19; Eileen Gambrill and Theodore Stein, *Supervision in Child Welfare: A Training Manual* (Berkeley, CA: University Extension Publications, June 1978), 99-135.
13. Pike et al., op. cit.; Theodore Stein, Eileen Gambrill, and Kermit Wiltse, *Children in Foster Homes: Achieving Continuity of Care* (New York, NY: Praeger Publishers, 1978), 21.
14. Other goals have been identified. See Pike et al., op. cit; Martha Jones and John Biesecker, *Permanency Planning Guide for Children and Youth Services* (Millersville, PA: Training Resources in Permanent Planning, 1979); Paul Kuczkowski, *Permanent Planning in Maryland: A Manual for the Foster Care Worker* (Baltimore, MD: Maryland Foster Care Impact Demonstration Project, August 1978).
15. Forrest Mercer, *Case Management in Social Services: Foster Care* (Richmond, VA: Virginia Department of Welfare, Division of Social Services, n.d.), VIII-6-VIII-7.
16. This information is adapted from Finley and Rothe, *The Handbook for Service Plan Development*, op. cit., 26-33.
17. Anthony Maluccio and Wilma Marlow, "The Case for the Contract," *Social Work* 19 (Janaury 1974): 28-36; Jim Brady, "Advantages and Problems of Using Written Contracts," *Social Work* 27 (May 1982): 275.
18. John McGowan and Christine Deyss, *Permanency Planning: A Casework Handbook* (New York, NY: Welfare Research Inc., March 1979), 66; Brady, op. cit.
19. Maluccio and Marlow, op. cit., 34-35; Brady, op. cit.
20. Maluccio and Marlow, ibid.; Gambrill and Stein, "Decision Making," op. cit., 115-116.
21. See Callard and Morin, op. cit.; McGowan and Deyss, op. cit., 49-54; Commonwealth of Pennsylvania, "Foster Family Care Service for Children," *Social Services Manual*, Chapter 11, Section 31, Effective Date 7/1/80, 6-8; American Public Welfare Association, *Standards for Foster Family Services Systems for Public Agencies*, DHEW Publication No. (OHDS) 79-30231 (Washington, DC: U.S. Department of Health, Education and Welfare, 1979), 29-31.
22. See Mercer, op. cit., Section VIII; Pike et al., op. cit., 48-52; McGowan and Deyss, op. cit., 66-71; South Carolina Department of Social Services, *Manual of Children and Family Services*, Chapter 08, "Permanency Planning," 1981; Susan Downs and Catherine Taylor, eds., *Permanent Planning in Foster Care: Resources for Training* (Portland, OR: Regional Research Institute for Human Services, 1978), Unit 1, Module 5.

23. See Stein, Gambrill, and Wiltse, op. cit., 114-116, 181-193; Gambrill and Stein, "Decision Making," op. cit., 115-116, 118, 123-125; Maluccio and Marlow, op. cit.; Theodore Stein, Eileen Gambrill, and Kermit Wiltse, "The Use of Contracts," *Public Welfare* 32 (Fall 1974): 20-25.
24. For example, in South Carolina, a first week planning conference with parents is to be held within 5 days from the date of initial placement. See South Carolina, op. cit., 52-53.
25. New York State policy requires this. See Administrative Letter 76-ADM 100; see also American Public Welfare Association, op. cit., 30.
26. Gambrill and Stein, *Supervision*, op. cit., 154-155.
27. Alaska Division of Family and Youth Services, *Program Manual*, n.d., 96.
28. For a discussion of some issues related to confidentiality, see Janet Moore-Kirkland and Karen Vice Irey, "A Reappraisal of Confidentiality," *Social Work* 26 (July 1981): 319-322.
29. Mercer, op. cit., VIII-8.
30. See South Carolina manual, op. cit.
31. Mercer, op. cit., VIII-19.
32. See Kentucky Department of Human Resources, *Community Services to Families and Children: Foster Care*, 1978; Pennsylvania *Social Services Manual*, op. cit.
33. For detailed discussion of implementations, see Pike et al., op. cit.; Jones and Biesecker, op. cit.; South Carolina manual, op. cit.; Kentucky manual, op. cit.
34. These reasons are identified by Finley and Rothe, op. cit., 43-44; McGowan and Deyss, op. cit., 6, 25; Downs and Taylor, op. cit., Section 1.6.3.
35. Finley and Rothe, op. cit., 44-48; Pike et al., op. cit., 8; McGowan and Deyss, op. cit., 38.
36. Cheryl Bradley, *A Caseworker's Guide to the Law of Permanency in New York State* (Albany, NY: School of Social Welfare, State University of New York at Albany, 1978), 56-57.
37. David Fanshel, "Parental Visiting of Children in Foster Care: Key to Discharge?" *Social Service Review* 49 (December 1975), 493-514.
38. See American Public Welfare Association, op. cit., 5-6.
39. This categorization was suggested by "The Skills of the Community Organizer," mimeo. (New York, NY: Columbia University School of Social Work, 1972).
40. For a discussion of sharing case responsibility, see Theodore Stein, Eileen Gambrill, and Kermit Wiltse, "Dividing Case Management in Foster Family Cases," *Child Welfare* LVI (May 1977): 321-331.
41. Stein, Gambrill, and Wiltse, *Children in Foster Homes*, op. cit.; Susan Downs et al., *Foster Care Reform in the 70's: Final Report of the Permanency Planning Dissemination Project* (Portland, OR: Regional Research Institute for Human Services, 1981).
42. Bernice Madison and Michael Schapiro, *New Perspectives on Child Welfare: Services, Staffing, Delivery System* (San Francisco, CA: 1973), 149.
43. Pamela Marr, "Foster Care Teamwork Comes to Kansas," *Case Record* 5 (January 1981): 1-2.

44. Ibid., 2.
45. National Association of Social Workers, "Placement Decided by Team," *Practice Digest* 4 (December 1981): 23-24.
46. Another model is used in Fort Worth, Texas. See Helen Grape, "Fort Worth's Permanent Planning Team," *Case Record* 3 (November 1979): 1, 3-4.
47. Donald Brieland et al., *The Team Model of Social Work Practice* (Syracuse, NY: Syracuse University of Social Work, Division of Continuing Education and Manpower Development, 1973); Marr, op. cit.; Madison and Schapiro, op. cit.; Susan Lonsdale et al., eds., *Teamwork in the Personal Social Services and Health Care: British and American Perspectives* (Syracuse, NY: Syracuse University School of Social Work, Division of Continuing Education and Manpower Development, 1980); Gambrill and Stein, *Supervision*, op. cit., 156; Callard and Morin, op. cit., 20-22; Michael Baugh, "Team-Shared Caseloads—A Way to Survive in Child Protection," *Adoption Report* 7 (Spring 1982): 1,5; Wells, op. cit., 6-7; Grape, ibid.
48. Marr, op. cit., 2; National Association of Social Workers, op. cit.; Baugh, op. cit.

4

INTERAGENCY COOPERATION AND COORDINATION

Karen Schimke

Children enter foster care for many and varied reasons, but parents' problems are often the principal cause.[1] The problems of the parents are often complex, and a range of services is required to ameliorate them. It is unusual for a single child welfare agency to provide all of these services. Most commonly, some of the needed services are available only through formal community resources, such as day care centers, family counseling agencies, mental health or health clinics, drug and alcohol abuse programs, employment counseling, and homemaker programs, and from informal resources such as relatives, neighbors, self-help groups, and community organizations. Moreover, many families are already known to one or more community programs before they become involved with the foster care system.[2]

In addition to the nonavailability of some services, any child welfare worker serving families can report a long list of problems in working with existing service providers.[3] They may be inaccessible because of distance, fees, hours, eligibility requirements, or language barriers. Some caseworkers have stopped trying to organize an array of services for families because they find the coordination problems burdensome and overwhelming.[4] Workers from different agencies may disagree on treatment plans, quibble about outreach, refuse to share information, or mistrust each other's competence. Some existing services may not be known to many of the child welfare workers.

Effective interagency coordination could overcome many of these problems. *Interagency coordination is the formalization, at the administrative level, of linkages among resources. Linkages facilitate the most effective provision of services needed by families to resolve specific problems.* Linkages also ensure communication and cooperation among workers from different agencies. Coordination can "eliminate fragmentation, gaps, and occasional unnecessary duplication in service provisions, enhance access to services generally and improve the delivery of services to the client or consumer."[5]

The process of developing interagency coordination involves

- assessing the service needs of parents and children, and the gaps in existing resources
- formalizing arrangements among agencies regarding the coordination of resources and the cooperation of workers
- developing an inventory of community resources
- facilitating the use of the inventory
- maintaining and evaluating the working relationships, the services, and the inventory

An administrative decision must be made concerning who in the agency is responsible for developing interagency coordination. Each agency, according primarily to its size and resources, will find it necessary to handle job assignments differently. The administrator may have to create a special staff position or assign tasks to program staff members, case managers, and/or supervisors. Interagency coordination requires agency commitment, attention to detail, and administrative oversight to assure that the activities are carried out.

Almost every agency has one or more staff members who are well known around the agency because of their knowledge of community resources. Long before agencies became involved in deliberate, organized efforts to coordinate services, these persons were seen by others as "walking service inventories." This kind of interest and ability can be enhanced through administrative assignments, participation in agency training sessions, and interagency projects. The ability to advance interagency coordination and develop linkages should be rewarded.

Caseworkers benefit from the successful development of interagency coordination. It enables them to effectively identify, coordinate, and monitor the services provided to families. Further, it eliminates "reinventing the wheel" each time a service is needed by a parent. So much of the preliminary work has been done that it is possible for caseworkers to make referrals quickly and successfully without wasting time and energy. Generally, caseworkers should not be given extensive responsibility for agency coordination. However, they must be consulted during the needs assessment process, since they are most familiar with the service needs of families and with many of the existing resources. Caseworkers should also contribute to the design and distribution of the resource inventory, as they will make the most use of it. Finally, because caseworkers work closely with many service programs, they must play a key role in the evaluation of these programs.

Parent involvement in the process of developing interagency coordination is both appropriate and necessary. Families may be in the best position to identify needs, to describe the pros and cons of existing services, and to make suggestions regarding needed services. Parents can contribute to program evaluation during meetings with their caseworkers, through responses to questionnaires and surveys, and during group meetings and parent education classes. Agencies committed to using informal resources to assist parents need parents' help to identify resources and assess their effectiveness.

Many agencies, especially public agencies, have developed mandated planning processes with built-in opportunities for public involvement. Professionals, however, tend to be the most active participants. Since consumers of services are in the best position to react to service delivery, they should be encouraged to participate in the opportunities for involvement.

THE PROCESS OF DEVELOPING INTERAGENCY COORDINATION

The activities necessary to ensure communication, cooperation, and coordination between child welfare agencies and other resources cannot be strictly chronological. Some must be accomplished before others can take place; some can be undertaken simultaneously.

Conducting a Needs Assessment

As noted earlier, a needs assessment in the first step.[6] During the assessment

- service needs of families are identified and described
- available formal and informal community resources are identified and categorized
- service gaps are identified, and a plan for addressing them is developed

The needs assessment is an information-gathering and question-asking process. It is essential that caseworkers and parents be involved in it. In addition, representatives from community agencies, "experts," and any individuals who might be sources of pertinent information should be contacted.

The questions, What do we need? What have we got? What shall we do?, should be answered.

Special attention must be given to understanding service needs that arise because of ethnic and/or cultural diversity.[7] This aspect of the needs assessment is particularly important since such a large proportion of the families served by foster care programs represent many racial, ethnic, and cultural groups. Because many agencies have not overcome obstacles related to cultural differences, some families have not received any services; services that have been received have often been ineffective (see fig. 4.0).

Once service needs are described, resources must be identified that respond to lifestyle and attitudinal differences, and be provided in languages other than English by persons from similar backgrounds.

The second part of the needs assessment involves identifying and categorizing community resources. Careful exploration is required to identify existing formal resources and ascertain whether they can be used by families. The existence of a service does not assure its availability or accessibility. Close examination may reveal long waiting lists, restrictive referral criteria, and long-established practices that prevent entry, such as delayed responses to initial inquiries, and complex application forms. Agencies must look carefully for policies and practices that are likely to prevent parents from using specific resources. Modifying such policies and practices should be proposed during this phase of the needs assessment.

It is especially important to explore all possible services. Families require assistance that cannot be provided by social service agencies alone. Health, educational, legal, and employment resources are examples. Informal resources, such as relatives, neighbors, and community groups, can also meet critical needs of families. A growing body of literature contains details of how informal resources can be found, and descriptions of methods for working with them.[9]

Some rural communities have found ways to adapt already existing resources to help families. For example, banks may provide credit counseling; schools can be tapped for testing, counseling, and other services; and churches may provide food, money, and other resources.[10] (See fig. 4.1).

Once information is obtained about available resources, it can be categorized in a number of ways.[12] For example, resources can be grouped by kinds of services provided, that is, social services, mental health, legal, health, education, and income maintenance. They can be organized by geographic areas or the service needs of families. The categorization must be done carefully, since it forms the framework for the resource inventory.

FIGURE 4.0
The Influence of Cultural Diversity on Service Needs

A young Korean mother was receiving help from a child welfare agency because she was perceived as having problems caring for her baby. The public health nurse was concerned about the mother leaving the baby lying on his back in his crib too often, because his head was becoming flat. The nurse thought this was an indication of child neglect. Another staff member with some background in Oriental culture reviewed the case, and noted the fact that, in some Oriental cultures, a flat head is a sign of beauty and is desirable.[8]

Identifying needed services that are not currently available is the last step of the needs assessment. The development of new programs or the expansion of existing resources becomes necessary. The child welfare agency must decide if it can take responsibility for meeting the unmet needs, or if it is more appropriate to encourage another resource to do so (see chap. 2).

This places the public child welfare agency in a powerful position. It can offer to formalize linkages with responsive organizations, as the following example illustrates (see fig. 4.2).

Public child welfare agencies are in a unique position in their communities to encourage program development and/or modification in order to eliminate gaps in existing services.

Formalizing Linkages Among Agencies

Once community resources have been identified and evaluated, the agency is ready to pursue the second step in the process of developing interagency coordination—the formalization of linkages with other agencies. In the past, this step has not received the attention it requires. Resources were often identified, but formal linkages were not created. Little effort was given to establishing boundaries or to developing working relationships. These activities, however, are the foundation upon which interagency coordination rests.[14]

A linking mechanism is "an exchange procedure that permits two or more agencies to coordinate their efforts, thus increasing the likelihood that each will achieve its objectives."[15] Interagency coordination is facilitated through a variety of "programmatic, staff, administrative and fiscal linking mechanisms."[16] The advantages of formalized linkages have been described:

FIGURE 4.1
Underutilized Resources for Families

A permanency planning notebook developed in New York State suggests that there are many resources agencies rarely think about using, despite their obvious value. Among them:

- Large companies are often very generous in loaning staff or resources. The personnel manager may be able to do group employment counseling, or a company bus may be used for transportation.

- Church youth groups may volunteer recreational or babysitting support as a group project.

- Church groups often contribute cash outright for emergency food or fuel.

- Service groups can be tapped for particular projects, such as winterizing a home or providing transportation.

- Home economists may offer training sessions on inexpensive food preparation and wise budgeting.

- Nursing schools may be enlisted to provide infant care seminars.

- Colleges may offer free dental or health services by students.

- A grocery store manager or consumer consultant may explain the use of food stamps and improved shopping skills.

- Membership in local recreational groups, e.g., a softball team, can offer a new sphere of friends and influences.

- If available, case aides can provide transportation, e.g., from rural to urban areas for evaluation.

- Medicaid may be able to provide transportation money.

- One family under treatment can often help another, peer assistance sometimes being accepted more readily than professional intervention.

- Friends or relatives who have a continuing relationship with the client may provide encouragement and assistance.[11]

FIGURE 4.2
Developing Linkages Between Public Child Welfare Agencies and Responsive Organizations

A needs assessment conducted by a large metropolitan child welfare agency in 1975 revealed a serious lack of placements for adolescents with special needs. The agency determined that the community-based group home was the optimal type of placement. A brief "request for proposal" (RFP) was disseminated to all of the agencies that had contracts with this public child welfare agency. The RFP described how this critical need was discovered, and included a detailed listing of components essential to these new programs. The broad dissemination of the RFP resulted in a number of responses from agencies that were seldom interested in establishing new programs.[13]

Exchanges improve services to clients and facilitate organizational management. From a service perspective, exchanges increase the likelihood of continuity of care for clients, and the probability that services offered by different agencies to the same clients will complement each other. From the agency's point of view, exchanges increase both the efficiency and the effectiveness of their services by reducing the need for each agency to provide every service that a client might need. Exchanges make it possible to provide a full range of needed services.[17]

To assess the appropriateness of the services provided by a resource, it is worthwhile for agency staff representative(s) to make personal contact. This also gives the staff of the resource an opportunity to meet agency staff and familiarize themselves with the child welfare agency's services. It may be necessary to overcome the stigma that public child welfare agencies often have that causes other agencies to be unwilling to work with them.[18]

Linkages should be formalized in writing. Written interagency agreements prevent many service delivery problems that have been barriers to quality service provision to families and that have made interagency coordination efforts difficult. Specifically:

Responsiveness to the service needs of families will be clearly enhanced.

Agreements can resolve problems related to availability and accessibility of resources by including provisions for aggressive outreach, evening and weekend hours, home visits, follow-up on missed appointments, and child care, enabling families who in the past have been labeled "hard to reach" to actually use these services. Because agreements contain comprehensive descriptions of services, as well as information about referrals and criteria for acceptance for service, child welfare workers should be able to successfully connect parents to resources that will be able to work with them without making the parents feel they are getting a "runaround." Because agreements state who has responsibility for service planning, provision, and monitoring and evaluation, accountability to parents for service quality and effectiveness should improve. Finally, when agreements contain provisions concerning confidentiality and information sharing, parents can be assured that information about their family is given only to those individuals who are working together in the family's behalf.

Accountability of the resource agency to the child welfare agency for effective services to parents will increase.

Written agreements state expectations and mechanisms of operation in well-defined terms. For example, how service planning will occur, what aspects of service provision each agency will be responsible for, and how authority and decision making will be handled are all dealt with in agreements. Mechanisms for reporting, holding conferences, and modifying service plans are described. Responsibility for coordinating, monitoring, and evaluating services to parents is delineated. Agreements also tell how these provisions of the agreements will be enforced, and in some cases may even include sanctions. When agencies clearly know what their obligations are, how they should be carried out, and what consequences can result if they do not comply with provisions, they are far more likely to do what is expected of them. Adherence to agreement provisions will improve communication between workers and ensure a coordinated, complementary service effort in behalf of clients.

A written agreement *must* exist between agencies when services are purchased. A purchase-of-service (POS) agreement is a legally binding contract.[19] In addition to the provisions noted above, a POS agreement spells out payment mechanisms and the documentation necessary for billing purposes. It is more likely to emphasize the purchasing agency's ultimate responsibility for decision making, monitoring, and evaluation. It is also more likely to address contract enforcement and possible sanctions when the contract is not adhered to. Possible sanctions include withholding partial payment, reducing referrals to the agency, and ultimate termination of the agreement. POS contracts that could serve as models are available through many state public welfare agencies and through the federal Department of Health and Human Services. These agreements, however, tend to focus on fiscal and administrative issues, leaving programmatic details to worker discretion. POS agreements would be strengthened by the addition of provisions concerning program issues, such as referrals, case management, and case conferences.[20] When services are not purchased, written agreements are still valuable instruments for the reasons discussed earlier, especially when the resource is likely to be used by many of the parents served by the child welfare agency. One may question why agencies would want to get involved in the preparation of a written interagency agreement when payment will not be exchanged. Like public agencies, other community resources are also concerned about quality service, better communication, and service coordination. And they too have to deal with resource limitations. But formalizing interagency coordination in writing ensures the most effective and efficient provision of services, and the benefits far outweigh the difficulties associated with preparation of agreements.

The Lower East Side Family Union (LESFU) in New York City frequently uses interagency agreements with neighborhood resources. The agreement between LESFU and Henry Street Settlement appears in appendix C.

A major barrier to formalizing linkages has been concern about protecting the family's right to confidentiality. Agencies having joint responsibility for services to a child and his or her family often hesitate to share specific information gathered during service contacts.

The purchasing agency may be unwilling to provide information obtained during an initial assessment except where it directly relates to the family's need for the contracted service. On one hand, the agency may insist, however, that because it is ultimately responsible for the child, and is paying for the service, its staff should receive a complete report of interactions between the parent or child and the staff of the provider agency. On the other hand, the agency providing the purchased service may argue that its staff needs the full assessment report to work effectively with clients. The provider may also assert that the purchasing agency should trust the summary reports and conclusions of the provider agency and not require details about the interactions with the client—the concern being that sharing this information will violate the client-worker relationship.

What information is shared and with whom must depend on the objectives to be achieved through the use of the service and the permanency goals for the child in care. For example, when an agency refers parents to a parent education program, the program staff will need to know the objectives that should be achieved by the parents' participation, and the time frames set. It is inappropriate and unnecessary to reveal the circumstances surrounding the child's placement in care or the development status of the child. It is equally inappropriate for the parent education program to reveal to the referring agency personal communications between staff members and parents that are not germane to the parent's progress. It is generally possible to protect the client's right to confidentiality while ensuring that information needed to achieve permanency for the child is conveyed.

Potential areas of disagreement concerning the sharing of information among agencies must be resolved before formalizing linkages. What type of information will be provided and who will be the specific individuals supplying and receiving information must be established. And this must be made absolutely clear to the family, including an explanation of the reasons why this information will be shared.

Many informal resources may be appropriate for only one parent or perhaps a small group of parents. Formalized interagency agreements with these resources are usually unnecessary. These resources should be involved, however, in developing written agreements at the case level. (See fig. 4.3.) (See also chapter 3 on case management.)

Developing a Resource Inventory

The two steps of the process of developing interagency coordination described thus far—conducting a needs assessment and formalizing linkages between agencies—form the basis for the third step: developing a resource inventory. The resource inventory is a compilation of information about community resources. Included in the inventory is descriptive detail about resources, whether from formal or informal systems. At a minimum, each entry includes:

- full description of the agency, organization, or resource, and the kinds of services it provides
- description of the referral process, name of contact person(s), kinds of clients served, and number who may be referred
- information about the accessibility of the resource, such as hours of operation, proximity to public transportation, facilities for child care, use of home visits, and number of staff members who are bilingual and what languages they speak
- description of payment mechanisms and cost of units of service

Any additional information that will help the staff to identify appropriate resources for families should be included. Two examples of inventory sheets showing pertinent content appear below (see figs. 4.4 and 4.5). However, any format helpful to agency staff can be used

FIGURE 4.3
Extent of Interagency Service Agreements

1. description of services to be provided, including treatment modalities, outreach activities, and home visits

2. number of clients who can be served; description of the referral process; criteria for service eligibility

3. explanation of case management process:
    a. how service planning will occur
    b. responsibilities of each agency for service provision
    c. handling of authority and decision-making questions
    d. methods for reporting, holding conferences, and modifying the service plan for a particular child and family
    e. other linking/integrating mechanisms used (on-site deployment of staff, joint planning sessions)

4. guidelines for sharing information between agencies, and rules of confidentiality

5. procedures for documentation of services, for the purposes of service record keeping, accountability, court reports, and billing*

6. procedures for assessing the quality and outcomes of the services provided

7. criteria for terminating the service agreement for a particular child and family

8. sanctions for inadequate compliance with agreement

9. criteria and process for terminating interagency agreements

*In agreements concerning purchase of service, mechanisms for payments should be stipulated.[21]

for compiling the information. Where applicable, a copy of the POS or interagency agreement should be included.

Many communities have a directory of community services. The resource inventory developed by the agency, however, will be far more helpful to its staff. It includes details of arrangements developed specifically for staff use, as well as descriptive matter that is much more complete. Thus, the inventory enables the worker to easily iden-

FIGURE 4.4
Inventory of Information to Include in Program Resource File[22]

Name of organization/agency:

Address:

Telephone

Contact person(s):

Type of service: _____ Substitute care _____ Protective

_____ Supportive _____ Supplementary

Specific services offered:
1.
2.
3.
4.
5.
6.

Eligibility requirements:

Financial arrangements (fees charged, methods of collection, etc.):

Estimate of number of available referral openings per month:

---

tify other resources that might help parents, and guides the process of connecting parents to resources. Where written agreements are included, it also facilitates the case management process.

Facilitating Use of the Inventory

To maximize use of the inventory, it must be easily accessible to staff. An agency can readily keep a centralized inventory, but it should include copies of selected inventory sheets in all worker manuals, or provide inventories to each supervisory unit or team.

Agencies can also increase the use of the inventory in several other ways.

Staff meetings

Most agencies hold regular staff meetings. Information available in the resource inventory, including written agreements and POS con-

FIGURE 4.5
Program Resource File: 3 x 5 Card Format[23]

(Front)

Name of Agency: Mudville Family Service

Address: Diamond Drive   Phone: 987-6543

Contact Person(s): Ronald Casey

Eligibility Requirements: Residence in Mudville area
Financial Arrangements: Fees charged on basis of ability to pay
Number of Referral Openings: Usually can be up to five clients with special needs per month

Special:

—Has caseworker (Jennie Cook) who has five adopted children and is sensitive to special-needs children

—Sensitive to ethnic issues

(Back)

Services Offered	Description of Service
1. Pre-placement assessment	Uses group methods
2. Adoptive Services	Handles all work including legal work
3. Post-Adoptive follow-up	— Up to five years after placement — Has group sessions with adoptive parents
4. Family Counseling	— Standard procedures
5. Testing	— Works cooperatively with the Child Guidance Clinic

---

tracts, can be discussed at unit and division level staff meetings. For example, an agency or resource that has been especially helpful to parents can be highlighted during each meeting. A person from the resource can be present to review services and to answer any questions. Although this is time consuming, the potential benefits are substantial and the time is well spent.

Training and staff development

Special training sessions on community services, POS contracts, and written agreements can be organized. Joint training involving staff members from the child welfare agency and an agency with which a POS contract or written agreement exists enhances coordination by increasing the likelihood that workers from both agencies will operate in accordance with the agreements.[24] A special training session that focuses on the inventory itself—why it was developed, what it contains, and how it should be used—is important.

Special events

Special events involving staff from several agencies provide workers with opportunities to get acquainted and develop personal relationships. After one such occasion, a worker remarked, "I had no idea that they see families; next time I need to refer, I will try them." These events not only enhance cooperation but also create a broadened and much needed support system for workers from both agencies.

Resource inventories may be made available to parents as well as workers. It is important that parents be informed about the resource inventory. Parents in need of particular services can review the pertinent sheets in the inventory and then consider with their worker which resource should be contacted. This reflects the agency's belief that parents are capable of making decisions and that they have the right to help choose their own service provider. Parents given this opportunity may well have greater investment in successful service outcomes.

Maintaining and Evaluating the Linkages and the Resource Inventory

The final step in the process of developing interagency coordination consists of maintaining and evaluating the linkages and the resource inventory itself. This is a fairly complex task because linkages between agencies are not easy to promote or maintain. These relationships require continual attention. Disagreements must be mediated both among and within the agencies involved, and a good deal of time and energy is necessary.[25] Evaluation requires assessing the interagency relationships, the resources being provided, and the inventory.

Following are the three critical tasks that must be accomplished.

First, all information in the inventory about any particular resource must be kept current. Periodic visits with the provider may be required along with receipt of information from the referring staff about changes in the provider agency. If, for example, a contact person leaves the resource and another is identified, it is important that the inventoried information be changed and the staff made aware of it.

Second, it is necessary to add information about new resources to expand the array of available services. Agencies will therefore need a mechanism for identifying new programs that should be described in the inventory. The identification of new programs may lead to the development of written agreements formalizing linkages among the agencies.

Third, monitoring and evaluation are required to assure the continuing use and effectiveness of inventoried resources. A procedure is needed for receiving and recording how provider agency services are working and how agreements are being followed.

Caseworkers are usually the most knowledgeable individuals about the resources included in the inventory. They are aware of which programs do an excellent job helping parents resolve problems, as well as those programs that fail to live up to expectations (see fig. 4.6). Although workers may have pertinent information, there may be no established mechanism for conveying it to administrative staff. Caseworkers must be given ample opportunities to share their information with the administration. It is especially important to encourage feedback about problems that impede the provision of effective services to parents, so that these problems are discussed and resolved as quickly as possible.

Administration can encourage feedback in the following ways:

1. Inventory sheets can contain blank spaces for notations about problems and/or other concerns regarding an agreement or a resource. Or, a feedback form could be developed for each resource in the inventory. Both would be reviewed periodically to collect and examine information.
2. Time can be allocated during staff meetings for discussion of staff experiences with resources and/or agreements. These discussions should be managed carefully to keep them from becoming nonproductive gripe sessions.
3. Administration can request information via memo about specific programs, or resources in general. The best time to issue such a memo would be just before the review process for a particular agreement.
4. Supervisors should be a conduit of information from caseworkers to administration regarding how interagency coordination is working and how resources are being used.

FIGURE 4.6
Example of How Resource Inventories Can Fail

Several workers at the public child welfare agency had referred families to a local mental health clinic for family therapy. Initially, the therapist had agreed to participate on the team and in the decision-making and evaluation process. However, he failed to attend case conferences and refused to share any information about the progress made by the families with whom he worked. This input was often a critical factor when the decision to return a child home was being considered. When the resource inventory was checked, a few workers found that the therapist's behavior was inconsistent with provisions in the POS.

Parents, as well as staff, should evaluate the services they are receiving. Parents are in an excellent position to discuss positive and negative features of community resources. Although there may be times when the information they provide should be balanced against other problems that are affecting them, parents can usually offer valid observations on the helpfulness of a program.

It is also necessary to learn from the resources used by the child welfare agency how they feel the agreement or relationship is working. For example, there may be dissatisfaction with the way referrals are made or how service provision is monitored.

Problems can occur in many areas, from failure to serve the number and kinds of parents agreed upon, to disputes and breakdowns in relationships over specific case management decisions. Because most possible areas where difficulties may occur are addressed in POS contracts and written interagency agreements, a mechanism is already in place for resolving differences. Whenever there are problems, there must be an opportunity for all participants to try to resolve the difficulties.

Information obtained for evaluation purposes from caseworkers, parents, and community agencies must be used very carefully. Negative information should not automatically lead to the imposition of sanctions or the discontinuation of agreements. Instead, problems should be investigated further to ascertain if they really do exist. If they do, changes in the agreement linking the two agencies or recommendations to modify specific agency policies should be considered before any decision to terminate the formal linkage. In any event, all feedback, both positive and negative, should be taken into account when agreements and contracts are renegotiated.

SUMMARY

Reported here are the ways in which an agency can assure the delivery of quality services to parents, facilitate its use of community resources, and develop and manage interagency coordination. Coordination of services, and cooperation and communication between agencies, are critical dimensions of a sound service delivery system. To achieve this end, the agency has to engage in a process that consists of conducting a needs assessment, developing formalized linkages among agencies, and preparing a resource inventory that is maintained and monitored.

Families require a wide range of problem-focused, well-coordinated services in order to resolve the problems that resulted in foster care placement so that their children can return home. Interagency coordination and cooperation enable the child welfare agency to effectively achieve those goals.

NOTES

1. Shirley Jenkins and Elaine Norman, *Filial Deprivation and Foster Care* (New York, NY: Columbia University Press, 1972); Alan Gruber, *Children in Foster Care: Destitute, Neglected, Betrayed* (New York, NY: Human Sciences Press, 1978); Edmund Sherman, Reneee Neuman, and Ann Shyne, *Children Adrift in Foster Care: A Study of Alternative Approaches* (New York, NY: Child Welfare League of America, 1973); Child Welfare League of America, *Standards for Foster Family Service*, rev. ed. (New York, NY: Child Welfare League of America, 1975), 3-4.
2. Jenkins and Norman, op. cit.; Mary Ann Jones, Renee Neuman, and Ann Shyne, *A Second Chance for Families: Evaluation of a Program to Reduce Foster Care* (New York, NY: Child Welfare League of America, 1976).
3. See Susan Downs, *Foster Care Reform in the 70's: Final Report of the Permanency Planning Dissemination Project* (Portland, OR: Regional Research Institute for Human Services, 1981). Comparable problems concerning interagency collaboration aimed at preventing problems among junior high school students are identified in "Cooperation and Its Perils," *Practice Digest* 3 (September 1980):19.
4. Bertram Beck, "A Practitioner's View of Management in Social Work," in *Training Social Welfare Managers: Social Work—Business School Cooperation*, edited by George Brager and Megan McLaughlin (New York, NY: Columbia University School of Social Work, 1979).
5. Alfred Kahn and Sheila Kamerman, *Social Services in International Perspective: The Emergence of the Sixth System* (Washington, DC: Social and Rehabilitation Service, Office of Planning, Research and Evaluation, Department of Health, Education and Welfare, 1977), 405.
6. For a more detailed discussion of the needs assessment, see American

Public Welfare Association, *Standards for Foster Family Services Systems for Public Agencies*, DHEW Publication No. (OHDS) 79-30231 (Washington, DC: U.S. Department of Health, Education and Welfare 1979), 13.
7. Shirley Jenkins, *The Ethnic Dilemma in Social Services* (New York, NY: Free Press, 1981); Shirley Jenkins and Barbara Morrison, *Ethnicity and Child Welfare: An Annotated Bibliography* (New York, NY: Columbia University School of Social Work, 1974).
8. The essential elements in this case example were provided by Dr. Steven Rosenberg of the Intensive Services to Families at Risk Project, sponsored by the Meyers Children's Rehabilitation Center in Omaha, and funded as a Prevention Demonstration Project by the U.S. Department of Health and Human Services.
9. See, for example, Alice Collins and Diane Pancoast, *Natural Helping Networks: A Strategy for Prevention* (Washington, DC: National Association of Social Workers, 1976); Charles Horejsi, Anne Bertsche, and Frank Clark, *Social Work Practice with Parents of Children in Foster Care: A Handbook* (Springfield, IL: Charles C Thomas, 1981), 145-174; Jack McGowan and Christine Deyss, *Permanency Planning: A Casework Handbook* (Albany, NY: Welfare Research, Inc., 1978), 57-59.
10. Author's conversation with Dan DeLong, Wyoming Department of Public Assistance and Social Services, 1981.
11. McGowan and Deyss, op. cit., 58.
12. Armand Lauffer, *Resources for Child Placement and Other Human Services* (Beverly Hills, CA: Sage Human Service Guides, 1979) 37-52.
13. Example provided by editor.
14. American Public Welfare Association, op. cit., 10.
15. Lauffer, op. cit. 55.
16. Ibid.
17. Ibid.
18. Author's conversation with Von Raiford, Tennessee Department of Human Services, in 1981.
19. Lauffer, op. cit.
20. For a complete discussion of the programmatic, fiscal, and administrative aspects of written purchase-of-service agreements, see American Public Welfare Association, op. cit. 46-47.
21. This list is adapted from American Public Welfare Association, op. cit.
22. Lauffer, op. cit., 47.
23. Lauffer, op. cit., 48.
24. Kenneth Krause, "Interagency Training: A Cooperative Approach to Staff Development," *Child Welfare* 56 (June 1977): 361-367.
25. Lauffer, op. cit.

INTRODUCTION TO CHAPTERS 5 AND 6

Working with parents in the ways this volume sets forth may be new to staff members at all levels within an agency. Many lack the appropriate knowledge and/or skills. Others may hold beliefs, attitudes, or values about parents of children in care that will inhibit their work with parents.

As discussed by Blumenthal and Weinberg in chapter 2, parent involvement is limited without strong administrative support and commitment to its philosophy. But effective supervision and training are also crucial to its implementation. And administrators' views of the importance of supervision and training, and the degree to which they are made available, will determine the effectiveness of parent involvement.

Although supervisors will retain many of the same responsibilities they had in the past, they must be conscious of new activities that will be occurring between worker, parent, and/or child, and be capable of preparing their workers and supporting them in these new responsibilities.

Peg Hess, in chapter 5, identifies and discusses many of the added responsibilities supervisors must assume. These responsibilities are classified as administrative, educational, and supportive.

Carla Overberger's chapter on training (chapter 6) explores the relationship between an agency's goals for its services to families and training goals. She relates the importance of training to working with parents, discusses who should be trained, and identifies methods for establishing and carrying out training programs.

When administrators set funding priorities, training is usually one of the first resources to be considered nonessential, and new burdens are placed on the supervisor. Although the supervisor may be able to teach staff necessary skills for working with parents, and give support to staff, in-depth training in a variety of parent involvement issues is also important. Supervisors either lack time to provide in-depth training or were not trained in involving parents and lack skills or resources. The primary responsibilities of supervisors regarding training include identifying gaps in workers' skills and following up on and enhancing training received by the staff.

5
SUPERVISION

Peg Hess

The presumption of total involvement of parents of foster children during all phases of the placement process represents a major shift in policy and practice for the majority of child welfare agencies.[1] For some, current policies and procedures have anticipated and will support the necessary innovations in practice. For others, the change is beginning to occur in practice as one component of permanency planning but it is not yet mandated or fully supported by agency policies and procedures. Although supported by social work theory and ethics, practice-relevant research, and national legislation, this major change will not come without struggle, resistance, and uncertainty. The philosophy of total parent involvement, however, promotes challenging and exciting opportunities for child welfare personnel as well as the children and families whom they serve. This chapter examines the role of the agency foster care supervisor.* The supervisory position between line staff and administration affords perhaps the most potent opportunity to maximize the benefits of increased parent involvement for both agency personnel and families.

Typically, the foster care supervisor is an "administrative officer, occupying a position of managerial responsibility, who is given authority to direct, regulate, and evaluate the work of others and who is accountable for the work performed. . . . The supervisor's ultimate objective is to deliver to agency clients the best possible service, both quantitatively and qualitatively, *in accordance with agency policies and procedures*" [emphasis added].[2] Therefore, the supervisor's ability to implement parent involvement as an essential component of work with families of children in foster care is in large part contingent upon the agency administration's explicit mandate to do so. Once given this

---

*Although titles may vary from agency to agency, the position discussed involves supervisory or management responsibilities for agency staff members who provide services to families whose children are at risk of, or are in placement out-of-home, or are receiving services following family reunification.

mandate to involve parents actively during the preplacement, placement, and postplacement periods, the foster care supervisor's responsibilities can be expected to expand, paralleling expansion of workers' activities in behalf of parents.

The foster care supervisor relates to a number of constituent groups: (1) clients served by the agency; (2) line staff assigned to the supervisor; (3) foster parents and other child care staff members; (4) agency administration and those financial and legal bodies under whose auspices the agency functions; and (5) the professional community. Responsiveness to the demands, expectations, and needs of these constituencies requires not only professional knowledge, skill, and judgment, but also the authority to command resources. As agencies implement a philosophy of total parent involvement, the foster care supervisor must reexamine the following areas for consistency of focus: legislative and agency policy, agency program and procedures, practitioners' approaches, community resources, and supervisory methods.

As this focus develops, several current trends are expected to occur more widely. First, the relationship between foster care workers and parents of children in care will become more visible; goals and tasks will be clearly defined and specifically related to minimum standards of child care. Second, appropriateness of goals and progress toward task accomplishment will be openly and regularly reviewed, within and outside the agency; parents, workers, and designated others will be held accountable for accomplishing these tasks. Third, in the majority of instances there will be a relationship between parents of children in care and foster parents (or other child care staff) based on their shared parenting responsibilities. This relationship will be directed to mutual planning and decision making and will support the child's continuing identification with his or her parents while in temporary care. Fourth, intra-agency organizational boundaries may shift as greater collaboration between protective service workers, foster care workers, foster parents, homemakers, legal staff, and aftercare workers is required to assure continuity of service to parents and children. Fifth, the supervisor-supervisee dyad will increasingly rely upon the process of shared group or team decision making regarding case plans, providing relief from the burden of making difficult case decisions alone, but requiring willingness to risk exposure of one's work. Finally, the delegation of authority within the agency, traditionally structured through the bureaucratic hierarchy, will be redefined. Some of the new processes, by their very nature, create changes in the distribution of authority. These include the increased parent participation in decisions regarding their children's future, their own goals, and the agency's services, and the expanded monitoring of, and intervention in, workers' case planning from the supervisor-worker dyad to both internal and external review systems. Within the context of these general changes, the foster care supervisor can anticipate changes in her or his responsibilities to the constituent groups listed earlier.

The familiar supervisory functions (administrative, educational, and supportive)[3] are presented in this chapter as an organizing framework for examination of these issues and are followed by a general discussion of supervisory methods. The three functions have been differentiated as follows:

> Administrative supervision provides the organizational structure and access to agency resources that facilitate the workers' job; educational supervision provides the knowledge and skills required for it; supportive supervision provides the psychological and interpersonal supplies that enable the worker to mobilize the emotional energy needed for effective job performance. Administrative supervision is concerned with organizational barriers to effective service; educational supervision is concerned with ignorance barriers to effective service; supportive supervision is concerned with emotional barriers to effective service.[4]

MAJOR FUNCTIONS OF THE SUPERVISOR

Administrative Supervision

For the foster care supervisor involved in implementing parent involvement as an essential component of work with families of children in foster care, the functions of administrative supervision relate to

- mastering the rationale and content of federal, state, and agency policies regarding goals, standards, and procedures affecting parent participation in foster care services, and participating in agency policy formulation
- interpreting policy to supervisees on a day-to-day basis, and coordinating and monitoring policy implementation, including attending to case planning and preparation for internal and external reviews
- assigning cases and assuring coverage, identifying foster care workers' and other team members' training needs, and evaluating supervisee performance
- facilitating and channeling communication among the constituent groups responsible for, and involved in, the foster care service

At first glance, these responsibilities do not appear to differ markedly from the traditional responsibilities of the foster care supervisor. However, implicit in the administrative functioning of the child welfare supervisor committed to increased parent involvement is an awareness of, and attention to, the effect of all decision making—both case-specific and system-wide—upon the expansion, maintenance, or restriction of parent involvement, and subsequently, upon the options available to children in care. The word *committed* is intentionally selected to describe an attitudinal and value stance of the supervisor. The minimum expectation for agency supervisors in the area of policy implementation regarding parent involvement is an openness to the possibilities inherent in such efforts and an awareness of their own biases toward change. If the supervisor's convictions are inconsistent with the agency's thrust toward increased parent involvement, the supervisor probably will be unable to assist workers in implementing agency policy.

Mastery of Policy and Participation in Policy Formulation

> I always assumed that laws and policies were the concern of someone else—my supervisor, or director of the agency. Now that I am a supervisor, I realize that everything that we do or don't do for clients in the child welfare division is related to laws requiring that children be protected, and parents don't get shafted.
>
> Foster Care Supervisor
> State Public Welfare Agency

That is the bottom line in the balancing of children's and parents' rights—assuring that children are protected and parents "don't get shafted." The current emphasis on parent involvement attempts to balance increased public and professional reactions to multiple sources of harm to children with recognition of the primacy of the parent-child relationship and of its importance as a natural resource for permanency.

Policy provides supervisors and workers the context within which case decisions must be made. Agency manuals, state juvenile codes, and published summaries of state and national legislation can assist supervisors in comprehending the legislation and policy from which their authority is derived. Often, however, even the manuals require interpretation for day-to-day practice decisions. Agency administrative and legal personnel can assist supervisors in anticipating practice decisions that will require knowledge of policy and its legislative sources.

Through the administrative functions described below, the supervisor develops a practical perspective on agency policy, including its usefulness in accomplishing organizational goals and its impact upon both agency personnel and clients served. The supervisor must use this perspective to formulate recommended policy changes.[5]

Interpreting Policy and Coordinating and Monitoring Policy Implementation

The legal rights retained by parents of children in foster care, and the responsibilities assigned to them, vary from state to state.[6] Therefore, agencies nationwide vary in the implementation of new or revised policies regarding parent involvement. Current practice literature and legislation, however, define several minimum acceptable standards for parent involvement.[7] These standards establish guidelines for future policy and practice in case planning and subsequent service, in the lives of the children while in placement, and in review of case progress and service delivery. The supervisor must assist workers in translating state- and agency-specific policy into practice behaviors consistent with the minimum acceptable standards, and advocate for policy revision when state or agency policies do not support practice consistent with these standards.

In case planning, for example, the minimum acceptable level of parent involvement would require that parents have been informed before placement of the reasons for the child's impending placement and that the reasons conform with the concept of minimum sufficient level of care.[8] This concept is a useful tool for supervisor and workers in establishing specific agency criteria against which to judge case objectives and progress.

The author has used this concept in assisting foster care workers with the development of criteria for initial case planning and decision making. In many instances the workers' standards for case progress reflect ideal standards of care that agencies have no legal right to require. Only with explicit parent agreement can ideal standards become case goals. Workers must be able to clarify for themselves, then for their clients, the rationale for children's placements—that is, minimum standards of parent care are not being met—and to pursue more specifically the behavioral changes that have to take place before children return home. Clarity in the purpose and limits of the agency's intervention is an important precursor to effective parent involvement in case planning.

Supervisors are responsible for monitoring workers' adherence to standards concerning parent involvement. Therefore, a regularly scheduled review either between supervisor and individual workers or within the unit of supervisor-supervisees must examine case-specific compliance with standards. This includes assuring that workers are informing parents of options, involving parents in determining case goals and plans, and specifying timetables for task accomplishment and case review.

Frequent, regular parent visitation and participation in the continuing life of the child while in placement are also minimum acceptable standards for parent involvement. Workers are typically more hesitant to encourage parents to be involved with their children while in placement than to involve them in the case planning for their children. Parent-child contact often brings into focus the difficulties existing within the relationship; in addition, the necessity of protecting some children through supervised visits frequently places a demand upon workers. A framework for developing criteria for making decisions regarding parent-child contact can be established by exploring with workers the importance of parent-child attachments.[9] Within this context, the importance of continued enactment of the role of parent by parents during placement can be understood, and the policy supporting such involvement interpreted.

Parent participation in case review is a standard of minimum involvement explicitly included in the Adoption Assistance and Child Welfare Act of 1980, Public Law 96-272.[10] Participation is a logical extension of parent-agency contracting for services to be delivered. It is intended to ensure that reasonable obstacles to parents' progress are considered; that sufficient services are being provided to the child, parents, and foster parents; and that procedural safeguards with respect to the rights of parents, family, and child are applied.

However, as agencies implement internal reviews and comply with legislative requirements for external reviews,[11] the supervisor assumes several administrative responsibilities:

- clarifying the purpose and authority of each reviewing system (such as administrative, judicial, citizen)
- assuring that prepared case documentation reflects an objective, current record of worker's, parents', and others' efforts and of services offered, while protecting client confidentiality
- assuring that persons required or permitted to attend the review hearing are informed of the review date
- providing information about the review process to workers and other team members, including parents
- providing support to team members
- attending reviews to provide information to reviewers and to support participants
- assuring that review recommendations or decisions are subsequently clarified to all affected persons

The supervisor, therefore, must be familiar with both policy and case activity; be active in assisting workers and others in anticipating the nature and probable consequences of the review; and be vigilant in monitoring compliance subsequent to the review.

Case Assignments and Coverage, Identification of Training Needs, and Performance Evaluation

> We have a new case assigned to the unit—a single mother with two children. She seems very attached to her daughter, but has no interest in her son, who has spent most of his life in the hospital. Both were placed because of serious physical and medical neglect. According to the children's doctor, the mother is depressed, possibly suicidal. They will go to the foster home sometime this week, and protective services has asked that we involve the mother in developing a permanent plan. Marcia, since you have had some real successes in helping parents explore their reactions to their children and you have worked closely with this foster family before, what is your reaction to taking primary responsibility for this case?

Marcia's response to this question, primarily a question of case assignment and coverage, probably will reflect not only her current workload, but also her personal response to the family situation, her confidence in her skill level, her previous experiences with this foster family, and her satisfaction at the positive ongoing performance evaluation implied in the supervisor's reference to her "real successes." Although functionally separate, the three supervisory responsibilities listed above—case assignment and coverage, identification of foster care workers' and others' training needs, and evaluation of supervisee performance—are intricately related. Each task requires recognition of supervisees' current levels of knowledge, skill, and judgment, as well as their capacities for professional development.

When assigning cases, the supervisor must balance workers' needs for task diversity with probability of success in any specific assignment. As workers' tasks are performed—for example, engaging the mother in exploring options and identifying goals for herself and her children, coordinating parent-child visits, and involving the foster mother and mother in sharing parenting—training needed by workers will become apparent. Successful case outcomes and worker effectiveness depend in part on the supervisor's ability to assign cases within the range of capacities of specific workers and the supervisor's willingness to give priority to identifying the additional training needs of the workers.

Assignments of tasks too difficult for the worker and a lack of feedback on performance are major factors contributing to worker burnout.[12] Even experienced workers, when confronted with shifts in agency expectations regarding parent involvement, may need considerable supervisory assistance in dealing with what is experienced as increasingly complex assignments, and may require more frequent specific feedback concerning job performance. Performance evaluation, too often viewed as a dreaded annual event, is most helpful to workers when feedback occurs frequently and when workers actively participate in identifying both case-specific and general performance difficulties and related training needs. A helpful tool in this process is the use of worker-supervisor contracts concerning case assignments, particularly those that require new skills.[13]

Facilitating and Channeling Communication

Workers must rely on the resources within their agencies and the broader community (see chap. 4) to provide service consistent with standards of minimally acceptable parent involvement. Issues frequently emerge regarding access to these services and collaboration among service providers. The supervisor may serve as a link between supervisees and a number of systems, both internal and external to the agency, regarding client and worker resource needs and difficulties relating to service delivery. The supervisor is in a position to identify the adequacy of community programs and their policies.[14]

He or she can then channel communication within the agency and the community regarding both client and worker resource needs or access difficulties, as well as difficulties relating to policy. For example, the supervisor may participate on review boards and community task forces, prepare documentation of parent-staff needs and difficulties for agency administration and board members, and participate in professional forums seeking to define the service needs of parents of children at risk. Through the channeling of such information from supervisees and other team members, including parents, to agency administration and other constituent groups, the documented need of each case is expanded to a level at which response may affect service to many.

The supervisor channels information from agency administration and service providers to supervisees and other team members as well, either remaining in a linkage role or facilitating direct communication between groups or individuals. The supervisor also collaborates in developing new channels of communication, such as parent advisory groups, agency-sponsored workshops, and community task forces. For example, as foster parents share the parenting role more actively with parents of children in their care, supervisors, workers, and other team members must have an opportunity to hear and respond to their concerns, reactions, and suggestions.

EDUCATIONAL SUPERVISION

What additional training topics or areas of knowledge would be helpful to you in performing your job?

Everything.

(Foster Care Worker's Reply on Agency Training Evaluation Form)

Because there are so few areas of professional knowledge and skill *not* drawn upon by the competent foster care worker, the educational function of the supervisor is a critical one. Fortunately, a wealth of educational resources is available to assist the supervisor in this task.

This discussion defines in a general way the major areas of knowledge and skill included in the "everything" needed by the worker to give timely and helpful service to individual parents and children. Methods of educational supervision are examined in the final section of the chapter.

Inservice training and educational supervision as specific forms of staff development have been differentiated as follows:

> In-service training refers to planned, formal training provided to a delimited group of agency personnel who have the same job classification or the same job responsibilities. Educational supervision is a still more specific kind of staff development. Here, training is directed to the needs of a particular worker carrying a particular case load, encountering particular problems and needing some individualized program of education.[15]

The areas of knowledge and skill discussed here can be assumed to pertain both to the planning of foster care worker training (see chap. 6) and the provision of educational supervision. Generally, these areas include:

- knowledge of agency policy, procedures, standards, and auspices under which the agency functions, and knowledge of community resources
- knowledge of the demonstration projects and research findings concerning permanency planning and parent involvement
- knowledge regarding children and families
- knowledge regarding, and skill in, basic professional social work practice

Each of these areas will be reviewed briefly, with emphasis on their relevance for educational supervision.

Agency Auspices, Policy, Procedures, Standards, and Community Resources

Information in these areas is always an important aspect of new worker orientation. But the changes in, or reinterpretation of, agency policy to expand the roles of parents, require continuing supervisory attention to agency auspices, policy, procedures, and standards, and to current information regarding the resources beyond the agency. Educational supervision is usually most meaningful for workers when specific case dilemmas are examined within the context of agency policy, and where applicable, state or federal legislation. For example, a worker preparing for a review hearing before a child's return home may be reminded of the continuing social and professional tension between children's and parents' rights. Through such discussion, the review process may be approached less as a personally threatening adversarial experience and more as a mechanism intended to protect the rights of both parents and children, as well as to protect the worker and the employing agency from actions that deprive clients of those rights.

Supervisory review of case plans allows for review of the overall mandates of the child welfare system as well as of agency-specific policy. Knowledge in these areas enhances the worker's ability to engage in the development of the agency's approach to parent involvement and to anticipate and respond to organizational difficulties encountered by workers in their clients' behalf.

The delivery of comprehensive services to families also requires knowledge of resources beyond the agency. Supervisors may assist workers in developing and maintaining a system through which specific current information regarding community resources, service requirements, and contact persons can be located and easily updated (see chap. 4).

Permanency Planning and Parent Involvement Projects

Knowledge of practice guidelines emerging from demonstration projects and studies in the area of family-focused services further support and clarify any one agency's efforts to increase parent participation as an essential component of service. Therefore, as supervisors and workers implement their agency's approach to increased parent involvement, familiarity with project publications, such as the numerous guides of the Oregon Project,[16] and with comparative analyses and critiques of projects' results and study findings,[17] will be helpful. In attempting to replicate or utilize findings of demonstration projects, agency personnel must be attentive to "special circumstances" affecting the outcomes,[18] for example, project-agency differences in populations served, location and resources, legal and agency mandates, and skill levels of workers.

A perspective on current practice developments can be gained from looking backward as well.[19] Parent participation in the definition of problems and goals is not a new technique, but rather "the most demanding aspect of social work practice. It is the most violated principle of practice."[20] Although the immediacy of case decisions often limits theoretical discussions between supervisors and workers, reference to both the "new" and the "old" professional experiences with parent involvement offers a strong foundation upon which specific case, program, and policy dilemmas can be examined.

Knowledge About Children and Families

Foster care supervisors and workers rely on three general areas of knowledge about children and families: the predictable stages of child development and predictable stresses of parenting, the problems that contribute to family dysfunction and subsequently to child placement, and the impact of separation upon families.

The predictable stages and stresses

Knowledge of the predictable stages of child development and predictable demands and stresses of parenting forms the basis of workers' ability to assess family members' needs and difficulties and assist them in formulating goals. For example, out of this basic framework comes the workers' crucial awareness of the importance of the parent-child attachment. Knowledge of the child's age-related understanding of the consequences of behaviors or of cause-effect relationships enables workers to help families deal with individual children's reactions to placement and to select age-appropriate explanations of the purpose and probable outcome of placement.

In assisting workers in case-specific assessment, planning, and interventions, supervisors will draw upon family development and family systems theories concerning the predictable stresses and demands of parenting and family life. Although therapeutic interventions with the family system may be provided through referral, workers' ability to be helpful to specific families will depend on their knowledge of roles within family systems. When determining particular case interventions, supervisors and workers must always consider the consequences of possible interventions upon the family system as a whole.

Problems contributing to family dysfunction

A worker assigned to 25 cases would most likely encounter a minimum of 25 different problem combinations. The parent-child relationship is typically affected by problems such as unemployment, poverty, severe or chronic physical illness, substance abuse, emotional stress, marital conflict, and geographic and social isolation.[21] Thus, supervisor and worker knowledge sufficient to identify problem areas, as well as the relationships between problems, is basic to the task of engaging individual clients in problem definition and formulation of goals. The supervisor's vantage point affords both knowledge of typical problem areas across caseloads and educational resources (professional literature, audiovisual resources, consultants) with which supervisee learning needs can be matched.

Impact of separation

Foster care services focus not only on the reality of temporary parent-child separation, but also the possibility of voluntary or involuntary termination of parental rights. Therefore, supervisors and workers must be aware of the continual themes of actual and anticipatory loss and grief. Knowledge of the stages of grief may be gained through training. But case-specific anticipation and detection of the meaning of separation to each individual parent and child, as well as of family patterns related to separation and loss, necessarily occur through the process of educational supervision. The translation of this knowledge into hearing and responding to often obscure client messages is a sophisticated skill necessary not only in involving parents in planning for placement, but also in maintaining contact with the child and exploring goals for the parents' future relationship with the child. Development of workers' ability to hear, understand, and accept a parent's decision to be permanently separated from the child is as crucial to facilitating the partnership between parent and agency as is the development of workers' commitment to reunification of families.

Basic Knowledge and Skill in Professional Social Work Practice

As a social work educator and practitioner, the author's bias is that the heart of the "everything" needed by foster care workers lies in this area. It is significant for the profession of social work that certain skills have consistently emerged as effective practice in permanency planning projects.[22] They are engaging the client, assessing and defining the problem with the client, developing mutual goals for service, clarifying tasks and responsibilities, and involving the client actively in service delivery and evaluation. The use of explicit contracts as an essential component of parent involvement draws upon these basic social work skills in problem solving.

In addition to these basic social work skills, the supervisee is likely to require case-specific assistance with the differential implementation of social work roles, including advocate, broker, mediator, counselor, enabler, collaborator, educator, and evaluator. Delivery of comprehensive services depends upon worker knowledge of, and skill in, implementing social work roles creatively.

Foster care workers must also become knowledgeable about decision making, team practice, and themselves. A major function of the foster care worker is to "be willing to make decisions and to exercise judgment in doing so."[23] The decisions often require the ability to identify risks being taken. Therefore, skills in applying knowledge to anticipate consequences of case-specific decisions and interventions (or professional judgment) is crucial. Nurturing in each worker the ability to balance perspectives when parents' and children's interests conflict; to decide which of several important activities should be given priority; to not only cope, but be helpful, in situations that are potentially dangerous; and to know when to seek supervisory assistance is an educational task of central importance. Mutual supervisor-worker identification of case-specific risks, of the information required to anticipate the degree of risk, and of the criteria for making decisions is an educational process that enhances the worker's ability to make professional judgments. Professional judgment is not only required for decisions pertaining to specific cases, but also in setting priorities among cases. Although permanency planning projects have provided some guidelines for setting priorities within caseloads,[24] helping the worker develop the ability to assess individual client readiness to engage will be especially useful.

The utility of shared decision making, or the team approach, has been emphasized as a major component in implementing a permanency planning process.[25] In implementing the team approach, supervisors and workers draw upon knowledge of group process and dynamics, including the typical developmental stages of small working groups, leadership and communication patterns within small groups, scapegoating in groups, and resolution of group conflicts.

Finally, the continuing development of self-awareness is a critical goal and product of educational supervision. A worker's responses to agency policy, the often inherently conflicting needs of persons involved in the placement process, clients' problems, the dearth of adequate and responsible resources, and, often, lack of training for the job at hand, must be examined as they relate to the worker's use of self in the helping process. Awareness of personal values and attitudes that interfere with helpful service to families or that bias case decisions is a critical first step toward assuring that personal reactions do not determine case outcome. Workers will need assistance in recognizing the potential impact not only of their own attitudes but also those of other team members upon case decisions and outcomes.[26]

Neither the supervisor nor the foster care worker can be expected to know "everything." Workers' access to professional literature; to colleagues' professional experiences; to professional education; and to workshops, conferences, and inservice training will support and supplement the resources provided through educational supervision.

SUPPORTIVE SUPERVISION

Attention to the personal aspects of the social worker's responsibilities is the essence of the supportive function of supervision: "Supportive supervision is concerned with emotional barriers to effective service."[27] For the foster care worker actively involved with parents, children, and foster parents, as well as with a wide assortment of public and private resources, the primary emotional barriers to effective service are associated with frequent, intense, job-related stress.

The sources of stress vary, depending upon the setting, the worker's assignments, and the individual needs and characteristics of the worker. There are, however, as illustrated below, a number of predictable job-related stresses that the foster care supervisor must openly recognize and directly respond to.

Complexity of Client Difficulties

> Don't get me wrong, I went back to school to get a degree and came back to this agency to the same job because I love this work—I wouldn't want to do anything else. But sometimes it feels as if it will never end, as if the change comes in such small steps you'll miss it if you aren't paying attention. And the problems. I am always amazed at the strength people have to go on, with the problems they have to face. I have learned that parents depend on me for hope, and sometimes I can't see where the hope is.

Interpersonal Relationships with Clients

> I don't think I can stand to go back one more time. Going with her to the hospital to supervise the visits, looking at that child who will never be

able to see or talk, and knowing that her mother let someone do that to her. I just have to come back here and tell someone how angry I am at her.

I know I could terminate with the Rogers, but they've done so well since the children have gone home, I feel so proud. I can't imagine saying goodbye to them. They are so important to me.

Acknowledged Lack of Skill

Each time I meet with Mrs. Riley, she has changed her mind again. I always have the feeling that if I just knew better how to help her understand where each choice is likely to take her we could begin to make some progress.

The only time, really, that I talk with the Grant kids is in the car. Then I'm thinking about where we're going or whether they are undoing their seat belts and it's hard to find out how they feel about all this. I watch Tim talking with the kids he works with, and I think, "How does he know what to say to them? How does he get them to talk with him so easily?"

Decision Making and Risk Taking

From the first minute I am assigned a case until the last word of dictation, there is one decision after another. Some are easy, some are impossible, and they all matter. The hardest decisions are the ones you have to make without knowing, for sure, everything you need to know. Those are the ones you have to wait out, hoping you don't see your name in the newspaper. I look at the file on a new case and it makes me tired just thinking about it.

Own Values and Attitudes

I've been trying so hard to get Jimmy's foster parents to be more positive about his parents. She told me folks who hurt their kids don't deserve to get them back. It's hard for me to help her see things differently, because I feel a pull between what I believe are Jimmy's parents' rights to have him back and Jimmy's rights to have a good home, whatever that is.

Lack of Professional Status

You know what she said? Right in front of me, she said that I couldn't possibly understand, I was just a welfare worker. I hear it in their voices when I call, they're the professionals and I'm just a welfare worker. And she's the one who didn't send us the report she promised! I don't think they understand that kids can't wait forever.

Increased Visibility of Worker Case Activity

I always get very anxious when one of my cases is up for administrative review. Even when I'm sure I have done everything humanly possible, I worry what they will say. And when I *can* think of things I might have done and haven't, then I really worry! It's so public.

Environment of the Workplace

I have hours of dictation to do on this week's work, and there is nowhere I can have the quiet and privacy to think.

I've driven over 1000 miles this month. Here in our county, everything's so spread out, it takes all my time and energy just getting people together.

These workers' comments illustrate only some of the feelings that lead to "putting the case in the bottom drawer." Unattended, reactions associated with these stresses build up and symptoms of burnout become identifiable: distancing of clients, constant feelings of helplessness, physical deterioration (such as frequent illnesses), suspicious attitudes, inappropriate risk taking, and changes in work attendance.[28] Supervisors must be constantly alert for signs of worker stress and burnout, and maintain as a high priority helping staff reduce—or live with—workplace stresses.

Supervisory responses to workers' reactions to stress include, first and foremost, an attitude and climate of openness, acceptance, and readiness to listen. Without *explicit* permission, encouragement, and opportunities to ventilate and explore emotional reactions, workers may protectively deny their feelings. When feelings are denied, important emotional barriers to service cannot be examined.

Other supervisory responses include encouragement, acknowledging the "normalcy" of reactions, sharing own experiences, recognizing both achievement and realistic situational limits, inspiring hope, and mutual problem solving regarding stressful situations. Mutual problem solving may result in other supportive supervisory behaviors. For instance, supervisors may accompany workers when situations are extremely difficult or when the authority of the supervisor's position would support the worker's role. Such actions not only support the worker emotionally, but also allow the supervisor to be a buffer in the worker's interactions with parents, foster parents, and others. The supervisor and worker may move together from exploring the emotional aspects of the stressful situation to examining the educational needs clarified by the experience, such as developing skills of time management and self-care, or identifying dilemmas in interpreting agency policy in a specific situation. Thus, a critical complement to the supportive function is the supervisor's ability to respond competently and in a timely manner in the educational and administrative roles.

Beyond the responsibility of intervening in the supervisory relationship, the supervisor is responsible for identifying and/or developing supportive resources within the work environment, including mechanisms for shared decision making, peer support, time-out breaks, and compensatory time. Shared decision making is a major component of successful family-focused work, because implicit in this process are powerful supportive elements:

> Team decision making provides emotional support for workers. In the process of case review, frustrations can be shared, the impact of the case on the worker explored, and encouragement, compliments, and suggestions given. The isolation that contributes to worker burnout is greatly decreased and worker morale and collegiality enhanced. . . . Team decision making may provide a new perspective on situations that seem unresolvable. Failing that, support can be given to the worker in the difficult conclusion that no further case progress can occur.[29]

For most supervisors, the supportive function is that aspect of middle management most similar to the helping role that attracted her or him to the profession. Although the supervisor's interpersonal helping responses to the supervisee are critical, the supervisor also has organizational influence within the work environment in relation to workers, and provides or facilitates access to educational resources, such as consultation, to better prepare them for the task at hand.[30] (As broker, mediator, and advocate for workers, the supervisor asserts that supervisees deserve not only the support of the individual supervisor, but institutional support as well.)

The possibility of increased job-related stress after implementation of a philosophy of total parent involvement emphasizes the importance of a critical management ethics issue: humaneness of the workplace. It is clear that agency expectations regarding increased parent involvement place new demands on foster care workers. For example, workers must more efficiently mobilize a variety of resources to support families' efforts as well as actively engage parents in decision making. This process must be paralleled and supported by increased agency mobilization of resources to support employees' professional efforts and increased mutuality of workers in decision making.[31] Supervisory advocacy in behalf of both workers and clients for increased agency responsiveness is an ethical responsibility clearly within the supportive function.

SUPERVISORY METHODS

Discussion of supervisory methods brings us again to the issue of authority. Different supervisory methods can be examined in terms of the authority the supervisor maintains, shares, or delegates to others in the supervisory process. As noted earlier, one change necessarily accompanying a focus upon increased parent involvement is the redefinition of authority traditionally structured within the bureaucratic hierarchy.

Supervisory approaches will necessarily be influenced by the two general areas of power that legitimate and enable authority: formal power and functional power.[32] Formal power relates specifically to the supervisor's position and ability to require compliance through both rewards and punishments as well as through claiming the delegated authority of position. The power of professional competence and the interpersonal relationship between the supervisor and the supervisee constitute functional power. Authority derived from formal power will be referred to here as the authority of position; functional power as the authority of competence.

Supervisory methods are selected with regard to the supervisor's knowledge and skill and the relative anticipated effectiveness of each method with a specific supervisee or group of supervisees at a point in time. For example, the approach or combination of approaches that may most effectively support an inexperienced worker may be counterproductive with that same worker 6 months later.

Three general types of supervisory approaches are briefly reviewed here: tutorial, consultative, and team. The emphasis of the discussion is on teamwork, since that is the method most frequently reported as an essential component of supervision in permanency planning.

Tutorial

Traditionally, the tutorial approach has been the most frequently used method of social work supervison.[33] The explicit supervisory authority implied in the tutorial approach allows for individualized attention when concerns regarding worker skill, knowledge, or judgment arise, and when assurance of confidentiality is required. Although responsibility for developing the supervisory agenda is shared, and worker discretion in making day-to-day case decisions may be recognized, authority of position and of competence resides with the supervisor.

The tutorial approach is helpful to new or inexperienced workers, as well as experienced workers who at times may require or request this form of assistance. For example, when case crises require prompt, administratively supported decisions, unscheduled tutorial conferences provide a mechanism for confirming policy interpretation, reviewing intervention options, and eliciting emotional support for risk taking.

The major disadvantage of exclusive use of the tutorial model lies in the inevitable limits in interpersonal and knowledge resources of any one individual supervisor. Exclusive reliance on this method not only restricts the resources of the worker, but also places an unnecessary stress upon the supervisor to "have all the answers."

Consultation

Consultation to supervisees regarding specific policy, program, or practice issues may be requested from agency personnel or other professionals on a one-to-one and/or group basis. Through the use of consultation, the supervisor shares or delegates authority in clearly defined areas in which the consultant has expertise. Therefore, the consultant may supplement or even accomplish aspects of both the educational and supportive tasks of the supervisor. Tasks included in the administrative function, however, are not incorporated into the consultant-supervisee relationship and must be accomplished through other methods.[34]

Consultation takes many forms. It may occur with individual professional experts as well as with professional colleagues. Consultation with peers occurs both informally and formally. Peer group supervision is defined most accurately as a form of consultation:

> In peer group supervision there is no designated supervisor, and all the members of the group participate as equals.... As in the consultation model, it must be clear to all the members that they are under no obligation to act in accord with the ideas proposed in the group discussion of their case.[35]

This freedom from obligation "to act in accord with the ideas proposed" characterizes the supervisees' role with consultants and distinguishes the supervisee's relationship with the consultant from the supervisor-supervisee relationship. The supervisor assists workers in clarifying areas in which individual or group consultation would be helpful, in identifying experts in those areas, in arranging for consultation, and in appropriately integrating the consultant's ideas into subsequent practice decisions and activity.

Given the complicated nature of foster care services, worker access to a variety of consultant experts as educational and supportive resources is critical. Consultation from peers, agency personnel, and other community professionals provides not only knowledge, information, and expertise, but inspiration, new perspectives, and hope.

Team

Team decision making has emerged as an essential element of family-focused foster care service delivery.[36] (See chap. 3, p. 89.) Possible variations in team purpose, composition, and delegated authority have not, however, been adequately differentiated, nor have the possible consequences of these variations for the roles of workers or supervisors been fully explored.

Three general team types have been reported as conducive to provision of family-focused services: the case management team,[37] the social services or decision-making team,[38] and the specialized agency service team.[39]

The *case management team* consists of persons actively involved in determining an individual case plan and in providing case services. Such a team then is uniquely formed and includes the agency social worker assigned to work with a family as primary worker or case manager; the clients, including parents and child; and others directly involved in service provision. Most frequently, the case management team is an interagency team.

Purposes of this team type include defining the problems that place a specific child at risk, determining case goals and objectives, negotiating tasks and responsibilities, setting a timetable for task completion, and meeting regularly for collaboration and review of progress. An agency social worker, as case manager, has responsibility to coordinate and monitor service, facilitate communication among team members, and document task accomplishment. In using this model, some of the traditional supervisory administrative functions will be shared with other team members.

Although charged with case-specific decision making, the case management team is not intended to provide educational supervision or attend to management tasks that cut across workers' caseloads. Other supervisory methods must be utilized to accomplish these functions. Supervisors must be permitted to attend and actively participate in the decision-making process of case management teams. However, the demands of time and schedule are likely to require the development of means to share responsibility for each team's productivity other than regular supervisory participation.

The second general team type is the *social services or decision-making team*—a group of individuals, including a supervisor or team leader,[40] who maintain separate caseloads but are as a group responsible to plan, review, monitor, and evaluate service to the group's total shared client population. A group of primary workers or "case managers" and their supervisor may constitute such a team. Team members share responsibility for initial case assessment and assignment, review of difficulties related to specific case coordination and progress, exploration of professional intervention alternatives, and mutual support. The team may detect service needs and barriers common to the client population and formulate recommended programmatic responses.

Although designated agency employees constitute the core team membership, this team's boundaries may be fluid. Others involved in case planning and service delivery, including family members, foster parents, and other professionals within and beyond the agency, may actively participate at critical decision points.

The primary goal of the social services or decision-making team is assurance of effective service delivery for the total group of clients served by individual team members.[41] This goal is accomplished through the team's attention to specifically shared or delegated administrative, educational, and supportive supervisory tasks. This team is differentiated from peer group supervision, tutorial group supervision, and case management teams by the number of functions (administrative, educational, and supportive) and the nature of authority (of position and of competence) each supervisee shares with the supervisor.

Implementation of this team structure inevitably has a direct impact on the definition of supervisory responsibilities. Although the decision-making team may be delegated many supervisory functions, others necessarily remain with the team's supervisor. For example, the tasks of linking the team and the agency administration, coordinating management tasks between team meetings, and attending to specific worker performance are assigned to the supervisor to assure continuity and efficiency of management.

The third general team type, the *specialized agency service team*, incorporates elements of the other two. An intra-agency team, its members deliver specialized services to shared clients who may or may not be defined as team members. Rather than each worker performing generic tasks with individually assigned clients, a team of workers performs specialized tasks with shared clients. For example:

> One worker might deal with the biological parents, while another worker with the child in the foster home. Sometimes, several workers would deal with the demands of a difficult parent. Teaming also allowed for specialization of such tasks as writing court reports. The legal writer was responsible for polishing rough drafts submitted by other members and handling matters related to the court process. The administrative workers kept track of administrative details, and also led the team meetings until a supervisor assigned to the unit took over this function.[42]

In this regard, this team incorporates elements of the case management team (specialization) and decision-making team (responsibility for review and monitoring case goals and progress for a total client population).

Within any one setting, one or more team types might be used to actively encourage parent involvement. The impact of various team structures upon supervisory responsibilities, therefore, depends upon the team's purpose, composition, and agency-delegated authority empowering the team to accomplish its purpose. When elements of the supervisory functions are delegated to or shared with a team structure, clarity regarding the relationship between the supervisor and team members, and specific supervisory responsibilities, must be reached. The latter, however, can be expected to include acquainting workers with the stages of team development and examining obstacles to team building.

SELECTION OF METHODS

The use of the tutorial, consultation, and team supervisory methods has been discussed in terms of the functions or tasks each method usually achieves. In implementing the philosophy of total parent involvement, supervisory methods can be weighed with regard to their utility in a particular agency setting. The following chart (fig. 5.0), in comparing supervisory methods, assumes general supervisor, consultant, and team member competence. Shaded blocks convey clear advantages in achieving a particular function; an asterisk denotes that the approach is useful, but needs to be supplemented with other approaches; unmarked blocks denote an approach that is less likely to accomplish the associated function than are others.

The degree of association depicted here will vary considerably from setting to setting; however, the chart is an attempt to illustrate (1) that a number of different supervisory formats may accomplish any one specific supervisory function; and (2) that no one supervisory approach used exclusively can predictably achieve all supervisory functions.

For example, the individual tutorial approach can be expected to be a productive method generally for accomplishing the administrative and supportive functions. To meet supervisee educational needs, however, particularly in a complicated service such as foster care, the individual tutorial can be supplemented through use of agency personnel or others as consultants and/or through teams.

Although necessarily combined with other supervisory methods, both case management and social service decision-making teams offer important advantages that support the implementation of the philosophy of total parent involvement. Both rely on the process of shared decision making; both provide a structure for review of case progress and for monitoring service provision. Therefore, it is recommended that agency administrators, supervisors, and foster care workers experiment with both team approaches to determine comparative effectiveness of each method in their particular settings.

FIGURE 5.0 Relative Utility of Supervisory Methods in Accomplishing Supervisory Function Related to Implementation of Total Parent Involvement

<table>
<tr><th rowspan="3">Supervisory Functions</th><th colspan="7">Supervisory Methods/Approaches</th></tr>
<tr><th colspan="2">Tutorial</th><th colspan="2">Consultation</th><th rowspan="2">Case Manage</th><th rowspan="2">Team Decision Making</th><th rowspan="2">Special Service</th></tr>
<tr><th>Individual</th><th>Group</th><th>Individual</th><th>Group</th></tr>
<tr><td colspan="8">ADMINISTRATIVE</td></tr>
<tr><td>Interpret, Monitor/Coordinate Policy Implementation, Participate Policy Development</td><td>▓</td><td>▓</td><td></td><td></td><td>*</td><td>▓</td><td>▓</td></tr>
<tr><td>Case Assignments, Coverage</td><td>▓</td><td>▓</td><td></td><td></td><td></td><td>▓</td><td>▓</td></tr>
<tr><td>Identification of Training Needs</td><td>▓</td><td>▓</td><td>*</td><td>*</td><td>*</td><td>▓</td><td>▓</td></tr>
<tr><td>Performance Evaluation</td><td>▓</td><td>*</td><td></td><td></td><td>*</td><td>*</td><td>*</td></tr>
<tr><td>Channeling Communication within Agency</td><td>▓</td><td>▓</td><td>*</td><td>*</td><td>*</td><td>▓</td><td>▓</td></tr>
<tr><td>Outside Agency</td><td>*</td><td>*</td><td>*</td><td>*</td><td>▓</td><td>*</td><td>*</td></tr>
<tr><td colspan="8">EDUCATIONAL</td></tr>
<tr><td>Agency Policy, etc.</td><td>▓</td><td>▓</td><td>*</td><td>*</td><td>*</td><td>▓</td><td>▓</td></tr>
<tr><td>Parent Involvement Projects</td><td>*</td><td>*</td><td>*</td><td>*</td><td>*</td><td>*</td><td>*</td></tr>
<tr><td>Child/Family</td><td>*</td><td>*</td><td>*</td><td>*</td><td>*</td><td>*</td><td>*</td></tr>
<tr><td>Social Work Practice</td><td>*</td><td>*</td><td>*</td><td>*</td><td>*</td><td>*</td><td>*</td></tr>
<tr><td>Prevent, Reduce Job-Related Stress</td><td>▓</td><td>▓</td><td>*</td><td>*</td><td>▓</td><td>▓</td><td>▓</td></tr>
</table>

Case management teams are not typically defined as a supervisory technique. As they are currently being used, however, they do provide an important format for assuring opportunities for active parent involvement, collaboration and support among service providers, identification of resource needs, case-specific documentation of workers' performance, and shared decision making. But the productiveness of this structure over time depends on the development of effective means to tie in the case management teams with the agency. This is essential if services to the general client population are to be monitored, and educational resources provided to supervisees. Monitoring and resource development are management functions that case-specific teams cannot address. Implementation of case management teams requires agency-developed guidelines concerning the delegated/shared authority of supervisor and case manager, and the accountability of the team to the agency and other constituencies.

The social services decision-making team has been found to be useful in examining a group of workers' cases, and therefore is a productive forum for initial case assessment and assignment, for review of critical case decisions and service provision, for discussion of alternative professional interventions, for worker support, for identification of barriers to effective service delivery across caseloads, and for formulating recommended strategies for dealing with such barriers. Through this team process, inexperienced workers are provided with training as well as specific professional supervision regarding their cases. Experienced workers are provided a collegial climate and the opportunity to contribute to the professional development of their peers. The decision-making team is an internal agency mechanism accounting for consistency of focus among policy, program, practice, and supervision. Because the social services team defines its core membership as intra-agency, however, the team structure does not assure the degree of interagency communication and involvement provided through the case management team. Therefore, greater worker initiative may be required in that area.

Both team types additionally encourage workers' active participation in the agency's permanency efforts. Team identification of policy and practice dilemmas or gaps, based on review of similar client problems or needs, can result in development of innovative practice approaches or programs within the agency and in revision of policy.[43]

In rural areas, the use of case management and social service decision-making teams may be complicated by distance and by the small numbers of workers. In urban public agencies, the size of caseloads may initially complicate implementation of team approaches. Such situations obviously call for creativity in modifying models to fit the purpose, the place, and the persons involved.

As illustrated in figure 5.0, the use of case management and social service decision-making teams will be necessarily supplemented by other approaches. Availability of individual and/or group tutorial as well as individual and/or group consultation assures that workers' needs for clarity of administrative mandate, for specific feedback related to job performance, for confidential exploration of personal job-related stress, and for current information about particular client problems or practice approaches are met.

Open, regular, mutual examination by supervisor and supervisees of the relative effectiveness of supervisory approaches is particularly important when the expectations of the agency regarding practice approaches and case outcomes are in transition. At such times, it becomes imperative that *all* administrative, educational, and supportive supervisory functions are attended to.

SUMMARY

Changes in service emphasis or service models may require changes in supervisory structure and method. Hesitation to restructure supervision and case management, particularly through the use of teams, often reflects supervisory and agency administrative concerns regarding potential loss of power or authority. It is important to acknowledge that emphasis on parent involvement recognizes parents' competence regarding their own goals and capacities. Similarly, emphasis on sharing management decisions with workers recognizes their experience, expertise, and investment in providing effective professional service. Thus, expanding parents' and workers' authority within the case management and supervisory structure further strengthens rather than weakens the supervisor's authority by broadening the boundaries of her or his expertise and maximizing opportunities for successful outcomes for families.

Changes in supervisory structure and method, and the need for supervisory practice knowledge and skill to support increased parent involvement, will require supervisory access to training, resources, and agency support. As experienced staff members with seniority, supervisors have often relied for long periods of time on former agency policies and practice approaches for direction.[44] Therefore, the recommended shifts in foster care practice may meet barriers if supervisors are not afforded opportunities to explore and understand the rationale for increased participation of parents of children in care, as well as opportunities to develop the knowledge and skills necessary to accomplish the many complicated supervisory functions described in this chapter. Theirs is a potent position. Supervisors must have opportunities to strengthen their knowledge and skills, agency administrative support to strengthen their commitment, and resources and authority to maximize the benefits of increased parent involvement for both agency personnel and children and families.

NOTES

1. See Karen Blumenthal, chapter 1 of this volume.
2. Alfred Kadushin, *Supervision in Social Work* (New York, NY: Columbia University Press, 1976), 21.
3. Ibid., entire volume.
4. Ibid., 200-201
5. See Stephen Holloway, "Up the Hierarchy: From Clinician to Administrator," *Administration in Social Work* 4 (Winter 1980): 1-14; and Neil A. Cohen and Gary B. Rhodes, "Social Work Supervision: A View Toward Leadership Style and Job Orientation in Education and Practice," *Administration in Social Work* 1 (Fall 1977): 281-291, for discussion of components of supervisor skill in influencing agency administration.
6. Blumenthal, op. cit., 1.
7. For example, see "CWLA's Statement on Foster Care Services," *Child Welfare* 58 (January 1979): 49-50; Mary Ann Jones, Stephen Magura, and Ann W. Shyne, "Effective Practice with Families in Protective and Preventive Services: What Works?" *Child Welfare* 50 (February 1981): 67-80; *Case Record* 4 (August 1980); Anthony Maluccio and Paula Sinanoglu, eds., *The Challenge of Partnership: Working with Parents of Children in Foster Care* (New York, NY: Child Welfare League of America, 1981); Charles A. Rapp and John Poertner, "Reducing Foster Care: Critical Factors and Administrative Strategies," *Administration in Social Work* 2 (Fall 1978): 335-346; Victor Pike et al., *Permanent Planning for Children in Foster Care: A Handbook for Social Workers*, DHHS Publication No. (OHDS) 80-30124 (Washington, DC: U.S. Department of Health and Human Services, Children's Bureau, 1977); Public Law 96-272, "Adoption Assistance and Child Welfare Act of 1980."
8. The minimum sufficient level of care is a social standard; it is the minimum care necessary for a child's growth and development. Judgments made by this standard are necessarily relative and in part set by local, current standards. For further discussion of this concept see: Susan Downs and Catherine Taylor, *Permanent Planning in Foster Care: Resources for Training*, DHHS Publication No. (OHDS) 81-30290 (Washington, DC: U.S. Department of Health and Human Services, Children's Bureau, 1980), 1, 2, 13; and Pike et al., op. cit., 14.
9. See Peg Hess, "Parent-Child Attachment Concept: Crucial for Permanency Planning," *Social Casework* 63 (January 1982): 46-53; Selma Fraiberg, *Every Child's Birthright: In Defense of Mothering* (New York, NY: Basic Books, Inc., 1977); Vera Fahlberg, *Attachment and Separation* (Lansing,

MI: Department of Social Services, 1979); Ner Littner, "The Importance of the Natural Parents to the Child in Placement," *Child Welfare* 54 (March 1975): 175-181.
10. Fact sheets that describe the mandates of this law are available. Write for "Public Law 96-272 Resource Folder," Child Welfare League of America, New York, NY (1981).
11. The full effect of implementing case reviews is not yet known; see Stephen Magura and W. Eugene Claburn, "Foster Care Review: A Critique of Concept and Method," *Journal of Social Welfare* 5 (Fall 1978): 25-34; Jane Park Cutler and Richard W. Bateman, "Foster Care Case Review: Can It Make a Difference?" *Public Welfare* 38 (Fall 1980): 45-61; Virginia LaFalce Krymow, "Obstacles Encountered in Permanent Planning for Foster Children," *Child Welfare* 58 (February 1979): 97-103; American Public Welfare Association, "Service Planning and Case Review," *Standards for Foster Family Services Systems for Public Agencies*, DHEW Publication No. (OHDS) 79-30231 (Washington, DC: U.S. Department of Health, Education, and Welfare, Children's Bureau, 1979), 29-33.
12. Michael R. Daley, "Preventing Worker Burnout in Child Welfare," *Child Welfare* LVIII (July/August 1979): 443-450.
13. In addition to assuring clarity regarding expected worker tasks and level of performance, such contracts should specify supervisory responsibility for education, support, agency resource allocation, and administrative backup. Additionally, such agreements provide documentation of supervisee effort, progress, and achievement helpful in subsequent performance evaluation. See Thomas D. Morton and P. David Kurtz, "Educational Supervision: A Learning Theory Approach," *Social Casework* 61 (April 1980): 240-246.
14. See Leonard Schneiderman, "A Social Action Model for the Social Work Practitioner," *Social Casework* 46 (October 1965): 491.
15. Alfred Kadushin, op. cit., 126.
16. See Pike et al., op. cit.; Downs and Taylor, op. cit.; Arthur Emlen et al., *Overcoming Barriers to Planning for Children in Foster Care*, DHEW Publication No. (OHDS) 78-30138 (Washington, DC: U.S. Department of Health, Education and Welfare, Children's Bureau, 1978); Susan Whitelow Downs et al., *Foster Care Reform in the 70's: Final Report of the Permanency Planning Dissemination Project* (Portland, OR: Regional Research Institute for Human Services, 1981).
17. For example, Jones, Magura, and Shyne, op. cit.; Maluccio and Sinanoglu, op. cit.; Rapp and Poertner, op. cit.; Magura and Claburn, op. cit.; Anthony N. Maluccio, Edith Fein, Jane Hamilton, Jo Lynn Klier, and Darryl Ward, "Beyond Permanency Planning," *Child Welfare* LIV (November 1980): 515-530; Ronald Rooney, "Permanency Planning: Boon for All Children?" *Social Work* 27 (March 1982): 152-158.
18. Rooney, op. cit., 156.
19. For example, see Alice Overton et al., *The Casework Notebook* (St. Paul, MN: Greater St. Paul Community Chest and Councils, 1957).
20. Beulah Compton, "The Family-Centered Project Revisited," paper presented at the Council on Social Work Education Annual Program Meet-

ing, March 1981. Mimeo. Available from Dr. Compton, Indiana University School of Social Work, Indianapolis, IN.
21. See Paula Sinanoglu, "Working With Parents: Selected Issues and Trends as Reflected in the Literature," in Maluccio and Sinanoglu, op. cit., for a concise review of the types of family problems contributing to out-of-home placement.
22. See notes 7, 17, 19, and 20.
23. Pike et. al., op. cit., 6.
24. For example, see Paul Kuczkowski, *Permanent Planning in Maryland: A Manual for the Foster Care Worker*, mimeo. (Baltimore, MD: Maryland Foster Care Impact Demonstration Project, August 1978), 13; John McGowan and Christine Deyss, *Permanency Planning: A Casework Handbook* (Albany, NY: Welfare Research Inc., March 1979): 114-126.
25. See *Case Record*, op. cit., 2. For content regarding group problem-solving, see Naomi Brill, *Teamwork: Working Together in the Human Services* (New York, NY: J.B. Lippincott Company, 1976); Herbert Thielen, *Dynamics of Groups at Work* (Chicago, IL: University of Chicago Press, 1963).
26. Differences between workers' and foster parents' attitudes, for example, can be expected to affect decisions regarding involvement of parents in decision making about their placed child and visitation. A foster care attitude assessment scale and self-score have been developed for use with workers, foster parents, and others to heighten awareness of attitudes and their probable impact on decision making. See appendix E.
27. Kadushin, op. cit., 200-201.
28. Class lecture notes shared by colleagues Mary Kapur, "Child Welfare Service Delivery Systems," Indiana School of Social Work, Fall 1981. See also Daley, op. cit.; Martha Bramhall and Susan Ezell, "Are You in Danger of Burning Out?" "Working Your Way Out of Burnout," and "How Agencies Can Prevent Burnout," *Public Welfare* (3-part series) 39 (Winter, Spring, Summer 1981); Edward Davis and Marjie Barrett, "Supervision for Management of Worker Stress," *Administration in Social Work* 5 (Spring 1981): 55-64; Marjie Barrett and J. McKelvey, "Stresses and Strains on the Child Welfare Worker: Typologies for Assessment," *Child Welfare* 59 (May 1980): 277-285.
29. Kate Mullins and Peg Hess, "Achieving Quality Services in Public Agencies Through Team Practice and Consultation: A Lesson in Curriculum Development," paper presented at the Council on Social Work Education Annual Program Meeting, New York, NY, March 1982, 11-12, mimeo.
30. This would include supervisory involvement in policy formulation with regard to flextime and/or compensation time; employee benefits; salary levels; career advancement; institutional racism, sexism, and ageism.
31. A crucial condition in implementing new policies in involvement of staff members who will be carrying out the policies. Participation in the various stages of implementation of strategies increases staff investment in such strategies. See Rapp and Poertner, op. cit., 345.
32. See Kadushin, op. cit., 91-115, for a review of supervisory authority and sources of power.

33. Kadushin, op. cit., 320. Also see Kenneth Watson, "Differential Supervision," *Social Work* 18 (November 1973): 80–88, for comparison of the tutorial and other supervision models; Emily Jean McFadden, "Helping the Inexperienced Worker in the Public Child Welfare Agency: A Case Study," *Child Welfare* LIV (May 1975): 319–329, for description of combined individual tutorial and consultation with an inexperienced worker.
34. Watson, op. cit. 83–84; also see Florence Whiteman Kaslow et al., *Supervision, Consultation and Staff Training in the Helping Professions* (San Francisco, CA: Jossey-Bass Publishers, 1977), xv.
35. Watson, op. cit., 85.
36. See *Case Record*, op. cit.
37. See chapter 3 in this volume; see also Compton, op. cit., 6–10, for an excellent discussion of the "one-family—one-worker concept" and concerns regarding case management. For reviews of the literature regarding case management, see Susan Wells, "Bibliography: Case Management," and Susan Wells, "Case Management and Child Welfare," mimeo., (Los Angeles, CA: Region IX Child Welfare Training Center, UCLA School of Child Welfare, 1980).
38. See Mullins and Hess, op. cit.; Watson, op. cit.; *Case Record*, op. cit.
39. See Willard Richan, "Personnel Issues in Child Welfare," in *Child Welfare Strategies in the Coming Years*, DHEW Publication No. (OHDS) 78-30158 (Washington, DC; U.S. Department of Health, Education and Welfare, Children's Bureau, 1978); Michael Bough, "Team-Shared Caseloads—A Way to Survive in Child Protection," *Adoption Report* 7 (Spring 1982): 1, 5.
40. This model appears to be workable with the supervisor participating "in the team's formal work equally with the other team members" while "designated by the agency as leader" (Mullins and Hess, op. cit., 10), or with team accountability divided between a participating nonsupervisory team leader and a nonparticipating administrator (Watson, op. cit., 85–86).
41. Mullins and Hess, op. cit., 9–10.
42. Baugh, op. cit., 1.
43. For example, see Peg Hess and Linda Williams, "Group Orientation for Parents of Children in Foster Family Care," *Child Welfare* LXI (September/October 1982): 456–466.
44. See Pauline Zischka, "The Effect of Burnout on Permanency Planning and the Middle Management Supervisor in Child Welfare Services," *Child Welfare* LX (November 1981): 611–616.

6
TRAINING

Carla Overberger

Because working with parents and involving them in services requires staff to be knowledgeable in many areas, use new skills, and modify attitudes concerning the families with whom they work, staff development and, particularly, preservice and inservice training must be essential components of foster care programs. It is the agency's responsibility to provide these components if staff members are required to implement changing policies in their daily practice.

Staff development is an administrative process; its aims are to improve attitudes, enable staff to think critically and make sound judgments, and support their desire to learn.[1] Training is one facet of staff development; it is designed to teach skills appropriate to the tasks the staff must perform.[2] Before carrying out a training program, it is important to identify and review existing staff development resources that complement the training. These include:

- regular, formalized staff meetings
- orientation programs
- teams of workers that share decision-making responsibility
- budget allocations for staff to attend conferences or workshops
- consultation and supervision from trained professionals in the agency
- peer consultation
- committees or special projects that involve staff members from other agencies and professional organizations
- staff membership in professional associations
- provision of educational leaves
- an agency library[3]

A good training program is built on already existing training and staff development activities within the agency, and recognizes that there are many ways to help staff develop a knowledge base, learn new skills, and modify attitudes. Training is only one means, although an important one.

Training related to parent involvement should be directed to caseworkers, supervisors, administrators, foster parents, child care workers, case aides, and volunteers. It should

- sensitize the staff to the special needs, feelings, and qualities of parents involved in the foster care system
- help the staff to identify and confront their own feelings and attitudes toward parents
- enhance skills in working with parents, particularly in assessing parental needs and strengths and helping to resolve family problems
- clarify the importance of team work and help staff members work as a team
- impress upon the staff the importance of early decision making
- expose participants to innovative methods and programs that emphasize services to parents[4]

Many factors in the child welfare field contribute to the critical need for training—a high level of staff turnover, the high proportion of untrained and inexperienced staff, a lack of clarity concerning the roles of those involved in planning for and providing services, changes in child welfare practice, and inadequate preparation by schools of social work of those entering the child welfare field.[5] Training, however, is not the sole resource for addressing major problems.[6] It can facilitate organizational changes or support other activities designed to solve these problems, but alone, its impact is limited.[7] Many problems must be resolved by administrative decision; others are more appropriately addressed through training efforts. For example, policies and procedures must be established by administrative mandate; learning how to implement them is the subject of training efforts. The use of teams in a decision-making process is an administrative decision; learning how to work effectively as a team is a training goal. The use of written service agreements with parents is an administrative decision; learning how to develop and modify service agreements is a training responsibility. Training can be a solution to organizational problems, but because of the expense involved, it is essential to determine if there may be alternative, less costly ways of addressing these problems.

For most agencies, the focus on parent involvement throughout the foster care process requires new efforts. It produces new roles for foster parents and child care workers, new methods for negotiating differences of opinions, and new tasks for workers. The purpose of this chapter is to examine administrative responsibilities for developing a strong training program to facilitate agencies' efforts. Four questions are addressed:

1. What should training accomplish?
2. Who should be trained?
3. What resources should be used to create training programs?
4. What are the responsibilities of the trainer in developing a specific training program?

WHAT SHOULD TRAINING ACCOMPLISH?

In the broadest sense, training must develop the knowledge, skills, and appropriate attitudes for working with parents, attributes now largely lacking in many staff members.

Knowledge

Knowledge refers to the factual information and understanding that staff members must be made aware of:

- current, critical child welfare public policy issues
- variations in family structures and lifestyles
- the sources and nature of stress experienced by multiproblem families
- tasks associated with good parenting and the worker's role in making good parenting possible
- the effects of separation, loss, and disruption upon children and parents
- the goals of foster care services
- the permanency planning philosophy
- the importance of parents to children
- the relationship of parent involvement to return home
- the effects of cultural, ethnic, and religious differences on the provision of services
- the rights and responsibilities of parents, children, foster parents, child care workers, and other staff members
- the range of services, approaches, and community resources available to meet the needs of children and families
- legal issues and procedures that affect families[8]

Most training programs contain a component for participants to enhance their knowledge. When knowledge is the training objective, it should be related to actual job performance (see fig. 6.0).

FIGURE 6.0
Conveying Knowledge

In Tennessee, a group of social workers met to staff cases with a professor from a school of social work. Case consultation was the method used to impart basic knowledge about attachment and separation, child development, and the cycles of abusing families. The staff gained help with specific cases while developing a knowledge base for working with clients.[9]

Skill Development

Before knowledge can be applied to work with parents, the staff must learn specific skills. Many skills are complex, such as being able to form nonjudgmental relationships with parents, use a new treatment technique, assess family problems and strengths, design appropriate service plans, coordinate community resources, and use the team approach in decision making; some skills are relatively uncomplicated, such as using a new form or resource inventory.[10] Training teaches new skills and strengthens existing ones. It provides an opportunity to practice skills in a learning environment before using them on the job. Complex skills usually have to be taught over time, with appropriate feedback provided as the skills are practiced on the job. It is often assumed that once a particular skill has been demonstrated in a training session, and staff members have had exposure to it, they will be able, if they are willing, to apply it on the job. For most people, repeated practice and feedback are essential to consolidate new skills (see fig. 6.1).

Attitude Shaping

Attitude shaping refers to a planned effort to encourage individuals to rethink their beliefs and/or values about parents, family relationships, foster parents, and foster care based upon knowledge they acquire. The goal of attitude shaping is to influence the trainees' behavior toward the other parties involved in the foster care system. Policies can mandate specific changes in practice; however, unless staff members understand why the new practice is important and have a positive attitude toward it, they will not effectively carry out changes.

Attitude shaping is usually most successful when issues of values, attitudes, and beliefs are presented in a training session related to

---

FIGURE 6.1
Acquiring Skills

One trainer suggested to her group that each participant select only one case in which to practice a new technique for working with resistant parents, and to continue applying the technique even if it did not seem successful. At the next session, they were able to discuss difficulties they had, but were also able to become more familiar with the activity and consider applying it to two additional cases.

---

knowledge or skill acquisition. For example, many workers believe that parent-child visiting disrupts the foster care placement and therefore should be limited. When provided with information about parent-child attachments, normal grief reactions to separation from parents, and the role of parent-child visiting in facilitating discharge, staff members may still consider the visiting disruptive but are more likely to understand why it should not be limited. If training also teaches workers skills that will enable them to handle negative behaviors that are a result of visits, they are even more likely to accept the concept that visits should not be limited.

Attitude surveys have been developed to assess staff attitudes concerning parent involvement (see appendix E). Workers' responses to statements can be explored, myths can be dispelled with factual knowledge, and feelings may be modified when staff members become more competent in using essential skills.

TRAINING GOALS

Before a training program is developed, administrative staff must determine its goals and must obtain the staff's commitment to them. Training goals give direction to the training program and must be consonant with the overall goals of the agency, which in turn must be clear to the staff. Once there is agreement about what should occur as a result of the training, other decisions about the training program can be made.

It may be a training goal to prepare workers to accept or take on responsibilities related to a change in agency operations, or the goal may have to do with the development of specific skills unrelated to a change in agency policy. Examples of training goals include:

- to increase the staff's knowledge of various family structures and lifestyles, strengths, and needs
- to sensitize workers to the importance of parents as significant resources to their children in care
- to sensitize foster parents and child care workers to the needs and feelings of parents
- to heighten staff sensitivity to racial, cultural, and religious factors that affect the provision of child welfare services to various populations
- to increase staff skills for assessing the strengths and needs of children and families
- to provide staff with the basic skills necessary for interpersonal communications with, and interviewing of, parents
- to enable workers to develop service plans, including outcomes, objectives, responsibilities, and time frames, and to monitor and evaluate the service plan
- to foster the team approach in decision making, planning, and helping parents make decisions about the future of their children
- to enable the staff to facilitate parent-child visiting and obtain appropriate services for families
- to teach staff how to document reports and forms in a clear and informative way[11]

A training program is unlikely to encompass this quantity and variety of goals unless it is designed to run for an extended period of time. For time-limited training efforts, areas of the greatest need must be identified and pertinent training goals developed.

COMMITMENT

Training goals are an important component of a *formalized staff development plan*, whether for a single agency or an entire state system. Formalized plans give direction to the staff and further their commitment to the training effort.

Lack of commitment to the training effort can prevent the training from taking place or have a significantly negative impact on how much the training can accomplish if it does take place. If supervisors are unfamiliar with the training being received by their workers, for example, they may fail to support a new way of working.

Gathering support requires political sensitivity and creative ingenuity. For example, workers may resist the training because they may feel their professionalism is being questioned. They may also argue that the training is not germane to their caseload, that it is based on idealistic notions rather than realistic expectations.

Support for new training programs may be gained by

- establishing a time-limited task force, consisting of critical actors in the system, to review or establish training goals and recommend what resources should be used, who should be trained, and how the training should be evaluated
- creating a training team consisting of potential recipients of training, such as foster parents, caseworkers, child care workers, and supervisors
- meeting with administrators, policy setters, and supervisors to explain the training plan
- presenting the training plan at a staff meeting for discussion and revision before it is consolidated and implemented
- presenting the training program to significant board members and budget personnel

Participants are most likely to commit themselves to training when they understand how they will benefit from it. Individuals are often more ready to support training activities if they or their peers have contributed to the plan (see fig. 6.2).

Mandatory training does not ensure staff commitment or support. Staff members may attend because they are required to, not because they are particularly interested in the training. The challenge to the trainer and administrators is to convey the benefit of the program in a way that opens participants to the ideas being presented.

EVALUATION

To determine if the training has accomplished what it set out to do, the formalized staff development plan must have a means of evaluation. Since there are many techniques available for evaluation, those who plan the training should work with the trainer to decide the best way to evaluate the training effort.[15]

One format is known as evaluation by objectives. This requires that the administrator, in conjunction with the trainer, first specify what he or she wants the trainees to be able to do differently as a result of the training. For example, as a result of the program, participants should be able to

- identify the stages of grief that parents and children experience following separation, and the ways that they can be helped to move through them

CHAPTER 6: TRAINING 153

FIGURE 6.2
Gaining Commitment to Training

In North Dakota, a team effort, involving foster parents, supervisors, caseworkers, an educator, and others, designed a successful training program. Their input was critical in avoiding turnover of experienced, effective workers, supervisors, and foster parents.[12]

The Institute for the Study of Children and Families at Eastern Michigan University developed training course outlines. Each location where the program is run, however, may have an advisory board made up of parents, foster parents, and trainers to tailor the general design to their needs and conduct the training. This assures local commitment to a training program developed for broad use.[13]

In Kansas, selected foster care supervisors and caseworkers from each county were trained together in permanency planning philosophy and techniques in a central location. They returned to their counties as a training team, promoted the early intervention philosophy, and trained the remainder of the staff in the new techniques.[14]

- demonstrate how to involve the family in setting specific, feasible priorities for case objectives
- demonstrate the active listening and focusing skills used to convey empathy with, and acceptance of, parents
- identify points during an interview at which the values of the parents and worker are in conflict or are blocking the helping process, and demonstrate what can be done to resolve the problem
- identify the barriers to returning children to their families
- write a written service agreement
- demonstrate skills in handling parents' resistance to entering into a service agreement
- select appropriate service models for various family situations
- complete a written service plan for inclusion in the case record
- document diligent efforts to strengthen parents' ties with their children[16]

Any evaluation should assess whether these outcomes have been achieved. Pretests and posttests can be used. Outcomes that can be demonstrated at the end of training (e.g., writing a service agreement) can be evaluated by the trainer. Other outcomes might be observed on the job by supervisors or other designated staff members. Although evaluation can be time consuming, there is no other way to determine if the time and money invested in training have been justified or whether to provide further training.

Training also produces results that benefit the agency even though they are not explicitly stated in the goals or objectives.[17] Training creates an esprit de corps among participants, who often feel a strong sense of support and commitment that motivates them on the job after training. It often helps bridge existing communication gaps among participants (especially if the trainees are a heterogenous group) by giving them a better appreciation of their roles, responsibilities, and interrelationships. Finally, a portion of the training session is often set aside to plan strategies for implementing changes on the job.

SUMMARY OF WHAT TRAINING SHOULD ACCOMPLISH

Training should increase knowledge, enhance skills, and shape attitudes of participants in their practice with parents. Training content must be related as closely as possible to practice issues; to the realities confronting the trainees; and to the needs, qualifications, and expectations of trainees.[18] Since confusion and frustration commonly occur when new skills are learned that have limited application to expected job performance, administrators, with staff input, must be able to clearly specify training goals and outcomes, and be willing to have the training evaluated to ensure that it is successful. Any gains made by staff have to be reinforced and enriched through other learning opportunities.

WHO SHOULD BE TRAINED?

Once general agreement on training goals and desired outcomes has been reached, a decision must be made concerning participants. The choice of the target population will further refine goals and outcomes because some pertain only to particular categories of staff. Although there is a tendency to single out caseworkers as a primary target group, training of the other significant participants in the child welfare system—administrators, program managers, supervisors, child care workers, and foster parents—is needed.[19]

Agencies with limited training resources often have to set priorities by groups of staff, then either train all groups over time to use those trained first to train others (the "train-the-trainers" approach). There is no simple formula for determining who has the greatest need for training. The administrative staff must assess this issue and then decide if the group with the greatest need should be trained first, or if it is more desirable to train a particular group before training others because that group is the key to the implementation of new practices with parents.

Different approaches have been tried. For example, in South Carolina, protective service workers were trained first, foster care workers shortly thereafter.[20] In Michigan, a training program designed for one target group, foster parents, evolved into a broader program for supervisors and caseworkers when it became apparent that all of these groups needed the training if any one group was going to modify its practice with parents.[21]

Another issue administrators must consider is whether different staff groups should be trained together. Different levels of staff may be trained separately when controversial matters are being covered that could exacerbate existing organizational problems. In several states, caseworkers and foster parents have been trained separately, using the same general content, because of antagonisms that existed between the two groups.

To expose different levels of staff to one another and perhaps to use the sessions to help resolve existing organizational problems, it may be appropriate to provide some of the training separately and some jointly. For example, one agency scheduled content sessions separately for workers and foster parents although skill development sessions were attended jointly to promote their work together as a team. Training concerning the use of written service agreements might involve workers, supervisors, and clerical staff; an initial session discussing the purposes and formats of agreements could involve all three groups; training in procedures related to the specific responsibilities of each of these groups, however, should probably be conducted separately.

In still other instances, joint training has been used exclusively. In Kansas, foster parents and social workers were trained together in order to establish teamwork as a standard mode of practice (see fig. 6.3).

Joint training may be appropriate when all participants share the need for the same information. Possible combinations—foster parents and caseworkers; managers, supervisors, and caseworkers; child care workers and caseworkers; board members and line staff; caseworkers and clerical staff—should be assessed, comparing potential benefits and disadvantages. On the one hand, for example, possible advantages to training caseworkers and supervisors together are the opportunities to develop teamwork, confront different attitudes about new directions, and combine new directions and methods of accountability. On the other hand, the joint training might inhibit caseworker participation because of the supervisor's presence, create reluctance on the supervisor's part to acknowledge a lack of information, or result in a discussion of organizational problems irrelevant to the training.

FIGURE 6.3
Training for Foster Care Teamwork

As a part of the initial round of training, workshops on teamwork were presented at the Kansas State Association of Foster Parents (KSAFP) Regional Conferences at six locations. Several evening sessions on teamwork were also held for local foster parent groups throughout the state. A total of 74 hours of teamwork training was presented to 262 foster parents and 118 social workers. These sessions were particularly beneficial in highlighting the value of bringing social workers and foster parents together for training. Since teamwork depends upon cooperation, joint training can provide opportunities for breaking down barriers between foster parents and agencies, and for practicing teamwork skills. In July 1980, a 2-day seminar was held involving foster parents, caseworkers, and foster care administrators. The primary goal of the seminar was to form teams of foster parents and social workers who could return to their respective areas with the mission of implementing the team approach to foster care.[22]

WHAT RESOURCES SHOULD BE USED TO CREATE TRAINING PROGRAMS?

Resources include money, expertise, time, space, and equipment. There are never enough resources for training programs that will satisfy existing needs. All available resources must therefore be used as creatively as possible.

The Trainer

The most critical resource is the trainer. The trainer must be an individual who has

- training capacity and experience
- an appreciation of the working environment of the group of trainees
- credibility with those whom he or she trains[23]

The trainee should have expertise in the specific areas in which he or she is training. Practice experience in a child welfare setting will not always be necessary, since required knowledge and skills could be derived from research or administration.

Sometimes, prominent child welfare professionals are used to provide training. They usually possess the characteristics mentioned above; in addition, their reputation may attract attention. They may be knowledgeable about innovations in the field and can generate a great deal of enthusiasm.[24] Their fees, however, may be high; it may be difficult to arrange and schedule a training program with them; or they may be available only for limited time periods. Perhaps they may be unfamiliar with an individual state's program. Thus, the advantages and disadvantages of using a nationally known expert will have to be weighed.

Another common practice is to contract with private organizations for training. Some states have found that this enables them to provide a high quality of training.[25] Furthermore, it is sometimes easier to use Title XX training funds with a private contractor than to get an allocation of training money through the state agency.[26] Pennsylvania has developed a resource book that contains descriptions of training available from private contractors. The state allocates a share of Title XX training funds to each local department, which then can select the training package that can best meet its most pressing needs.[27]

Since training funds are at best limited, it is important to screen outside trainers carefully. The record of a trainer's experience, although relevant, is not sufficient for a decision. The trainer must be able to achieve the desired outcome of the specific training program. The content and techniques to be used, as well as the means of evaluating the results, should be discussed. One must also ascertain whether the trainer has the other essential qualities described earlier.

Some public and voluntary agencies have staff development units. But staff members in these units may not be familiar enough with parent involvement to train other staff members. It lowers costs markedly, however, to use a "train-the-trainers" approach, which would train a small cadre of individuals within these units who could then provide training statewide. Line workers and supervisors can also be used successfully as trainers, assuming they have the required expertise and can relate well to staff. All too frequently, the expertise that exists within the agency is overlooked. This can be the least expensive method of training provided that those staff members do not first have to be trained. If line staff members provide training, however, it is essential that their other work responsibilities be adjusted so that they can devote enough time to training.

Other Resources

To enhance any training effort, foster parents, parents, child care workers, and others should be engaged as cotrainers or resource persons. They can contribute a great deal through their special knowledge and life experiences.[28] Trainees often view them as the real experts because they have lived through what they are teaching (see fig. 6.4).

In light of the high cost of training in money, time, and energy, it is often unrealistic for child welfare agencies to conduct a full-scale training program on their own. A single agency may have resources to train staff members only once in several years, or have limited staff time to devote to planning training activities. Working cooperatively with other providers creates an opportunity to build community contacts, improve interagency coordination, upgrade the standards of professional conduct, exchange expertise at lower cost, and acquire access to more resources. Successful programs have used a wide range of local talent, including mental health experts, teachers, medical personnel, home economists, substance abuse counselors, and representatives from food stamp and family planning programs. Using local resources may also help in obtaining training funds from an external source, such as a foundation.

Possible disadvantages to working collaboratively, however, include the time needed to formally plan the training effort, the fact that many people must be involved in planning the training, and the difficulties involved in negotiating roles and responsibilities. State agencies charged with monitoring or promoting changes in services may be able to assist local agencies in coordinating their efforts and resources and overcoming some of these potential disadvantages. They may also have access to information about similar efforts being conducted elsewhere.

Packaged training materials are available from several national organizations and universities. These training programs have been designed and tested with staffs throughout the country and are available for local review and purchase. They may be tailored to meet the particulars of a local training effort. (See the annotated bibliography in appendix F for description of training materials.)

Courses offered by professional organizations, community colleges, undergraduate and graduate schools of social work, and postgraduate continuing education programs at social work schools may be germane to the training needs of caseworkers, foster parents, child care workers, and supervisors. Local community colleges often provide courses in child development and parenting skills that might be useful to foster parents and child care workers, as well as parents. Continuing education programs at schools of social work or other professional disciplines are designed to improve existing skills, such as conducting needs assessments and treating family problems. Agencies are sometimes able to reimburse individuals for the costs of attending appropriate courses.

FIGURE 6.4
Using Foster Parents in the Foster Parent Education Program at Eastern Michigan University

The structure of the classes in the Foster Parent Education Program reflected two basic philosophical premises of the program: (1) collectively, a group of foster parents have most of the answers to any question about fostering, and (2) foster parents learn best from sharing ideas with one another.

Classes were small (20–25), and group discussion, home assignments, and role playing were the methods of teaching used throughout the sessions. The instructors came from a variety of backgrounds and professions, including social work, law, medicine, mental health, special education, and community service; about one-fourth of the instructors had experience as foster parents.[29]

Training resources such as space and equipment can be donated as a community service by local businesses, churches, or other organizations. Staff and board members who have access to these resources should be encouraged to take advantage of their contacts.

Money

The importance of training should make funding it a high priority budget allocation. But because it competes with many other important programs within agencies, training rarely receives an adequate allocation.

Until recently, money for training has been available to every state through Title XX and has filtered down to local agencies in different ways in different states. Since the Reagan administration has made dramatic cuts in this program, the future of federal training funds for child welfare is uncertain. These cutbacks bolster the arguments for using capable line staff, foster parents, child care staff, and parents as teachers; collaborating with other agencies; seeking training funds from other resources;[30] and identifying community resources that can make "in-kind" contributions to training efforts.

Limited money also requires agencies to compare the cost and effectiveness of the training. For example, the cost of a program to train ten staff members to use a new counseling technique that requires video equipment for immediate feedback may be too high for use with so small a group. Less costly ways of providing comparable training would have to be explored.

Moreover, the creative use of available dollars can expand resources. For example, a private agency budgeted only $50 per year for training for each staff member. To stretch their dollars, the staff combined the allocations to pay an outside consultant to train them in a new behavior management skill. They also produced a training program, one part of which was of interest to other local agencies. The fee charged to other agencies for participation in this program then covered the consultant's fee. Another agency made training of foster parent and parent groups a part of each caseworker's job description, and made it possible for them to assume this additional responsibility by setting up a rotating schedule. Packaged training programs can also stretch dollars because the cost of the material per participant is reduced over time as more staff members use the material.

WHAT ARE THE RESPONSIBILITIES OF THE TRAINER IN DEVELOPING A SPECIFIC TRAINING PROGRAM?

Although administrative personnel in conjunction with staff representatives are responsible for establishing much of the training program, decisions should be made by the trainer, with administrative approval, about the specific learning objectives of the training, the techniques to be used, and the evaluation to be conducted.

A specific learning objective specifies, for example:

—who	the foster parent
—will do what	demonstrates to foster parents proper discipline for 14-year-olds who run away
—under what conditions	in a role play
—with what level of skill	to the trainer's satisfaction, using the performance checklist provided by the trainer

It may take time to develop competence in specifying learning objectives. To be able, however, to make content applicable to the particular needs of any agency and to evaluate whether the training is successful, specific learning objectives must be identified. They tell the trainer and the trainee what is expected during and after the training.

There are many training techniques, and the trainer must be comfortable with them. The techniques used should be those most appropriate for achieving desired outcomes. Questions to help guide the choice of techniques include:

- Does the technique permit the group to interact comfortably with one another on common problems?
- Will participants be comfortable enough with it to take an active part in the session?
- Does the technique allow for both skill development and attitude shaping at the same time?

If the primary aim of the training is to augment staff members' knowledge about a specific area, then the use of programmed instruction, panels of speakers, lectures, reading/discussion groups, films, problem-solving groups, and case analysis could be beneficial. Common techniques used to teach skills include role plays, simulations, practice exercises, and audio and video feedback equipment. When the primary goal of training is attitude shaping or change, then attitude surveys, films, simulations, case methods, coaching, and retreats are useful.

When the technique does not meet the expectations of the group, an entire session can be wasted. For example, if the participants expect to sit and take notes on a presentation, they may be reluctant to participate in small group exercises and role playing. The group should be briefed in advance about the format that will be used.

As discussed earlier, the trainer must assume major responsibility for the design of the evaluation. When learning objectives are specified, the evaluation should clearly relate to these objectives. The trainer will also often be responsible for carrying out the evaluation and reporting the results.

SUMMARY

Training is an essential part of the process of changing the way in which child welfare agencies involve parents in their foster care programs. Although training cannot complete the total change process, it can foster the development of the skills, knowledge, and attitudes that staff members need to work in new ways with parents. Training is particularly valuable in reinforcing the importance of teamwork in making permanent plans for children in out-of-home care. Although budget cutbacks may impair the ability of agencies to provide formal, costly training programs, alternative resources should be sought that will enable agencies to provide quality training to all levels of staff.

NOTES

1. Carol H. Meyer, *Staff Development in Public Welfare Agencies* (New York, NY: Columbia University Press, 1966), 98.
2. Ibid., 99.
3. See Child Welfare League of America, *Standards for Foster Family Service*, rev. ed. (New York, NY: Child Welfare League of America, 1975), 93.
4. Anthony Maluccio, *Education for Practice with Parents of Children in Foster Care*, mimeo. (West Hartford, CT: The University of Connecticut School of Social Work, March 1980) 52-53.
5. Susan Whitelaw Downs et al., *Foster Care Reform in the 70's: Final Report of the Permanency Planning Dissemination Project* (Portland, OR: Regional Research Institute for Human Services, 1981) 5.13.
6. See, for example, Robert Mager and Peter Pipe, *Analyzing Performance Problems* (Belmont, CA: Fearon, 1970).
7. In a forum conducted by the Regional Research Institute for Human Services, field consultants recalled instances in which states had reduced caseloads in an effort to promote aggressive casework but failed to give workers the training they needed to make changes in how they used their time. See "Issues and Experiences in Permanent Planning: A Report on Seven Regional Work Sessions on Foster Care Reform" (Portland, OR: Regional Research Institute for Human Services, n.d.), 7.
8. An excellent source of ideas for knowledge content is *Child Welfare Training: Comprehensive Syllabus for a Child Welfare Training Program*, DHHS Publication No. (OHDS) 80-30276 (Washington, DC: U.S. Department of Health and Human Services, October 1980).
9. Peg Hess. Interview with author, 1981.
10. See *Comprehensive Syllabus*, op. cit., Unit 102, Module E, for more detailed discussion of these and other skills.
11. For additional examples, see Maluccio, op. cit.; *Comprehensive Syllabus*, op. cit.; Esther Dean Callard and Patricia Morin, *PACT: Parents and Children Together: An Alternative to Foster Care* (Detroit, MI: Wayne State University, 1979), 17-18; Roger Boothroyd and Jody Fitzpatrick, *An Assessment of Training Priorities: Implications of the Child Welfare Reform Act* (Albany, NY: Continuing Education Program, School of Social Welfare, State University of New York at Albany, July 1981); "Child Welfare Reform Act Training Program," (Stony Brook, NY: School of Social Welfare, State University of New York, 1981).
12. Don Schmid, Deputy Administrator, Children and Family Services, North Dakota. Interview with author, 1981.
13. Bruce Warren, Codirector, Institute for the Study of Children and Families, Eastern Michigan University, Ypsilanti, Michigan. Interview with author, 1981.
14. Pamela Marr, "Foster Care Teamwork Comes to Kansas," *Case Record* 5 (January 1981): 1-2.
15. For examples of descriptions of training evaluations, see Maluccio, op. cit., 167-192; Boothroyd and Fitzpatrick, op. cit.
16. Additional examples of outcomes are identified in *Comprehensive Syllabus*, op. cit.; Boothroyd and Fitzpatrick, op. cit.; Emily Jean McFad-

den, *Working with Natural Families: Instructor's Manual* (Ypsilanti, MI: Foster Parent Education Program, Eastern Michigan University, 1980); John McGowan and Christine Deyss, *Permanency Planning Training Resource* (Part I) (Albany, NY: Welfare Research, Inc., n.d.); Heather Craig et al., *Team Training; Manual II: A Foster Care Staff Development Curriculum* (Virginia Department of Welfare, n.d.).
17. *Issues and Experiences*, op. cit., 10.
18. Maluccio, op. cit., viii.
19. See Susan Whitelaw Downs, op. cit., 5.12.
20. Mack McGhee, South Carolina Department of Social Services, Foster Care. Interview with author, 1981.
21. Bruce Warren, op. cit.
22. Marr, op. cit.
23. See Maluccio, op. cit., viii; Susan Whitelaw Downs, op. cit., 513.
24. *Issues and Experiences*, op. cit., 9.
25. Ibid.
26. Ibid.
27. Pennsylvania Department of Public Welfare, *Prospectus: Training Activities for Children and Youth Services in Pennsylvania* (Harrisburg, PA: Office of Children, Youth and Families, n.d.). This resource book has been discontinued. Some users objected to being limited to the particular resources identified in the book.
28. Maluccio, op. cit., viii.
29. Eastern Michigan University, "Foster Parent Education Project Stresses Professional Development," *Case Record* 5 (January 1981): 1, 3.
30. Two potential resources for training funds are foundations and private industry.

APPENDIX A

Examples of Agency Policies, Procedures, Forms, and Training Relevant to Parent Involvement (by State)

I. *Service Planning*
   A. Virginia
      1. Service Planning Toward Return Home
         a. Developing Realistic, Achievable Service Plans
         b. Integrating the Agreements Into Service Planning
   B. Kentucky
      1. Parental Participation in Treatment Planning
      2. Treatment Planning Conferences
         a. Attendance
         b. Roles
         c. Narrative and Written Materials
         d. Initial Treatment Planning Conference
         e. Ongoing Treatment Planning Conference
   C. South Carolina
      1. Tasks of First Week Conference
      2. Preparation Tasks Required of the Presenting Worker
      3. Preparation of Parents for Case Conferences
      4. Preparing Other Attendees
   D. Pennsylvania
      1. Placement Service Plan

II. *Service Provision*
   A. Virginia
      1. Ongoing Casework Services
   B. Alaska
      1. Services to the Child's Family

III. *Parent-Child Visiting*
   A. South Carolina
      1. Parent-Child Visitation

       2. Role of Visitation in Treatment
       3. Frequency of Visits
       4. Parent-Child Visitation in Out-of-County Placements
       5. Visitation Settings
       6. Workers Follow-up to Parent-Child Visitation
       7. Cancellation of Visits
       8. Sibling Visitation
       9. Visitation Contract
     10. Distribution of the Visitation Contract
     11. Elements of the Visitation Contract
     12. Disruptive Visits
  B. Alaska
       1. Problems That May Arise Regarding Visitation
          a. When a Parent Cancels Visits or Arrives Late for Visits
          b. When Visits Create Problems

IV. *Review*
  A. Alaska
       1. Case Review
          a. Guidelines for Areas of Review
  B. Kentucky
       1. Administrative Review

V. *Forms*
  A. South Carolina
       1. Foster Care Review Summary Sheet
  B. Family Strengths

VI. *Training*

  A. Detailed Case Management Checklist for Children Headed for Restoration
  B. "The Worker's Perspective"

I. Service Planning
A. Virginia
SERVICE PLANNING TOWARD RETURN HOME

The service plan is a working tool which reflects the consensus between the worker and client as to the direction their efforts will take in order to achieve the mutually derived goals. It should be noted that most cases are thrown out of court because the plan was not written correctly the first time.

Developing Realistic, Achievable Service Plans

The development of a service plan that is a working tool is dependent on much initial work. There must be emphasis on mutual planning and agreement as to strengths and needs, mutual objective setting, and delineation of responsibilities. If the child has recently entered care, there must be agreement as to those factors that precipitated custody and those factors that must change in order for the parents to reach the minimum sufficient level to provide for this child. If the child is old enough, s/he should be involved in the joint planning process whenever possible. The process of service planning is one that is based on self-determination. The child who is involved in the planning process will have a better understanding of what is happening to him/her and why events occur in certain ways. Planning that is done with, rather than for, the child will help him/her to realistically participate in decisions about his/her future and will help to minimize the uncertainties about placement and anxiety about unknown situations.

When the conduct of the child is part of the reason for custody it is even more critical that all family members who can be involved enter into the planning process. Behaviors and needs worked on in isolation often can cause more distance in a family. Mutual responsibility and understanding will be difficult to achieve in a planning process that is isolated for each family member.

The evaluation of the goal of return home mandates that parents be given the opportunity to participate in planning, treatment, and rehabilitation that will lead to the child's return. For children coming into care the service plan that is developed within the first sixty days should contain short-term and longer-range objectives to facilitate return home. If a child has been in care and parental contact has been minimal or not maintained, the goal of return home must be worked on to provide the parents the opportunity to reach the minimum sufficient level. *The goal of return home cannot be eliminated until parental participation is sought and evaluated..*

Important points to consider in service planning include:

1. use of strength/need lists as developed in the assessment process;

[Reprinted from "Foster Care," in *Permanent Planning Handbook: Case Management in Social Services*, with permission from the publisher (Richmond, VA: Virginia Dept. of Welfare, n.d.).]

2. awareness of the length of time the child has already spent in care, and the need of the child for a permanent home;
3. the biological parents should be aware of the consequences for themselves and their children if they do not participate in a service and treatment plan;
4. parents should be aware that both you and the agency will support and evaluate their efforts;
5. parents should be aware of their ability to participate in making alternate plans for their children if they cannot return home;
6. the development of a service plan should lead to the clear delineation of roles and responsibilities and to the development of written agreements;
7. behavioral objectives should be set which focus on individual outcomes—the clarity of objectives permits meaningful client participation;
8. realistic target dates should be set that will work as frequent positive feedback to the client's progress;
9. regular evaluation of the service plan requires evaluating the objectives and steps mutually agreed upon by you and your client in the service plan/agreement;
10. revisions to the plan should be made as necessary when there is a need for change in objective(s), goal, services or service components.

Integrating the Agreements Into Service Planning

Written agreements should be an integrated part of the planning process. The written agreement will become a formalized way of direction, clarification and specification. Responsibilities of both the parents and the agency should be included.

B. Kentucky

PARENTAL PARTICIPATION IN TREATMENT PLANNING

The natural parents shall be notified of conferences and of their right to have an attorney present during these conferences. Notification shall include information on the purpose, time, and location of the conference and on who will be in attendance. Notification must be given early enough to insure that the natural parents will have an opportunity to attend, and the notification should be in a language the parents understand and, if illiterate, notification should be made in person. Conferences must be scheduled at mutually agreed upon times and locations.

Parents who do not attend the initial conference must receive a copy of the Synopsis and must be informed of their right to request another conference to revise it within ten (10) days of receipt. Upon the parents' timely request, the conference must be held within ten (10) days of the request.

If the parents disagree with part of the treatment plan, their specific objections are noted on the Synopsis on the same line as the objectionable component. In any case, parents must be advised of their right to file a Service or Civil Rights Complaint during the conference or upon their receipt of the Treatment Plan Synopsis and Visitation Agreement.

Parents have the right to participate fully in the development of the treatment plan by identifying their perception of their problems and the special needs of their child.

TREATMENT PLANNING CONFERENCES

Attendance

1. Required: family worker and Team Leader, foster care worker, homemaker (if appropriate), child's natural parents, and the child when age and level of understanding allow.
2. Recommended: outside persons knowledgeable about family or who will be involved in family's treatment plan.
3. Upon request: foster care worker's Team Leader, Social Service Supervisors, District Managers, and Specialists.
4. Any other person (e.g., foster parents, relatives, etc.) must have natural parents' permission to attend.
5. Foster parents should attend conferences involving children in long-term care when appropriate.

[Reprinted from *Bureau for Social Services Policies and Procedures Manual* (1981) with permission from Bureau for Social Services, Frankfort, KY.]

Roles

1. *Family Team Leader* is responsible for scheduling conferences, chairing the conferences, making necessary decisions, providing follow-up and monitoring, and providing copies of written material to appropriate persons. From the case conference discussion and narrative report, Team Leader will summarize all conferences on the Treatment Plan Synopsis Sheet.
2. *Family Worker and Team Leader* are responsible for all planning and decisions with input from the foster care worker and foster care Team Leader. The family worker, during conferences, must state the problems, why the child was removed, what the plans are, when the child will return to the natural family, provide Title XX information to the foster care worker, and share transportation responsibilities.
3. *Foster Care Worker* is responsible for locating a suitable placement, providing services to the child and foster family, providing input to the family worker for case planning, and sharing transportation responsibilities with the family worker.
4. *Foster Care Team Leader* is responsible for scheduling and chairing case conferences when parental rights have been terminated or when a child is in permanent substitute care.
   Note: Prior to the actual circuit court hearing terminating parental rights or prior to the actual signing of the permanent substitute care agreements by the foster parents and the Department, the responsibility for scheduling and chairing case conferences remains with the family services team leader.
5. *Social Services Supervisor* must attend the six (6) month conference to assist in the decision-making process and assure that progress continues toward permanent planning.
6. *Natural Parents* are responsible for stating their perceptions of the problems/condition which led to the child's removal. Additionally, the parents are expected to participate in the formulation of the treatment plan by providing input on the child's needs and by establishing goals for themselves. The parents will assist in the development of a visitation plan.
7. *Professionals from Other Agencies and Other Bureau Personnel* who have knowledge of the family may attend at the request and permission of the family Team Leader.
8. *Foster Parents* may attend conferences prior to six months of placement at the invitation of the family Team Leader only with the permission of the parents. After six months of placement, foster parents and relatives may attend at the invitation of the chairperson of the conference. When foster parents do not attend, their comments concerning the child's treatment plan must be solicited by the foster care worker prior to the conference and must be discussed during the conference.
9. *Foster Child* should attend all treatment planning conferences if he is of appropriate age and the discussions will not unnecessarily threaten his well-being. The participation of the adolescent child is vital.

Narrative and Written Materials

Copies of the Treatment Plan Synopsis must be given to the parents or caregivers and the child, if of appropriate age, at the end of each conference or as soon thereafter as possible. Foster parents are given a copy of the child's Synopsis *only*, and that copy must delete confidential information about the family. Other copies are circulated to appropriate agency personnel, the parents' representative upon their request, and the Bureau for Social Insurance when necessary for ongoing financial assistance.

Initial Treatment Planning Conference

The initial Treatment Planning Conference is held within one week [five (5) working days] of the child's initial placement in foster care. It is chaired by the Family Team Leader. During the conference, the initial goal for permanent placement is discussed and set, and a treatment plan to achieve it is developed. The following matters must be discussed at the initial treatment planning conference:

1. a description of the relevant history of the child, including a diagnostic statement about his family circumstances and special needs;
2. a description of the services offered or provided to help the child remain with his family;
3. a determination of the appropriateness of the child's placement, addressing the child's best interests, and special needs, the placement's restrictiveness, and its proximity to the parents' home, and if the current placement is determined inappropriate, describing the placement to be sought;
4. a statement of all requirements and recommendations of the court and a discussion of how those will be met;
5. an analysis of the circumstances and problems that necessitated the child's initial placement and the improvements necessary for the child's return home;
6. a summary of the objectives to be achieved during the child's placement, the services to be provided to the child, his parents, and his family, and a discussion of the appropriateness of these services in meeting the objectives and the child's special needs;
7. a statement of the supervisory arrangements planned to assure that the child receives proper care while in his placement, including services to the foster parents to facilitate and support the child's adjustment, and the supervisory arrangements planned to assure that the services to the child, his parents, or other appropriate family members to improve conditions in the parents' home are provided;
8. an estimated date by which a decision will be made to return the child to his parents or to seek an alternative permanent placement;
9. a description of the extent of participation by the child (if of appropriate age), his parents, and other relatives in the development of the plan.

At the finish of the discussion, the Family Team Leader prepares the Treatment Plan Synopsis for the parents or caregivers and for the child. Each synopsis must include:

1. a list of the specific problems the parents or the child face that are barriers to the child's return home, and a list of specific problems that are not barriers to return home but limit the child's optimal development;
2. a separate but corresponding list of the objectives which will lead to the resolution of each of these problems;
3. a separate but corresponding list of services to be provided to reach these objectives, and the persons responsible for providing them;
4. the objectives for which the parents or caregivers will be responsible;
5. the time frame in which all objectives will be accomplished.

A Visitation Agreement, according to guidelines set forth below, must be made.

Signatures of conference participants must be affixed to the original of the Treatment Plan Synopsis and Visitation Agreement as appropriate.

A date for the next conference must be set.

As soon after the conference as practicable, but no later than thirty (30) days following initial placement, the Family Team Leader will prepare a narrative, entitled "Initial Treatment Planning Conference Narrative," which contains:

1. necessary identifying information;
2. a summary of the tasks above, including a clear statement of the initial goal for permanent placement;
3. signature of the preparing team leader and date of preparation.

Upon the narrative's completion, the Synopsis and Visitation Agreement are attached, originals are filed in the family case record, and copies are sent to the committing court, to the parents, to the child, if of appropriate age, and to appropriate agency personnel.

Ongoing Treatment Planning Conference

Ongoing Treatment Planning Conferences are held as needed, but at intervals of no longer than ninety (90) days during the first six months of placement and no less frequently than every six months thereafter, until a permanent placement is achieved. Conferences are chaired by the Team Leader to review progress made by the parents and service providers toward achievement of objectives. Adherence to time frames for service and to the Visitation Agreement are also examined. The Team Leader insures that all necessary services have been and will continue to be provided to the parents, the child, and the foster family. Treatment Plan Synopses and Visitation Agreements are to be revised as necessary. The rights of parents to notice of participation in and representation at the conference remain the same as for the initial conference.

C. South Carolina

TASKS OF FIRST WEEK CONFERENCE

Specific tasks of the Conference are:

1. to establish the preliminary foster care goal—this task should include review of the preliminary goal developed by the Placement Committee;
2. to review with parents the list of "Legal Rights/Responsibilities of Natural and Legal Parents to the Placed Child";
3. to review with parents the list of "Agency's General Expectations of Natural/Legal Parents of the Placed Child";
4. to review list of "General Responsibilities of the Agency to the Placed Child";
5. to develop a written time-limited service agreement with the parents to be recorded on the "Parent-Agency Service Agreement";
6. to interpret to parents the Administrative Review and Foster Care Review Board process and to inform them of the on-going schedule for reviews;
7. to develop a written treatment/service agreement with/for the child to be recorded on the "Child's Service Agreement";
8. to develop a written visitation contract to be recorded on the "Visitation Contract";
9. to develop a written agreement for financial support to be recorded on the "Parent's Financial Support Agreement";
10. to review the findings and provisions of the Court Order with parents, if it is available;
11. to secure from parents any remaining information needed for the "Placement Planning Checklist" or the "Social History" (where applicable);
12. to complete with parents the "Child's Developmental History."

PREPARATION TASKS REQUIRED OF THE PRESENTING WORKER

Although both the Protective Service and Foster Care workers may be involved in the First Week Planning Conference and/or subsequent case conferences, a mutual agreement should be made concerning which worker will assume primary responsibility for preparing the parents and others for the conference. The "presenting worker" is designated as the worker responsible for preparation of the parents and other attendees.
The "presenting worker" will:

[Reprinted from *Permanency Planning Manual* (1981) with permission from Protective and Placement Services, South Carolina Dept. of Social Services, Columbia, SC.]

1. notify all parties of date, time, and location of case conference;
2. prepare the parents;
3. obtain a copy of the court order (if not available for First Week Conference, should be reviewed at next on-going case conference);
4. make the first week visit to the child and foster caregiver to:
   - solicit input of child and foster caregiver on visitation plans which will be finalized in "Visitation Contract" at First Week Planning Conference
   - solicit input of child and foster caregiver on treatment goals for the child which will be recorded on the "Child's Service Agreement" at the First Week Planning Conference
5. investigate treatment resources which may need to be used in treatment design at the conference;
6. obtain forms to be completed at the conference:
   - "Parent Agency Service Agreement"
   - "Child's Service Agreement"
   - "Child's Developmental History"
   - "Parent's Financial Support Agreement"
   - "Visitation Contract"
7. review case information with chairing supervisor and other attending worker(s) and clarify role responsibilities for conducting and recording the conference.

PREPARATION OF PARENTS FOR CASE CONFERENCES

If case conferences are to be useful in the treatment process, they must be planned, structured, and purposeful. The following preparations must be made:

1. written notice will be given the parents/prior caretakers of the date, time, and exact location of the conference;
2. explanation will be given the parents of the purpose and tasks of the conference;
3. the parents must be informed of who will be present and what they will do (In this regard, parents may be asked if they desire the attendance of another support professional with whom they may be involved in treatment.);
4. the parents must be informed of what will be expected of them in the conference, i.e., to share their plans and identify what they see as problems;
5. the worker should discuss with the parents their feelings/reactions to the conference;
6. any questions the parents have regarding the conference should be answered.

PREPARING OTHER ATTENDEES

1. obtain parents' written permission for non-agency professionals to attend;
2. explain the purpose and process of the conference;
3. give the date, time, and location;
4. explain who will be present and what their responsibilities are, i.e., giving information, planning, or observing;
5. inform the person of what portion of the conference he will attend.

D. Pennsylvania

This placement service plan reflects the fact that the public agency may be purchasing foster care services from a voluntary agency. It is being revised to strengthen the authority of the public agency.

PLACEMENT SERVICE PLAN

The placement service plan shall be developed in three phases. At each phase of the development of the plan and at all subsequent reviews, the parents and child shall have the right to be accompanied by a spokesperson of their choice.

In developing any phase of the placement service plan, the agency may offer services which are not directly related to the circumstances which necessitated the separation but which may be of benefit to the child and/or his/her parent(s). If accepted by the family, these services shall be identified in the placement service plan as ancillary services. Achievement of goals related to ancillary services shall not of themselves be considered a basis for continuation of placement.

The County Agency or other agency having legal custody shall be responsible for developing Phase I. The child's parent(s) and age-appropriate children shall be asked to cooperate with the County Agency or other agency having legal custody in completing Phase I, which shall include the following:

1. date on which child was separated from the family;
2. current address and phone number of the child's parent(s);
3. a family history;
4. a description of the specific circumstances which necessitated the placement;
5. the placement goal which will identify the type of permanent home being planned for the child;
6. the service objectives identifying the changes to be accomplished by the parent(s) and/or the child in order to achieve the placement goal;
7. identification of the agency to be responsible for directly providing the foster care service to the child and the parent(s).

Phase II shall be completed by the agency directly providing Foster Family Care Service. The child's parent(s) and age-appropriate children shall be asked to cooperate with the agency in completing Phase II of the plan.

Phase II of the plan shall contain the following points:

1. the specific actions to be taken by the agency to achieve the objectives of the plan and dates by which each objective will be accomplished;

[Reprinted from "Foster Family Care Service for Children," in *Pennsylvania Department of Public Welfare Regulations* (1980), with permission from the Pennsylvania Department of Public Welfare, Office of Children, Youth and Families, Harrisburg, PA.]

2. the specific actions to be taken by the parent(s) to correct the circumstances which led to separation, with dates by which each of these is to be accomplished;
3. the specific services and supports to be provided to the parent(s) and child by other agencies;
4. the anticipated length of the placement stated in number of months;
5. the plan for visitation of the child with parent(s), including the frequency of visits, location, and participants;
6. a statement describing the participation of parents and child in the development of Phase II, including an identification of the areas of agreement and disagreement.

Upon completion of the development of Phase II, the agency directly providing Foster Family Care Service shall submit the plan to the County Agency or other agency having legal custody. The agency shall indicate whether or not the parent(s) agree or disagree with Phase II of the plan and shall identify the specific areas of disagreement, if any.

The County Agency or agency with custody shall be responsible for completing Phase III of the plan, which shall include the following steps:

1. the County Agency with custody shall convene a face-to-face conference for the purpose of determining whether the plan as developed in Phase II shall be approved, at which the following parties shall be present:
   - the agency directly providing care, if different
   - the child's parent(s), unless they cannot be located, are unable or unwilling to attend, or have had parental rights terminated
   - the age-appropriate child unless he/she is unable or unwilling to attend
2. a representative of the County Agency or other agency having legal custody shall review Phase II as submitted by the agency directly providing Foster Family Care Service and determine if approval is appropriate. If approved the plan shall be *signed* by the representative of the County Agency or other agency having legal custody. If the representative of the County Agency or other agency having legal custody disapproves the plan, he/she shall obtain modification of the plan in cooperation with the above-specified parties to the plan;
3. parent(s) shall be asked to sign the approved plan as evidence of their agreement to the plan. Parent(s) shall be informed that they may refuse to sign the plan if they are not in agreement with any term of the plan. If the parent(s) do not sign the plan, the County Agency or other agency having legal custody shall assume that the parent(s) are in disagreement with the approved plan and shall follow the [designated] procedure.

The child's awareness of and participation in the development of the placement service plan shall be documented in the case record.

The agency shall consult the foster parent(s) and involve them in the planning as it relates to their role in accomplishing the objectives of the plan.

A copy of the placement service plan shall be provided by the County Agency or agency with custody to the following:

1. the family receiving service;
2. the court of jurisdiction;
3. the agency or agencies assuming direct service responsibility to the child and his/her parent(s).

II. Service Provision
A. Virginia

ONGOING CASEWORK SERVICES

For any plan to be successful, it is necessary for both you and the parents to stay actively involved. The demands on your time are enormous and it may be difficult to keep parents from getting discouraged or becoming disinterested when things do not happen right away. To help prevent the plan for returning the child from falling apart, keep in mind the following techniques:

1. Provide reasonable support to the parents to help them in their efforts to stabilize their situation and have their child returned. It is often difficult to decide how much you as the worker should do, and how much should be left up to the parents' own initiative. This decision should be based on your knowledge of the parents' capability, resourcefulness and sophistication. The less capable the parent, the more help s/he will need arranging appointments, transportation, etc. However, it is unrealistic to provide prolonged, massive support to a family before the child can be returned home because this probably means the family will need even more support after the child is returned.
2. Modify the plan when necessary and reasonable to help the parents achieve their goals. The parents will have to be reminded that the child cannot wait forever.
3. Keep track of the parents to prevent the parents from losing contact with the agency. You may have to make frequent trips to their home, leave messages with friends or neighbors, call other relatives, etc., but this kind of effort will prove that the agency made every effort to provide services and support the parents.
4. Investigate and use all available community resources that may be helpful in meeting the needs of the child and his/her parents to promote reunification. If you are a worker in a rural agency, you may not have a wealth of available resources, but you may know of informal helping systems that will help to compensate for the lack of organized community resources.
5. Follow up on all appointments made with the parents, whether the appointment was with you, the foster parents, or another agency. Getting immediate feedback can provide insight into progress or problems so that support can be given the parents (for following through with a clinic appointment, for example), or issues can be dealt with as they occur, if the parents fail to keep a scheduled appointment.

[Reprinted from "Foster Care," in *Permanent Planning Handbook: Case Management in Social Services*, with permission from the publisher (Richmond, VA: Virginia Dept. of Welfare, n.d.]

B. Alaska

SERVICES TO THE CHILD'S FAMILY

1. The purpose of providing services to families is to give parents all the support and service necessary for them to resume care of their children.
2. Services to Parents Shall Be Time-Limited to Ensure That Placement Does Not Continue Indefinitely.
   - Clearly defined short-term goals must be set with parents. (For example, "Go to at least two job interviews within the next week.")
   - A limit of one year or less, if possible, should be set for the change program as a whole. By the end of this time, expect either to return the child or develop another permanent plan for him.

[Reprinted from *Alaska Division of Family and Youth Services Program Manual* (1978) with permission from the Alaska Division of Family and Youth Services, Juneau, AK.]

III. Parent-Child Visitation
A. South Carolina

PARENT-CHILD VISITATION

When the foster care goal is to return the child to his natural family, treatment is directed at strengthening the family unit.

ROLE OF VISITATION IN TREATMENT

In such cases, the Agency is committed to a visitation policy aimed at maintaining continuity in the child's relationship with his parents and siblings. The importance of visitation must be interpreted to natural parents *and positively reinforced by the worker.*

The purpose of the parent-child-sibling visitation is to:

1. maintain the parent-child-sibling relationship;
2. prepare the family for reunification.

FREQUENCY OF VISITS

The frequency of visits between the placed child and his natural family will depend on factors such as the child's needs, circumstances of the parents, the child's age and sense of time, and sometimes, the order of the Court. In general, the following standards apply:

1. the frequency must be such that visits maintain or improve the child-parent relationship:
2. at least one visit between parents and child must occur within the first week of placement;
3. visits should occur at least every two (2) weeks in most cases in which the goal is to enhance the parent-child relationship;
4. any arrangement for less frequent visitation must have the written approval of the Chairing Supervisor of the First Week Planning Conference;
5. as treatment progresses and return home approaches, extended visits, such as weekends, should be arranged;
6. frequency of visitation must not depend totally on the worker's schedule.

[Reprinted from *Permanency Planning Manual* (1981) with permission from Protective and Placement Services, South Carolina Dept. of Social Services, Columbia, SC.]

PARENT-CHILD VISITATION IN OUT-OF-COUNTY PLACEMENTS

All parent-child visitation plans for children placed out of their home county must be approved on a case-by-case basis by the County Liaison assigned to the home county.

If the parents are involved and the goal is return of the child to his natural family, twice-a-month visitation between child and parents/family is recommended. If the parents must depend on the Agency for transportation to the visits, it is recommended that placement of the child not be made out-of-county unless special treatment needs of the child preclude local placement. In any event, if out-of-county placement is made and parents *cannot provide or arrange transportation for visits*, it is the Agency's responsibility to do so.

VISITATION SETTINGS

Every effort should be made to arrange meaningful visitation opportunities in a relaxed, natural setting. Office visits are not recommended.

Exception: Obvious exceptions to this standard would include cases where there is real concern for the child's safety or a need to control or structure the parent-child interaction during the visit.

WORKER'S FOLLOW-UP TO PARENT-CHILD VISITATION

It is the worker's responsibility to make prompt follow-up contact with the foster caregiver and the child, following parent-child visits, to secure information on what the visits mean to the child and how he adjusts following the visits.

CANCELLATION OF VISITS

Parent-child visits scheduled in Visitation Contracts should not be cancelled because of unexpected schedule conflicts of workers. When such a situation arises, it will be the responsibility of the supervisor to arrange for the scheduled visit to be held with assistance from another worker.

SIBLING VISITATION

In general, it is the responsibility of the supervising worker to arrange for regular, frequent visitation between siblings who are placed separately. This arrangement must be entered on the Visitation Contract.

VISITATION CONTRACT

A detailed Visitation Contract is to be cooperatively drawn up at the First Week Planning Conference and signed by the parents and each Conference member. If there are siblings placed separately, the Visitation Contract must be completed at this conference even if parents do not attend, and should address sibling visitation.

The Visitation Contract must be reviewed/renegotiated at all subsequent case conferences.

DISTRIBUTION OF THE VISITATION CONTRACT

A copy of the Visitation Contract must be distributed to:

1. the parent(s);
2. the foster caregiver;
3. the case record;
4. the child (if age-appropriate).

ELEMENTS OF THE VISITATION CONTRACT

Items to be included in the contract are:

1. time and place schedule;
2. frequency;
3. transportation details which will state who will be responsible for transportation for the parents and for the child;
4. individuals, other than natural parents, with whom the child may visit (i.e., siblings, relatives, etc.);
5. special parental or foster parent requests;
6. whether or not telephone calls or letters will be allowed between parents and child;
7. special responsibilities of any of the parties involved in visitation;
8. an advance notice clause for visit requests other than those regularly scheduled.

DISRUPTIVE VISITS

Parents have a right to visit with their child in foster care. However, in certain cases it may be necessary to carefully structure and supervise the visits. Children who are separated from their parents will inevitably experience anxiety and exhibit some symptoms (such as restlessness, stomach upsets, sleep disturbance, etc.) prior to and following visits. However, it is the worker's and the supervisor's responsibility:

1. to judge the difference between the child's normal anxiety responses to the parent-child visit and when visitation is having a destructive effect on the child. If expert written medical opinion recommends discontinuance of parent-child visits, a Court Order may be secured authorizing total discontinuance;
2. to identify specifically what parental behavior during visits is destructive (*example*: as when parents continuously make unrealistic promises to the child which they obviously cannot keep);
3. to discuss with the parent the inappropriate behavior, explain the effect of the behavior on the child, and structure the visitation so that the inappropriate behavior is avoided (*example*: explain to the parents that the worker will observe the visit and that if the parents resume making the promises the visit will be immediately terminated).

Note: If the foster care goal continues to be to return the child home, total discontinuance of visitation *or* infrequent visitation due to Agency decision is *not* appropriate and is *not* consistent with the stated goal.

B. Alaska

PROBLEMS THAT MAY ARISE REGARDING VISITATION

When Parents Cancel Visits or Arrive Late for Visits

Being late or canceling visits may reflect the parents' reluctance to visit.

1. The worker should explore the reasons why the parents canceled or were late.
2. The importance of visiting should be stressed.
3. Assistance should be offered to the parents in such a case; they should not be ignored.
4. If the reason for the failure to keep appointments was an unrealistic visiting plan, efforts should be made to rearrange the visiting time, location, or circumstance.
5. Only by aggressively reaching out to parents can the worker convince them how important visiting is.

When Visits Create Problems

1. Visits with parents can be stressful to children—they may be upset by their parents' unpredictable or disturbed behavior; they may be anxious prior to visits and unhappy, hostile or difficult to handle afterward.
2. Parents may also become hostile and critical toward the child, the Division or the substitute care provider. Others may be argumentative, uncooperative or unpredictable.
3. If visits create problems, the social service worker should work more closely with the child and the parents, and try to determine what factors might help to make the visits more satisfying to all. If there are certain behaviors on the parents' part which are unacceptable, these behaviors should be pointed out to the parents and the parents should be helped to change.
4. Parents may on occasion appear at a foster home or facility and demand to visit the child when drunk.
   - *Substitute care providers shall be informed they should not release the child to a drunken parent and should notify the worker of such attempts to see the child. All such attempts should be documented in the case record.*
   - *If the parent should become belligerent, substitute care providers shall be instructed to call the police or troopers, if warranted, for their protection.*

[Reprinted from Alaska Division of Family and Youth Services *Program Manual* (1978) with permission from the Alaska Division of Family and Youth Services, Juneau, AK.]

5. *If parents do not return a child after a scheduled visit, substitute care providers shall be instructed to notify the worker.*
   - *The worker shall investigate all such situations, and take necessary action to protect the child, if necessary.*
   - *If the child is placed by court order, the court shall be informed.*
6. Problematic behavior following visits should not be a reason to terminate visiting. For example, when a child cries, it doesn't mean he doesn't want to see his parents. Foster parents and other substitute care providers should be helped to understand this.
7. Only behavior on the part of parents which is clearly dangerous to others should be grounds for terminating visiting. If this behavior occurs, and supervisory approval is given for terminating visits, the case should be reassessed. That is, if parents' behavior is dangerous, consideration should be given to whether a goal of returning a child to this family continues to be realistic. If not, consideration of court action to seek termination of parental rights may be appropriate.

IV. Review
A. Alaska

CASE REVIEW

A mutual assessment of progress toward improved functioning and of the family's potential for change occurs continually during case management. Ongoing assessment will indicate if goals or plans are set too high for the family to achieve and should be broken down into more manageable steps, or if plans are not specific enough. It will also indicate to the family that we are serious in wanting the family to improve so that we will not need to continue to intervene, and may therefore help motivate them to try harder.

The worker should assist the family in recognizing the potential for removal of the child from his family if change is not achieved.

Review between parents and worker helps the parents to see what they have accomplished. Such a process encourages the constructive use of time as a therapeutic tool, helps the parents and worker to see clearly what they are trying to accomplish together, and serves to strengthen the worker-parent relationship.

Guidelines for Areas of Review

1. problems needing attention;
2. the role each parent is assuming in meeting the needs of the family;
3. the motivation of each parent in resolving family problems;
4. the support members of the family are giving to each other in reducing conflict and developing better understanding;
5. the abilities, talents, and skills of the parents and children that can be used constructively in resolving family problems;
6. areas in which the family is achieving success;
7. case goals that can be achieved by the direct effort of the social worker;
8. case goals that can be achieved by utilizing other resources;
9. the pace at which progress can be expected in specific areas;
10. changes that have occurred in the parents' expectations and treatment of the children;
11. improvement in appearances, health, school adjustment, and attitudes of the children;
12. reaction of the parents to the worker's relationship with the children;
13. the frequency with which family crises occur;
14. increased initiative and energy in the parents in their daily living;
15. the ability of the parents to relax in family relationships;
16. broader and/or more constructive involvements;
17. extent of the use of drugs and alcohol;
18. improvements in financial functioning by better planning and/or increase in income.

[Reprinted from *Alaska Division of Family and Youth Services Program Manual* (1978) with permission from the Alaska Division of Family and Youth Services, Juneau, AK.]

B. Kentucky

ADMINISTRATIVE REVIEW

After six (6) months of a child's placement, an Administrative Review must be called. The review is chaired by the Social Services Supervisor and, in addition to the Family Social Worker, Team Leader and Foster Care Worker, the attendance of a Bureau employee outside the supervisory channel of any of the other participants is necessary.

The parents or caregivers, and the child, if appropriate, must receive prior written notice of the time, place, and purpose of the review. The parents and the child have the right to be accompanied by a representative and must be so informed in the notice.

The child may be notified in person, and the foster parents should attend unless the parents, despite efforts made to help them understand the importance of their participation, object to the presence of the foster parents.

The review shall:

1. determine the continuing necessity for and appropriateness of the child's placement;
2. discuss the extent to which all parties have complied with the treatment plan and the objectives of the plan;
3. summarize the progress toward alleviating or mitigating the circumstances necessitating placement;
4. set a target date by which the child may be returned home or placed for adoption or other permanent placement.

The Administrative Review need not occur if the court reviews the case at similar intervals and addresses the four (4) points above in its hearings, recommendations, and orders.

Administrative Reviews must occur at the sixth month of placement and every six months thereafter. The Review may include the Ongoing Treatment Planning Conference scheduled for that time frame.

Each Administrative Review must generate a written report shared with all participants including the parents, subject to the parents' and child's confidentiality.

[Reprinted from *Bureau for Social Services Policies and Procedures Manual* (1981) with permission from Bureau for Social Services, Frankfort, KY.]

V. Forms
A. South Carolina

South Carolina
DEPARTMENT OF SOCIAL SERVICES

FOSTER CARE REVIEW SUMMARY SHEET

FOSTER CARE REVIEW SUMMARY SHEET

a. Name of Child:

b. Birthdate:

c. Race:

d. Sex:

e. Agency Case Number:

f. Parent (or Legal Guardian)

g. Relationship to Child:

h. Date Entered Foster Care:

i. Agency Supervising Foster Care Placement:

1. Location of Foster Care Placement:

   Name:

   Address:

j. Caseworker:

FOSTER CARE REVIEW SUMMARY SHEET (continued)

k. Caseworker Supervisor:

Telephone:

m. Reasons for Initial Foster Care Placement: (Be Specific)

n. Chronological History of Foster Care Placements Through Present Including Dates Indicating Length of Time in Each Placement and Reason for Termination of Each:

o. LEGAL STATUS OF THE CHILD

Was Current Placement in Foster Care Voluntary? (i.e., No Court Order)
☐ Yes ☐ No

Is the Child Legally Free for Adoption?
☐ Yes ☐ No

[Reprinted from *Permanency Planning Manual* (1981) with permission from Protective and Placement Services, South Carolina Dept. of Social Services, Columbia, SC.]

FOSTER CARE REVIEW SUMMARY SHEET (continued)

Who Has Legal Custody of the Child? (Name Specific Court or Agency)	Who Is Legally Responsible for the Child's Supervision? (Name Specific Court or Agency)

Other Facts Regarding Legal Status of Child:

p. Educational Information: (School, Grade, Level of Intellectual Functioning, Level of Social Functioning, etc.

q. Review Board No.	r. Review Board Chairperson:	s. Date of this Review	t. Date of Last Review

u. Special Needs of the Child: (Health—Physical, Mental, etc.)

FOSTER CARE REVIEW SUMMARY SHEET (continued)

v. Adjustment of Child in Foster Care, Especially in Present Placement (Include Child's Feelings of Self-Worth, Closeness to Foster Parents and to Other Children in Home, Friendships, and Activities):

w. Contacts: (Give Dates and Nature of the Following Contacts Since the Last Review)

　A. Contacts Between Parents/Relatives and Child:

　B. Contacts Between Child and Siblings:

　C. Contacts Between Parents/Relatives and Agency:

　D. Contacts Between Child and Agency:

x. Agency's Efforts to Contact Parents/Relatives:

FOSTER CARE REVIEW SUMMARY SHEET (continued)

y. Plan Set Up for Parents/Relatives (Including Referrals to Other Community Resources):

z. Progress of Parents/Relatives in Following Through With Plan:

aa. Does the Child Have Any Siblings in Placement? ☐ Yes   ☐ No

If Yes, Where?

bb. Long-Range Plans for the Child
   ☐ Return to Own Home
   ☐ Termination of Parental Rights
   ☐ Adoption (Not by Foster Parents)
   ☐ Foster Parent Adoption
   ☐ Foster Parent Custody
   ☐ Foster Parent Guardianship
   ☐ Permanent Foster Family
   ☐ Institutional Care
   ☐ Independent Living
   ☐ Other (Explain)

Are Any Siblings Living With Parents or Relatives?   ☐ Yes   ☐ No

cc. Reasons for Plan and Anticipated Time Required:

B. Family Strengths

Rating Scale of Level of Strengths
1 = adequate   3 = very good
2 = good   4 = excellent

Parenting Strengths
1. Adequate supervision of children   _____
2. Children well-disciplined   _____
3. Positive interaction between parent and
   child   _____
4. Adequate physical, psychological stimulation
   of children   _____
5. Affectionate with children   _____
6. Definite attachment to children   _____
7. Adequate knowledge of children's needs and
   age-appropriate behaviors   _____
8. Concerned about children's well-being,
   development, etc.   _____
9. Other _____

   _____
   _____
   _____

Parental Independence/Social Contacts Strengths
1. Independent decision making   _____
2. Motivated for change   _____
3. Emotionally, psychologically mature   _____
4. Presence of support system—available
   relatives/friends   _____
5. Other _____

   _____
   _____

Developmental Strengths of Children
1. Developmentally sound   _____
2. Emotionally sound   _____

[Reprinted from "Appendix L: Family Strengths," in *PACT—Parents and Children Together: An Alternative to Foster Care* (n.d.), with permission from Wayne State University, Detroit, MI.]

194 APPENDIX A

3. Intellectually sound   _____
4. Nutritionally sound   _____
5. Absence of early physical illness   _____
6. Adequate mastery of age-related skills   _____
7. Normal language development   _____
8. Absence of learning disabilities   _____
9. Socially mature for age   _____
10. Good physical tonus and shape   _____
11. Other _____

_____

_____

Environmental Strengths
1. Adequate living quarters   _____
2. Good housekeeping techniques   _____
3. Adequate stimulation from physical environs   _____
4. Other _____

_____

_____

Health-Related Strengths
Health Care
1. Consistent about health care   _____
2. Makes appropriate judgments about health problems   _____
3. Adequate family planning; use of contraception   _____
4. Adequate hygiene   _____
5. Presence of clean clothing   _____
6. Use and accessibility of free health care   _____
7. Other _____

_____

Physical Health of Parent
1. Good health status   _____
2. Energetic   _____

3. Other _____   _____
   _____
   _____
   _____

Mental Health of Parent
1. Psychologically sound   _____
2. Normal intellectual functioning _____
3. Absence of substance abuse   _____
4. Other _____   _____
   _____
   _____
   _____

Nutritional Strengths
1. Organized meal times   _____
2. Adequate food supply   _____
3. Nutritious meal preparation   _____
4. Other _____   _____
   _____
   _____

Financial Strengths
1. Has income (ADC, job, other)   _____
2. Has supplementary income (LTP, SSI, etc.) _____
3. Economical buying practices   _____
4. Adequate budgeting of money   _____
5. Able and willing to secure employment _____
6. Other _____   _____
   _____
   _____

Community Resource Strengths
1. Has transportation (car)   _____
2. Use and accessibility of transportation (bus, cab, etc.) _____

196 APPENDIX A

3. Consistent use of community resources _____
4. Other _____ _____

_____

_____

Social Service Strengths
1. Able to secure independently (ADC, etc.) _____
2. Knows ins-and-outs of social service system _____
3. Other _____

_____

_____

School-Related Strengths
1. Children attend school regularly _____
2. Get along well with peers _____
3. Age-appropriate grade level _____
4. Intellectually appropriate placement _____
5. Good communication between parent and school _____
6. Do well in studies _____
7. Other _____ _____

_____

_____

Conjugal Strengths
1. Lives harmoniously with mate _____
2. Mate contributes to household support _____
3. Other _____ _____

_____

_____

Foster Care Strengths
1. Regularly visits children in foster care _____
2. Wants children to remain in the home _____

3. Wants children to return home   _____
4. Other _____   _____
   _____
   _____
   _____

VI. Training
A. Detailed Case Management Checklist for Children Headed for Restoration

Yes	No	
		General Questions:
_____	_____	A decision to restore the child was made by the parent.
_____	_____	If the youngster is old enough to participate in planning, he/she is in agreement with this decision.
		Problem Selection:
_____	_____	A list has been made of problems requiring resolution. The source identifying each one has been noted.
_____	_____	Resolution of the problems identified directly concerns the well-being of the child, given that he or she is restored. Useful questions here are: (1) "Will the stability of the restoration be threatened if this problem is unresolved?" (2) "Would a judge or referee keep this child in care because the parent did not satisfy a certain criterion?" (3) "If left unchanged, will this harm the child?"
_____	_____	The client understands why each of the problems selected must be resolved.
_____	_____	The client was involved in problem selection.
_____	_____	Baseline data have been gathered for each problem that will serve as a reference point for evaluating change (indicate its location).
_____	_____	Baseline data have not been gathered, but a procedure has been described for evaluating progress in each problem area.
_____	_____	If collateral resources are involved in problem resolution, there is a clear plan for coordinating service delivery and exchanging information.

Yes	No	
		Contracts:
_____	_____	There is a written contract.
_____	_____	The contract has been signed by all involved parties.
_____	_____	A contract has been written but the client will not sign it.
_____	_____	The client has been given a copy of the contract whether or not he or she has signed.
_____	_____	The contract includes a clearly described schedule for parent-child visits (including time and place), with a plan to accelerate visits.

[Reprinted from *Supervision in Child Welfare: A Training Manual* (1978) with permission from the publisher (Berkeley, CA: University Extension Publication) and the authors, Eileen D. Gambrill and Theodore J. Stein.]

APPENDIX A 199

_____ _____ The visiting schedule is realistic, given the client's current visiting pattern.
_____ _____ There is a plan for ongoing assessment throughout the contract period.
_____ _____ Objectives are clearly described in each problem area.
_____ _____ Intermediate objectives are described for each area.
_____ _____ Client tasks during the contract period are clearly described (useful question: "Would I know what was expected of me if I were the client?").
_____ _____ Client tasks are developed in relation to client assets and environmental resources.
_____ _____ Caseworker tasks are clearly described.
_____ _____ The responsibilities of any community resources involved in the case are clearly spelled out.
_____ _____ The contract states the alternatives the worker will pursue (i.e., adoption, guardianship, planned long-term care) if identified objectives are not met.
_____ _____ If alternatives are unknown at the time a contract is written, the contract includes the statement: "Appropriate alternatives will be pursued if the client does not comply with this agreement."
_____ _____ The contract states the time limits for completion.
_____ _____ If the client has not complied with the terms of the contract, he or she has been afforded a second opportunity to do so.
_____ _____ The client has been offered a third opportunity to comply with the contract.
_____ _____ All steps involved in an intervention plan have been described in writing and are attached to the contract (if the child welfare worker is providing treatment services).
_____ _____ Degree of progress has been evaluated at regular intervals (documentation is available).
_____ _____ Intervention plans selected have been those most likely to succeed, based on currently available literature.
_____ _____ Any amendments to the contract are written and attached to the contract, and all involved parties have initialed the amendment.
_____ _____ There is only a verbal contract between worker and client.

B. The Worker's Perspective

Worker's Concerns, Attitudes, and Feelings About the Case
What concerns me the most about contact between this child and the child's parents?

What concerns me the most about contact between the child's birth parents and the foster parents?

Are these concerns based on facts, on intuition, or on a personal bias?

If these concerns are realistic, how can I plan to prevent problems?

Which of my personal attitudes and feelings are related to the parent-child decision to be made in this case?

How can I assure that my biases about the child, the birth family, and/or the foster parents do not affect my objectivity about the options available and about the implementation of the visitation plan?

Balancing the Needs and Concerns of Child, Birth Parents, and Foster Parents
Given the various perspectives (child's, birth parents', foster parents', and workers'), what modifications may be necessary in the preferred plans?

Are these reasons to set conditions on the nature of visitation (supervised visits), on persons involved, on frequency or length of visitation, on place of visiting, on tasks, or on foster parents' involvement?

Are these realistic reasons why visitation cannot occur in the birth or foster parents' homes? If so, what other options exist in the child's old or new neighborhoods?

What visiting focus would provide appropriate tasks or activities for child and parents to be involved together?

What assistance do parents and child need in being together? Can parents plan appropriate tasks or activities, provide sufficient supervision of child, talk with child about reactions to placement, avoid making unrealistic promises?

What assistance do foster parents need to support their level of involvement with birth parents around visitation and/or child's identification with birth parents?

How can I assist them in planning, preparing, and processing their activities in these areas?

Who is likely to disagree with this plan? For what reasons? Do I trust this person to comply with a plan despite disagreement with it?

[Reprinted from *Working with Birth and Foster Parents: Guide to Planning Parent-Child Visitation* (1982) with permission from the publisher (Knoxville, TN: The University of Tennessee School of Social Work) and the author, Peg Hess.]

How is the issue of trust likely to affect the implementation of this plan (worker–birth parents, worker–foster parents, birth parents–foster parents, etc.)?

If these visits are to be supervised, what assurance is there that this condition is fully complied with? What will my responsibilities be in monitoring this compliance?

What plan will meet the child's needs for maintaining or establishing the relationship with permanent caretaker?

Does the proposed plan meet agency policy?

Facilitating the Implementation of the Plan
Who should be expected to sign the contract/agreement regarding this visitation plan?

What guidelines will exist regarding changing the plan?

Who constitutes the "team" in delivering service to this child and the child's family?

How can I involve team members in reviewing and evaluating the plan as it is implemented?

What positive/negative outcomes can be predicted regarding this plan?

How can I prepare myself and others for these outcomes?

What guidelines will exist for documenting, evaluating, and reviewing the outcome of this plan?

Who must formally review this plan before it is implemented?

APPENDIX B

Sample Service Plans, Written Agreements, Behavioral Contracts, and Visiting Contracts

I. Service Plans
    A. Permanency Planning Form
    B. Service Plan Progress Monitoring

II. Written Agreements
    A. Parent-Agency Service Agreement
    B. Sample Agreement

III. Behavioral Contracts
    A. Restoration Agreement
    B. Sample Contract Between Client and Worker Regarding Trial Visit

IV. Visiting Contracts
    A. Visitation Contract

I. Service Plans
A. Permanency Planning Form

PERMANENCY PLANNING FORM
(For Case Intake and/or Initial Case Planning)

Child's Name: _____James Green_____

Child's Date of Birth: _____12/5_____

Date of Placement: _____6/20_____

Placement Location: _____Page boarding home_____

Case Number: _____CUS 12 108_____

Caseworker: _____Barbara Sutton_____

I. **Background of Case** *(Please state specific problems and services.)*

   A. Problem(s) that Resulted in Placement: __Child malnourished, confined to room__

   Voluntary or Court Placement? __Court__

   How Did Case Come to Agency's Attention? __Protective—Hotline__

   B. Services Provided to Parent(s) and Response to Services (Specify): __Foster care__

   C. Services Provided to Child and Response to Services: __Foster care—doing well; adjusted to home o.k.__

[Reprinted from *Permanency Planning: A Casework Handbook* (1979), by John M. McGowan and Christine S. Deyss, with permission from the publisher (Albany, NY: WRI).]

(This form was used for intake into "Foster Case Management: A Replication of the Oregon Project in New York." Guides for completing this form are available from WRI, Albany, NY.)

D. Parental Visits to Child:

	Approximate Frequency	Approximate Date of Last Visit
Mother	None	
Father	6–7/year	4/7
Other (specify whom)		

II. **Current Status of Family** *(Please state specific types of problems and services aimed at alleviating these problems.)*

    A. Current Problems/Obstacles to Returning the Child Home: Mother claims she can't and won't take any further responsibility for the child; she wants to surrender him. Father has history of emotional/psychiatric problems.

    B. Family Strengths and Weaknesses of Relevance to Returning the Child Home: Parents separated—father living with his parents; father doesn't recognize that he has any problems; unemployed.

III. **Services Presently Needed by Parent(s) and Child**

    A. Parent(s): Psychiatric evaluation—refer father for counseling/therapy; eventually, employment for father. Obtain psychiatric evaluations. Have father sign medical consent forms. Discuss surrender with mother.

    B. Child: Foster care; special class (to deal with delayed language and motor skills, emotional problems).

IV. Legal Status of Parent(s) and Child

A. Have any parental rights been terminated? ☐ Yes ☒ No
   If yes, indicate action taken below:

	Date of Action		
	Mother	Father*	Putative or Adjudicated Father
Voluntary Surrender	_____	_____	_____
Abandonment	_____	_____	_____
Permanent Neglect	_____	_____	_____
Mental Illness/ Mental Retardation	_____	_____	_____

B. Has either parent indicated interest in voluntarily surrendering the child?
   ☒ Yes ☐ No   If yes, who? __Mother__
   Are there presently legal grounds for termination of any parental rights through court action?
   ☐ Yes ☒ No   If yes, indicate grounds and date of referral to Legal Division:

	Date of Action		
	Mother	Father*	Putative or Adjudicated Father
Abandonment	_____	_____	_____
Permanent Neglect	_____	_____	_____
Mental Illness/ Mental Retardation	_____	_____	_____

C. If child is already legally freed, what is status of case?

Case referred to adoption unit	☐ Yes	☐ No
Child photo-listed for adoption	☐ Yes	☐ No
Adoptive home located	☐ Yes	☐ No
Child in adoptive placement	☐ Yes	☐ No

*Man to whom mother was married at time child was conceived or born.

If none of the above actions has occurred, please explain reason(s):

_____

_____

V. Long-Term Goal** *(check one)*

- [X] Return of child to parent/relative (specify to whom) __Father__
- [ ] Freeing of child and adoptive placement
- [ ] Placement of child legally freed for adoption
- [ ] Provision of care to enable a child of 14 years or older to achieve independent living, i.e., until child reaches age of majority
  How long would that be? _____ years
- [ ] Continued care beyond 18 years, with transfer to a suitable agency
  What agency/program should provide continued care? _____

VI. Placement Service Plan: *Short-Term and Intermediate Goals****

(What will be offered to meet the problems identified above—who, where, what, when? Type of action/services will vary considerably according to goal selected.)

A. Parent(s) (Plans may be different for mother and father.)

Short-term (achievable in 3 months): __Father—provide counseling and/or psychiatric treatment—Catholic Family Services and/or hospital outpatient psychiatric unit; make written service agreement.__

Mother—work on voluntary surrender.

Intermediate (achievable in 6 months): __Father—continue__

**When child first enters care, goal should be return home.

***The Social Service Law does not require proof of diligent efforts where a child has been abandoned for 6 months, or where there is psychiatric/psychological documentation that parental mental illness/mental retardation precludes return of the child.

If some specific immediate activity identified in this part of the placement plan will achieve the goal for a particular child (i.e., child can now be discharged, forwarded to adoption, etc.) that action when taken should be noted in the short-term or intermediate goal sections.

counseling/therapy; evaluate progress of service agreement. If counseling progressing o.k., begin OVR, evaluation/training.

B. Child

Short-Term (achievable in 3 months): Explore with Children's Hospital the possibility of individual sessions with child to deal with emotional adjustment. Contact Committee on the Handicapped regarding school placement.

Intermediate (achievable in 6 months): Evaluate school adjustment/progress. Action on recommendations of Children's Hospital and Committee on the Handicapped.

C. Visitation Plan (Specify who, where, frequency, and if supervised.)
With father every Saturday in father's home.

VII. Plan for Financial Support *(If no plan exists, explain why.)*
Father on P.A. ADC-FC for foster care.

VIII. Has a service agreement been prepared? *If yes, please attach. If no, give reason/explanation.*
Will be preparing service agreement during next month. Father refused to sign—8/7.

B. Service Plan Progress Monitoring

Child's Name: _James Green_   Time Period: _Jan_ to _Mar_

SERVICE PLAN PROGRESS MONITORING
(7-9 Months after Placement or of Diligent Effort)

Problem (Note Documentation)	Service (Where, When, Frequency)	Client Response Progress (Note Documentation)
Parent(s)		
Father—psychiatric problems (see 10/20 evaluation).	Catholic Family Services—1/wk	Attending almost every week. Written report in record.
	Dr. John Doe—1/mo.	Continuing medication
Employment		Father lost part-time job at car wash. Refused to go to OVR or employment service (2/10).
Visitation	1/wk at agency—supervised	Father missed last two appointments; had no excuse when asked why.
Child		
School placement	Resource teacher—3/wk	Functioning pretty well in class.
Emotional adjustment	Children's Hospital—play therapy every other week.	Responding well; will terminate soon (written report in record).
Foster home adjustment	Home visits regarding child every 3 weeks	Foster parents want to adopt if child cannot go home.

[Reprinted from *Permanency Planning: A Casework Handbook* (1979), by John M. McGowan and Christine S. Deyss, with permission from the publisher (Albany, NY: WRI).]

(This form was also used for monitoring for 1 to 3 months, 4 to 6 months, and 10 to 12 months; a different form was used for 13 to 15 months. Guidelines for completing these forms are available from WRI, Albandy, NY.)

> Record of Parental Contact with Child and Agency
>
> Mother—N/A (surrendered)
>
> Father—weekly visits until 2/7. Telephone call regarding missed visits on 2/16 and 2/23—no excuse offered (2/25).

At the end of 9 months, the child:

☐ Can return home
☐ Can be freed for adoption through voluntary surrender or abandonment
☐ Can be placed for adoption
☒ Requires continued foster care

Barbara Sutton	Betty Lane	4/1
Caseworker	Supervisor	Date

II. Written Agreements
A. Parent Agency Service Agreement

PARENT-AGENCY SERVICE AGREEMENT			
Parent's Name	Child's Name	Agreement Effective: From: To:	
The Parent-Agency Agreement is meant to identify objectives to be reached by parents, services to be provided to parents, and time frames for reaching objectives.			
Problem/Obstacle	Goal	Objective (Action Plan) / Parent / Worker	Expected Date To Achieve Objective	Results
The overall goal of this Agreement is to arrive at a Final Decision on permanent plans for _____ (Child's Name) within _____ (time frame)				
Parent's Signature:	Date:	Caseworker's Signature	Date:	

[Reprinted from *Permanency Planning Manual* (1981) with permission from Protective and Placement Services, South Carolina Dept. of Social Services, Columbia, SC.]

B. Sample Agreement

SAMPLE AGREEMENT

Agreement Between Betty Gault and Children's Services Division

The goal of this agreement is to assist Betty Gault in stabilizing her situation and improving the quality of her relationship to John and Florence Gault and to provide Children's Services Division with the information necessary to make the best possible permanent plan for John and Florence.

Children's Services Division's responsibility is to make a determination and subsequently a recommendation to the Juvenile Court as to whether John and Florence should be returned to their mother's custody. The caseworkers involved will evaluate Betty Gault's progress in several areas: ability to separate completely from James Gault and establish an independent living situation; stability of her living situation; quality of her relationship with her children; ability to meet her children's emotional and physical needs; emotional stability, including ability to control aggressive behavior.

This agreement will cover the period from September 1 through November 30. It is anticipated that it will be followed by a second three-month agreement. It is further anticipated that the entire evaluation period shall not exceed six months.

A. Children's Services Division's expectations of Betty Gault involve the following:

1. Betty Gault will maintain regular, weekly contact with a caseworker from Children's Services Division. Appointments will exclude other persons, and will be for the purpose of assisting Betty to meet the requirements of this agreement and to evaluate her progress. Betty will inform Martin Sims if she is unable to keep a scheduled appointment.

2. Betty Gault will maintain regular visits with her children. Visits will occur every other week for approximately one hour. The primary purpose of these visits is to improve the quality of the parent-child relationship. Children's Services Division will supervise these visits as needed and assess the effects of the visits on John and Florence. Depending upon the children's reactions to these visits, a modification of the visitation schedule could result.

3. Betty Gault will separate from all contact with James Gault. She will follow through on obtaining a divorce from him.

4. Betty Gault will obtain counseling. Counseling will occur on a weekly basis throughout the duration of this agreement. Betty Gault will release to Children's Services Division information concerning the frequency of her attendance at counseling sessions. In addition, Betty Gault will allow her counselor to release to Children's Services Division information concerning the progress she has made by engaging in counseling. This report will focus on Betty's ability to be an adequate parent to her two children. Specifically, does she have adequate parenting skills, sufficient emotional maturity, an ability to control her temper, a more positive self-image? Children's Services Division will not have access to specific information concerning the content of Betty's therapy sessions, but rather to an evaluation of her total progress.

[Reprinted from *Permanent Planning in Foster Care: Resources for Training* (1978) with permission from the Regional Research Institute for Human Services, Portland, OR.]

212 APPENDIX B

5. Betty Gault will begin to make steps toward an independent living arrangement. Before or during the month of September, she will obtain employment. Before or during the month of October, she will obtain housing independent of James Gault.

SIGNED:_____ DATED:_____

B. The caseworkers' responsibilities involve the following:

1. The caseworkers will keep all scheduled appointments. The caseworkers will inform Betty Gault in advance if they are unable to keep a scheduled appointment.

2. The caseworkers will provide partial supervision of the visits between Betty Gault and her children.

3. The caseworkers will provide whatever assistance is necessary to help Betty Gault meet the provisions as outlined in this agreement.

4. The caseworkers will conduct a thorough investigation concerning Betty Gault's past and present situation. This will be done in an effort to evaluate her capacity as a parent.

5. The caseworkers will continually evaluate Betty Gault's ability to provide a permanent home for John and Florence Gault. The caseworkers will keep Betty informed of their evaluation of her progress at any given time.

SIGNED:_____ DATED:_____

III. Behavioral Contracts
A. Restoration Agreement

RESTORATION AGREEMENT

This contract is entered into between _____, social worker for the Alameda Project of Children's Home Society, _____, child welfare worker, Alameda County Human Resources Agency, and _____, father of _____ and _____ _____, at present dependent children of the Alameda County Juvenile Court.

In keeping with the wish of the father of _____ and _____ to have his sons returned to his home on a 90-day trial basis, both _____ and _____ agree to recommend such a trial return to the Alameda County Juvenile Court, contingent upon attainment of the three goals listed below. It is understood by the father that failure to comply with these goals will result in a statement to the Alameda County Juvenile Court that, in the opinion of both social workers, such a return is not feasible at the present time. The general goals of the program are as follows:

1. The father is to visit his children on a regular schedule established by both social workers and the father (schedule attached).
2. The father agrees to be at his home, with his children, during the portion of each of these visits. The objective here is for the worker to observe and assess parent-child interaction (see attached plan for details).
3. The father agrees to establish a plan for substitute care for his children on any occasion on which he is absent from the home, other than those times when the children are attending public school (see attached plan for details).

This contract will be in effect for one month from January 27 to February 28. Signed:

Father	Social Worker, Alameda Project
Date	Child Welfare Worker, Alameda County Human Resources Agency

[From *Children in Foster Homes: Achieving Continuity of Care*, by Theodore J. Stein, Eileen D. Gambrill, and Kermit T. Wiltse. Copyright (c) 1978 Praeger Publishers. Reprinted by permission of Praeger Publishers.]

B. Sample Contract Between Client and Worker Regarding Trial Visit

Names and
Objective: This contract is entered into by Mr. C., social worker for _____ County Department of Social Services, and Ms. D., mother of J.D., at the present time a dependent child of the _____ Juvenile Court. The objective of this contract is to have J.D. reside in his mother's home for a two-week period, beginning on _____ through _____ .

Time Limits: This contract is in effect for eight weeks, beginning _____ and ending _____ .
During this period the mother agrees to visit with her son, and the worker agrees to observe a sample of these visits as per the following schedule:

Approximations: Ms. D. agrees to visit with her son on the following schedule:
    1. For the first four weeks, beginning _____, _____ Ms. D. will visit her son on Saturday from 9 A.M. to 5 P.M. Ms. D. will pick up her son at the foster home and return him to the foster home as per the above timetable.
    2. For the final four weeks, beginning _____, _____ Ms. D. will visit her son from 9 A.M. on Saturday through 5 P.M. on Sunday. Ms. D. will pick up her son at the foster home and return him to the foster home as per the above timetable.
Mr. C. the caseworker, agrees to do the following:
    1. To assist Ms. D. in developing a schedule of planned activities for visiting periods.
    2. To take Ms. D. food shopping for the weekend visits and to assist her in menu planning.
    3. To observe the mother and child for a minimum of _____ hours during these visits, the objectives of these observations being to identify both strengths and weaknesses in parent-child interaction. Should any problems be identified, they will be shared with the client, and the worker agrees to develop programs to resolve any problems that are identified.
    4. If no problems are identified, or if identified problems are either resolved or, in the worker's estimation, close enough to resolution so as to not threaten the stability of the trial visit, Mr. C. agrees to obtain an ex parte

[From *Children in Foster Homes: Achieving Continuity of Care*, by Theodore J. Stein, Eileen D. Gambrill, and Kermit T. Wiltse. Copyright (c) 1978 Praeger Publishers. Reprinted by permission of Praeger Publishers.]

order from the _____ Juvenile Court permitting J.D. to reside in his mother's house for the two-week period of time.

Cost: It is understood by Ms. D. that should she fail to maintain any of the above visits, or fail to participate in resolution of any identified problems, the planned two-week visit cannot take place.

    Signatures: _____
    Ms. D.

    _____
    Mr. C.

IV. Visiting Contracts
A. Visitation Contract

VISITATION CONTRACT	
CHILD'S NAME	PARENT'S NAME
\multicolumn{2}{l}{The Visitation Contract is intended to plan contracts between children in substitute care and their natural parents and/or extended families. It is also intended to define and protect the rights and responsibilities of the children, natural parents, foster caregivers, and the Agency.}	
TYPES OF CONTACTS:	CHILDREN MAY VISIT WITH:
FREQUENCY:	TIME:
LOCATION:	DURATION:
TRANSPORTATION FOR PARENTS:	TRANSPORTATION FOR CHILD:
SPECIAL REQUESTS: (made by parents, child, or foster caregivers)	OTHER:
\multicolumn{2}{l}{Special requests for visitation will be made at least _____ _____ in advance of the date. Any change in a schedule visit should be made with at least _____ _____ notice to all parties involved. This Contract, effective _____ is subject to review at any time at the request of the parties involved. This Contract will regularly be reviewed at all case review conferences.}	
PARENT DATE	CHILD DATE
WORKER(S) DATE	FOSTER CAREGIVER DATE

[Reprinted from *Permanency Planning Manual* (1981) with permission from Protective and Placement Services, South Carolina Dept. of Social Services, Columbia, SC.]

APPENDIX C

Interagency Agreement Between Lower East Side Family Union and Henry Street Settlement

LOWER EAST SIDE FAMILY UNION
57 Rivington Street
New York, New York 10002

HENRY STREET SETTLEMENT
265 Henry Street
New York, New York 10002

AGENCY CHILD DEVELOPMENT CONTRACT

In order to provide comprehensive services for children and families of the Lower East Side of Manhattan, the Henry Street Settlement agrees to enter into a contractual arrangement with the Lower East Side Family Union, a community-based child welfare agency, effective on June 1, 1975, to be periodically reviewed at the request of either the Settlement or the Union.

The purpose of this agreement is to develop higher quality, integrated services for community families, and by working together with these families, to strengthen the quality of child and family life in the community.

To realize the common goal of supporting existing family structures, the Settlement and the Family Union agree to the following forms of cooperation, which draws upon the unique strengths of each individual agency:

1. It is agreed that individual service contracts will be written by the Lower East Side Family Union and Henry Street Settlement for each family selected for services.

It is agreed that families to be considered for contractual agreements between the Lower East Side Family Union and Henry Street Settlement will

[Reprinted from "Lower East Side Family Union: A Social Invention," the Agency Child Development Contract, with permission from the executive director, (New York, NY: Lower East Side Family Union, n.d.)]

have a high risk of placement of one or more children and will be characterized by a highly uncertain quality of family life. Some examples of the families which might be selected are those with one or more of the following characteristics:

   a. have already indicated a desire to place their child;
   b. have a child who has formerly been in placement;
   c. have a child already living outside the home, either through formal placement or other informal arrangement;
   d. there is a mother with severe medical or psychiatric problems, and there is indication that the child is having problems in normal development;
   e. there is a child with severe psychiatric or physical impairment with which the family has been unable to cope;
   f. the parents are physically separated but no legal determination has been made;
   g. a child in the family has lived with different family members over the years;
   h. child abuse or maltreatment is suspected.

This list is neither inclusive nor exclusive. Families with none of the characteristics listed but experiencing other problems may be selected. Each case will be separately judged and selection for service will be based on mutual acceptance by Henry Street Settlement and the Lower East Side Family Union.

   2. For each of these families it is agreed that individual service contracts will be written by the Family Union and Henry Street Settlement, allowing those families to participate in Settlement programs within the guidelines and statutory regulations of the individual programs (e.g., fee schedule established for Day Care).

The Lower East Side Family Union will have responsibility for initiating steps to develop the individual contracts and for monitoring the contracts. Monitoring will involve taking all necessary steps to ensure that the plan agreed upon is carried out by all parties to the contract and will include periodically reconvening the parties to discuss progress made and new developments.

From time to time it will become necessary to modify or prematurely terminate a service plan. This shall be done only for compelling reasons and with the acquiescence of the monitoring agency.

Monitoring shall not include authority over the quality of work provided by Henry Street Settlement staff, assuming they are meeting the requirements of the contract.

Within the limitations of staffing, funding, research and agency policy, Henry Street Settlement and the Lower East Side Family Union agree that referrals made by either agency to the other will be given high priority for participation in their respective programs.

3. The Lower East Side Family Union and Henry Street Settlement staffs will develop jointly, and participate in, training sessions based on needs identified by the Family Union.

4. Family Union will make provisions for the exchange of relevant information and/or referrals through conferences and other agreed-upon means.

5. The Family Union will provide information and education about the Union's activities and resources to persons involved in the Settlement's programs. The Settlement will aid the Family Union in identifying and reaching potential members and will help the Union increase its membership.

6. The Family Union and Henry Street Settlement shall, from time to time, share in agency planning procedures in order to provide for more cost-effective services and prevention of duplicate overhead costs.

7. The Henry Street Settlement will assist the Family Union in its fundraising activities and grant applications but will bear no responsibility or liabilities for the expenditure of funds.

8. The Family Union will assist the Settlement in making recommendations for new programs and expanded areas of services to families in the community. The Family Union will also take a leadership role in suggesting public policy issues on which the Settlement and the Union may want to take further action.

9. The Henry Street Settlement staff will cooperate with efforts to develop a social history of the Lower East Side Family Union through discussions, meetings, and sharing of information with social history staff.

APPENDIX D

1. Age-Appropriate Activities for Parent-Child Visits
2. Levels of Involvement Between Parents and Foster Families

1. *Age-Appropriate Activities for Parent-Child Visits*

DEVELOPMENTALLY RELATED VISITATION ACTIVITIES

Stage	Developmental tasks	Developmentally related visitation activities
Infancy (0–2) Trust vs. mistrust	Develop primary attachment	Meeting basic needs (feeding, changing, holding, cuddling)
	Develop object permanence	Peek-a-boo games
	Basic motor development (sit, reach, stand, crawl, walk)	Help with standing, walking, etc., by holding hand, "come to me" games
	Word recognition	Naming objects, repeating name games, reading picture books
	Begin exploration and mastery of the environment	Child-proof environment; encourage exploration; taking walks; playing together with colorful, noisy, moving items

[Reprinted from "Work Sheet 4" in *Working with Birth and Foster Parents: Guide to Planning Parent-Child Visitation,* Trainer's Manual, with permission from the publisher (Knoxville, TN: The University of Tennessee School of Social Work, 1982).]

Stage	Developmental tasks	Developmentally related visitation activities
Toddler (2–4) Autonomy vs. shame/doubt	Develop impulse control	Making and consistently enforcing rules
	Language development	Reading simple stories; playing word games
	Imitation, fantasy play	"Let's pretend" games; encouraging imitative play by doing things together such as "clean house," "go to store"
	Large motor development (run, climb, dance)	Playing together at park; assist in learning to ride tricycle; dance together to music
	Small motor coordination	Draw together; string beads together
	Develop basic sense of time	Discuss visits and visit activities in terms of "after breakfast," "after lunch," "before supper," etc.
	Assert preferences	Allow choices in activities, clothes worn, foods eaten
Pre-school, Early school (5–7) Initiative vs. guilt	Sex role identification	Be open to discussing boy-girl physical differences. Be open to discussing child's perception of sex roles; read books about heroes together
	Begin development of conscience	Make and enforce consistent rules; discuss consequences of behavior
	Develop ability to solve problems	Encourage choices in activities
	Begin concrete operations (time, space, hierarchy)	Point out cause-effect
	Task completion	Plan activities with beginning, middle, end (as prepare, make cake, clean up)
	Play games with rules	Play simple games such as Candyland, Old Maid
	School entry	Shop for school clothes together; provide birth certificate, medical record

222 APPENDIX D

Stage	Developmental tasks	Developmentally related visitation activities
		required for school entry; go with child to visit school, playground prior to first day; accompany child on first day
School-aged (8–12) Industry vs. inferiority	Skill development (school, sports, special interests)	Help with homework; practice sports together; demonstrate support of special interests, as help with collections; go fishing; attend school conferences and activities
	Peer group development	Involve peers in visitation activity
	Team play	Attend team activities with child (child's team or observe team together)
	Develop self-awareness	Be open to providing feedback
	Preparation for puberty	Discuss physical changes expected; answer questions openly
Early adolescence (13–17) Group identity vs. alienation	Cope with physical changes	Help with attention re: personal appearance, such as shaving, buying cosmetics, bra; provide information re: physical changes
	Begin abstract thinking	Planning, discuss future; discuss politics, religious ideas
	Interest in heterosexual relationships, dating	Set clear rules, be open to discussing problems
	Become more independent of parents	Help learn to drive; delegate responsibility; allow to handle money
	Changes in peer group associations	Transport to peer activities; include peers in visitation plans
Late adolescence (18–22)	Separation from family	Encourage independence through actions such as help move to own

Stage	Developmental tasks	Developmentally related visitation activities
Identity vs. role diffusion		apartment, help apply for jobs
		Be aware of and tolerate independence-dependence conflict
	Develop life goals and values	Be open to discuss adolescent's options, "think through" together; share own experences as young adult
	Rework own identity and sex-role identity	
	Develop capacity for intimacy	

2. Levels of Involvement Between Parents and Foster Parents

FOSTER FAMILIES' INVOLVEMENT WITH BIRTH FAMILIES

Minimum Involvement

Foster Parents' Activities	Worker's Activities
1. talk with child regarding feelings about missing parents, help child with grief about separation from parents	talk with foster parent regarding child's and parents' reactions to child's separation; engage foster parent in understanding child's reactions and in planning to help child with grief
2. provide progress reports about child to parents through letters, sharing school papers, pictures, etc.	act as message bearer when appropriate; encourage child and foster parents to share information with parents
3. help child with gifts and cards for parents on special days	notify foster parent of special days (as parents' birthdays)
4. encourage parental participation in decision making by providing information about child to worker, requesting parental opinions, feedback through worker	discuss importance of continued parental input into decisions about the child; be available and willing to serve as message bearer and interpreter
5. prepare child for visits, encourage child's open expression of feelings about visits, transport to visits when no contact with birth parents	keep foster parents informed of visit plans, involve foster parents in exploring child's reactions to visits
6. seek information about child from birth parents through worker	provide foster parents with information about child, serve as message bearer to seek and report information about child from birth parents
7. share child by allowing child to spend special days with parents when requested	be available to foster parents to plan for special days; advocate and teach need for child-birth parents time together on special days; recognize and accept foster parents' reactions
8. refrain from demeaning child's parents to the child or to others	provide knowledge about birth parents to foster parents which may increase foster parents' empathy for

[Reprinted from "Work Sheet 10" in *Working with Birth and Foster Parents: Guide to Planning Parent-Child Visitation*, Trainer's Manual, with permission from the publisher (Knoxville, TN: The University of Tennessee School of Social Work, 1982).]

		birth parents; teach about child's need not to have others demean parents even when child is angry with them or disapproving of them
9.	cooperate in plans for child; if disagree with plans, share ideas with worker, not child	involve foster parents in planning and keep foster parents informed of progress and change in plans; be available to foster parents to discuss openly foster parents' reactions to plans
10.	respect the confidential nature of all information about the child and the child's family	inform foster parents of expectation that information regarding child and family be held in confidence and of the rationale for expectation; deal directly with inappropriate sharing of such information
11.	allow/encourage similar post-placement involvement (cards, letters, sharing pictures)	be available to plan and monitor such activities

Moderate Involvement

	Foster Parents' Activities	Worker's Activities
1.	allow/encourage phone calls between child and birth parents	plan limits for frequency, length of calls with birth parents, foster parents, and child; plan with foster parents about any expected problems
2.	transport children to visits where limited birth parent contact may occur, such as agency	be available to introduce, monitor, mediate
3.	allow/encourage visit in foster home with worker supervising visits	prepare child, birth and foster parents for possible reactions to situation, be available throughout visit; be available to process reactions following visits
4.	discuss decisions to be made about the child with birth parents on phone or in person	support foster parents' involvement of birth parents in decision making; be available to interpret, mediate when appropriate
5.	invite birth parents to attend activities such as school conferences and functions and clinic appointments with child and foster parents	assist foster parents, birth parents, and child in planning for activity and preparing for possible reactions; be available to process reactions following activity
6.	allow/encourage similar post-placement involvement	be available for discussion of reactions, assistance with limit setting, planning, monitoring

Maximum Involvement

Foster Parents' Activities	Worker's Activities
1. allow/encourage unsupervised visits in foster family home or visits with foster parents as supervisors	plan visits with child, foster and birth families; prepare for possible reactions, be available for processing, discussion of outcomes
2. coordinate visitation arrangements as agreed in the foster care plan	clarify roles with foster parents and support foster parents in roles agreed upon; be available for collaboration
3. invite birth parents to participate in foster family activities such as picnics and birthday parties	as above, participate in planning, preparing, processing
4. assist birth parents in development of parenting skills through teaching and modelling	participate in planning, preparing, processing; support foster parents in role as teachers and role models
5. encourage birth parents to visit with foster parents when child is not in home	participate in planning, preparing, processing
6. transport child to visits in birth families' home	as above
7. allow/encourage continued relationship with child/birth family post-placement	as above, and monitoring

APPENDIX E

Attitude Survey

FOSTER CARE WORKER ATTITUDE ASSESSMENT SCALE

This questionnaire is designed to assess public agency foster care workers' attitudes about their work roles, clients, and others involved in foster care services. Presented are a series of statements about beliefs which may be held. Please read each statement carefully and indicate how much you agree or disagree with each by *circling* the response categories which best express your opinions. Please keep in mind that since this is an attitude assessment, there are no right or wrong answers.

	Strongly Agree	Agree	Neutral	Disagree	Strongly Disagree
1. Natural parents should be encouraged to be more involved in making decisions about their children while their children are in placement.	SA	A	N	D	SD
2. Frequent visiting between foster children and their parents is of little value in the over-all treatment plan.	SA	A	N	D	SD
3. Foster parents should help foster children maintain their identification with their natural parents.	SA	A	N	D	SD
4. I find it easy to accept our agency's plans for foster					

[Reprinted from *Working with Birth and Foster Parents: Guide to Planning Parent-Child Visitation*, Desk Reference, with permission from the publisher (Knoxville: TN: The University of Tennessee School of Social Work, 1982).]

	Strongly Agree	Agree	Neutral	Disagree	Strongly Disagree
parents to be more involved with natural parents' visits with their children.	SA	A	N	D	SD
5. Contact with the natural parents is important for the child's adjustment in placement.	SA	A	N	D	SD
6. The agency's plans to increase foster parents' involvement in foster child/natural parent visits will not work.	SA	A	N	D	SD
7. In my opinion, natural parents have a right to visit their children at least once a week.	SA	A	N	D	SD
8. It is harder to keep good foster homes when foster parents are expected to be involved in parent/child visits.	SA	A	N	D	SD
9. Bringing foster and natural parents together causes problems for everyone.	SA	A	N	D	SD
10. Foster children who have frequent visits with their natural parents tend to have a clearer understanding of foster care.	SA	A	N	D	SD
11. When natural parents know where their children are placed, they inappropriately interfere with the child's life.	SA	A	N	D	SD
12. It is expecting too much of foster families to allow visiting in the foster homes.	SA	A	N	D	SD

13. It is helpful to a foster child when the child's

		Strongly Agree	Agree	Neutral	Disagree	Strongly Disagree
	natural parents and foster parents get along with each other.	SA	A	N	D	SD
14.	I do not believe it is important for foster parents, natural parents, and workers to work together in face-to-face situations.	SA	A	N	D	SD
15.	I expect that, in most cases, when foster parents are more involved in parent/child visits there will be major conflict between foster parents and natural parents over decisions made about the child.	SA	A	N	D	SD
16.	Most natural parents of children in foster care want to be good parents.	SA	A	N	D	SD
17.	Increasing foster parents' participation in natural parents' visits with children in my caseload is a threat to my authority as a foster care worker.	SA	A	N	D	SD
18.	Most foster children would prefer not to have regular visits with their natural parents.	SA	A	N	D	SD
19.	Involving foster parents in parent/child visits has many advantages.	SA	A	N	D	SD
20.	I believe it is important for children in placement to have frequent regular visits with their natural parents.	SA	A	N	D	SD
21.	When we let natural families visit their children in foster family homes, we are asking for trouble.	SA	A	N	D	SD

APPENDIX E

		Strongly Agree	Agree	Neutral	Disagree	Strongly Disagree
22.	Keeping the natural parents' image alive is an important part of the foster parents' job.	SA	A	N	D	SD
23.	With help, foster parents are usually able to understand natural parents.	SA	A	N	D	SD
24.	Foster parents have a lot to offer in the area of parenting skills that natural parents usually do not have the opportunity to take advantage of.	SA	A	N	D	SD
25.	Visiting helps foster children and their parents cope with their separation from each other.	SA	A	N	D	SD
26.	Children who have adjusted to foster care should not have that adjustment disturbed by visits from their parents.	SA	A	N	D	SD
27.	Parent/child visitation is an important part of the process of returning children to their parents.	SA	A	N	D	SD
28.	Most natural parents are very sad when their children are placed.	SA	A	N	D	SD
29.	It is not possible to lessen the mutual hostility between foster parents and natural parents.	SA	A	N	D	SD
30.	Frankly, most foster children would be better off not seeing their parents while in care.	SA	A	N	D	SD
31.	In my opinion, parents who have abused their children do not deserve to get their children back.	SA	A	N	D	SD
32.	When assisting with visiting, foster parents are able					

	Strongly Agree	Agree	Neutral	Disagree	Strongly Disagree
to model alternate ways of dealing with the child for natural parents.	SA	A	N	D	SD
33. Foster parents appreciate opportunities to work with natural parents on the child's behalf.	SA	A	N	D	SD

APPENDIX F

Annotated Bibliography

    I. Background Materials and Overviews
   II. Parent Involvement
       A. General
       B. Parent-Child Visiting
       C. Parent Groups
       D. Parent Handbooks
  III. Program Descriptions and Evaluations
  IV. Administration
   V. Permanency Planning
 VI. Foster Parent–Parent Contact
VII. Residential Care and Parent Involvement
VIII. Training
 IX. State Manuals

I. Background Materials and Overviews

American Public Welfare Association. *Standards for Foster Family Services Systems for Public Agencies and User's Guide.* Prepared for Children's Bureau, Administration for Children, Youth and Families. Rev. January 1979. (Send request for HHS Publication numbers (OHDS) 79-30231 and 79-30230, respectively, to LSDS, Department 76, Washington, DC 20241.) This volume includes sections on the rights of parents; service planning and case review; and preplacement, placement, and postplacement services.

Child Welfare League of America. *Standards for Foster Family Care.* New York, NY: Child Welfare League of America, 1975. This volume includes a chapter on services to parents.

Colon, Fernando, "Family Ties and Child Placement." *Family Process* 17 (September 1978): 289-311. [Reprinted in *Parents of Children in Placement: Perspectives and Programs*, edited by Paula Sinanoglu and Anthony Maluccio. New York, NY: Child Welfare League of America, 1981, 241-267.] The author examines the effects of current child placement practices on the child's ties to his or her family and, in some cases, foster families. The author concludes that the preservation of family ties, to whatever degree possible or appropriate, is basic to developing a sense of self.

Fanshel, David, and Shinn, Eugene. *Children in Foster Care—A Longitudinal Investigation.* New York, NY: Columbia University Press, 1978. This report of a substudy of a 5-year longitudinal study of foster care in New York City, conducted from 1965 to 1970 by the Columbia University School of Social Work, provides a comprehensive assessment of children in foster care. The children's characteristics and functioning were examined from the perspectives of program staff, foster care workers, teachers, and parents. (Three additional books were generated from this study. See Jenkins and Norman, and Shapiro.)

Hess, Peg, "Parent-Child Attachment Concept: Crucial for Permanency Planning." *Social Casework* 63 (January 1982): 46-53. The author examines the importance of the parent-child attachment to the development and implementation of permanent plans for foster children.

Horejsi, Charles. *Foster Family Care: A Handbook for Social Workers, Allied Professionals and Concerned Citizens.* Springfield, IL: Charles C Thomas, Inc., 1979. Horejsi answers questions about many different aspects of foster family care. There are separate chapters on parents and permanency planning.

Hubbell, Ruth. *Foster Care and Families: Conflicting Values and Policies.* Philadelphia PA: Temple University Press, 1981. This volume explores how and why foster care policy directives often have negative effects on the families they are intended to help. Policy components from the federal to the local level are examined.

Jenkins, Shirley, and Norman, Elaine. *Beyond Placement: Mothers View Foster Care.* New York, NY: Columbia University Press, 1974. A companion study to *Filial Deprivation and Foster Care* in which the authors explore the role expectations of mothers whose children have been placed in care in relation to caseworkers and mothers' perceptions of what a family means and how family constellations relate to household composition.

Jenkins, Shirley, and Norman, Elaine. *Filial Deprivation and Foster Care.* New York, NY: Columbia University Press, 1972. This is the first report of the parent substudy of the longitudinal research on foster care in New York City. It examines the effects of separation on parents of children in care.

Jolowicz, Almeda. "A Foster Child Needs His Own Parents." *The Child* 12 (August 1947): 18-21 [Reprinted in *Parents of Children in Placement* (see citation on p. 236), 55-63. A classic paper focusing on the importance of the parent to the child in placement.

Knitzer, Jane; Allen, MaryLee; and McGowan, Brenda. *Children Without Homes: An Examination of Public Responsibility to Children in Out-of-Home Care.* Washington, DC: Children's Defense Fund, 1978. This is an extensive nationwide analysis of service delivery systems for children placed out of their homes. It is based on intensive study of public policies and services in seven states and surveys of a broader sample of public officials in local probation and child welfare offices. Recommendations for change are included.

Krymow, Virginia La Falce. "Obstacles Encountered in Permanent Planning for Foster Children." *Child Welfare* LVIII (February 1979): 97-104. Although the author acknowledges the importance of permanency planning and foster care review, she also describes the difficulties involved in making decisions for particular groups of children.

Laird, Joan. "An Ecological Approach to Child Welfare: Issues of Family Identity and Continuity." In *Social Work Practice: People and Environments*, edited by Carel Germain. New York, NY: Columbia University Press, 1979, 174-209. [Reprinted in *Parents of Children in Placement* (see citation on p. 236), 97-126.] The author applies the ecological perspective to child welfare, emphasizing the importance of sustaining the child's connectedness to his or her family. She elaborates on ways to strengthen the family and preserve ties while a child is in substitute care: extensive attention to and involvement of the parents, and use of social supports and resources.

Littner, Ner. "The Importance of the Natural Parents to the Child in Placement." *Child Welfare* LIV (March 1975): 175-181. [Reprinted in *Parents of Children in Placement* (see citation on p. 236), 269-275.] The significance of the parents for the child is described from a psychoanalytic perspective. The author explains the importance of parental visits to the child, parents, and foster parents.

Maluccio, Anthony, and Fein, Edith. "Permanency Planning: A Redefinition." *Child Welfare* LXII (May/June 1983): 195-201. The authors provide a comprehensive definition of permanency planning and describe its major features in detail.

Maluccio, Anthony; Fein, Edith; Hamilton, Jane; Klier, Jo Lynn; and Ward, Darryl. "Beyond Permanency Planning." *Child Welfare* LIX (November 1980): 515-530. This article examines several aspects of permanency planning: its history, definition, research, and the impact it may have on delivery of child welfare services.

McGowan, Brenda, and Meezan, William. *Child Welfare: Current Dilemmas, Future Directions*. Itasca, IL: F.E. Peacock Publishers, Inc., 1983. This child welfare text analyzes the factors that created and perpetuated the current crisis in child welfare, and focuses on the service delivery issues with which the field must grapple in order to improve policy, service provision, and practice effectiveness.

Saville, Hugh. "Restoring a Balance: Parental Care—Foster Care." Paper presented at a workshop at the Child Welfare League Conference in Edmonton, Alberta, Canada, June 1, 1973. [Available through Informational Resource Services, Child Welfare League of America, 67 Irving Place, New York, NY 10003.] This presentation discusses several innovative aspects of foster care services, with particular attention to the crucial role of parents.

Shapiro, Deborah. *Agencies and Foster Children*. New York, NY: Columbia University Press, 1976. A substudy of Columbia University's longitudinal study of children in foster care, this volume presents a systematic picture of the agencies and workers involved in foster care. Of particular interest are findings relating to workers' attitudes toward parents and their impact on the outcome of service provision.

Triseliotis, John, ed., *New Developments in Foster Care and Adoption*. London, England: Routledge and Kegan Paul Ltd., 1980. This volume brings together the most recent developments in the field of foster care and adoption in Britain. The contributors cover a wide range of topics, including the views of parents and foster parents.

II. Parent Involvement

A. General

APPENDIX F 235

Fanshel, David. "The Availability and Capacities for Service Involvement of Parents of Foster Children." In *On the Road to Permanency: An Expanded Data Base for Service to Children in Foster Care*. New York, NY: Child Welfare League of America, 1982, 129-212. This chapter reports on a "mini-project" carried out in 1976-1977 with the cooperation of voluntary child welfare agencies in New York City. Data concerning the availability of parents for service contacts are examined.

Horejsi, Charles; Bertsche, Anne; and Clark, Frank. *Social Work Practice with Parents of Children in Foster Care: A Handbook*. Springfield, IL: Charles C Thomas, Inc., 1981. This is an invaluable resource for practitioners who work with parents. Using the question-and-answer format, Horejsi et al. answer questions about parents, parental visiting, parental rights and responsibilities, relationship building, assessment, service agreement, and resources.

Kufeldt, Kathleen. "Including Natural Parents in Temporary Foster Care: An Exploratory Study." *Children Today* 11 (September-October 1982): 14-16. This article discusses how parents, their children, foster parents and social workers feel about involving parents in foster care decisions. Their perceptions of the degree to which parents are actually included in some aspects of their children's lives are examined.

Maluccio, Anthony. "An Ecological Perspective on Practice with Parents of Children in Foster Care." In *The Challenge of Partnership: Working with Parents of Children in Foster Care*, edited by Anthony Maluccio and Paula Sinanoglu. New York, NY: Child Welfare League of America, 1981, 22-35. The ecological perspective, which stresses the dynamic transactions between people and their environments, is presented as a conceptual framework for practice with parents of children in foster care.

Maluccio, Anthony. "The Emerging Focus on Parents of Children in Placement." *Parents of Children in Placement* (see citation on p. 236), 5-14. The author reviews the emerging focus on parents. Following a brief discussion of the practice concerns and research findings that have helped stimulate this focus, he outlines the range of practice innovations in the field and the practice guidelines that are being developed or strengthened through increased activity in behalf of parents in many agency settings.

Maluccio, Anthony, and Sinanoglu, Paula, eds., *The Challenge of Partnership: Working with Parents of Children in Foster Care*. New York, NY: Child Welfare League of America, 1981. This collection of selected original papers concerning parents includes discussions of the ecological perspective on practice with parents, permanency planning with ambivalent parents, developing a parents organization, and new roles for foster parents.

Maluccio, Anthony, and Sinanoglu, Paula. "Social Work with Parents of Children in Foster Care: A Bibliography." *Child Welfare* LX (May 1981): 275-303. [Single copies may be ordered from the Publications Department, Child Welfare League of America, 67 Irving Place, New York, NY 10003.] This is an extensive bibliography (not annotated) of material concerning work with parents.

Sinanoglu, Paula. "Working with Parents: Selected Issues and Trends as Reflected in the Literature." *The Challenge of Partnership* (see citation above), 3-21. The author summarizes and analyzes selected issues, trends, and developments reflected in the literature on foster care. She concludes that while there is renewed emphasis on the family in child welfare, there are also continuing gaps and limitations in service delivery that must be addressed.

Sinanoglu, Paula, and Maluccio, Anthony. *Parents of Children in Foster Care: An Annotated Bibliography*. West Hartford, CT: Practitioner's Press, 1981. This annotated bibliography contains approximately 400 notations. It includes sections on legal issues, direct practice with parents, foster parent roles with parents, training and policy, program planning and evaluation, and administration.

Sinanoglu, Paula, and Maluccio, Anthony, eds. *Parents of Children in Placement: Perspectives and Programs.* New York, NY: Child Welfare League of America, 1981. This is a collection of selected readings on parents. Most are reprinted articles.

B. Parent-Child Visiting

Blumenthal, Karen, and Weinberg, Anita. "Issues Concerning Parental Visiting of Children in Foster Care." In *Foster Children in the Courts*, edited by Mark Hardin and G. Diane Dodson. Newton Upper Falls, MA: Butterworth Legal Publishers, 1983. The authors discuss the purposes of parent-child contact and several key visitation issues, including when visits should begin, what the frequency and length of contacts should be, who should be included in visits, and whether visits should be limited or terminated.

Fanshel, David. "Parental Visiting of Children in Foster Care: Key to Discharge?" *Social Service Review* 49 (December 1975): 493-514. [Reprinted in *Parents of Children in Placement* (see citation above), 277-299.] This article presents findings from the longitudinal study of foster care in New York City concerning parent-child visiting. High frequency of parental visiting is found to be significantly associated with discharge.

Fanshel, David. "Parental Visiting of Foster Children." In *On the Road to Permanency: An Expected Data Base for Service to Children in Foster Care.* New York, NY: Child Welfare League of America, 1982, 1-128. This chapter reports on a "mini-project" carried out in 1976-1977 with the cooperation of voluntary child welfare agencies in New York City. Data concerning many facets of parental visiting are examined.

Felker, Evelyn. "Maintaining Relationships with the Biological Family." In *Raising Other People's Kids: Successful Child-Rearing in the Restructured Family.* Grand Rapids, MI: William B. Eerdmans, 1981. In this chapter, the author discusses why foster parents should maintain relationships with the child's family, and how they can make parent-child visits more constructive.

Hess, Peg. *Working with Birth and Foster Parents: Trainer's Manual and Desk Reference.* Knoxville, TN: Office of Continuing Social Work Education, The University of Tennessee School of Social Work, 1838 Terrace Avenue, Knoxville, TN 37916, 1982. The *Trainer's Manual* was developed for use in training foster care workers and supervisors employed by the Tennessee State Department of Human Services. This excellent curriculum is designed to assist staff in increasing both the frequency of parent-child visits and the involvement of foster parents with parents, particularly in the area of visitation. The *Desk Reference* provides the materials trainees use in the training process, as well as other resources.

Special Services for Children. *Policy Statement on Parental Visiting.* New York City, Human Resources Administration, September 1975. [Available through Informational Resource Services, Child Welfare League of America, 67 Irving Place, New York, NY 10003. This statement is also reprinted as Appendix D in the Children's Defense Fund's *Children Without Homes* (see citation on p. 233).] This statement may serve as a model written policy statement regarding parental visiting. It addresses many critical issues in parent-child visiting, provides a rationale for its importance, and contains guidelines for the development of policy and good practice.

White, Mary. "Promoting Parent-Child Visiting in Foster Care: Continuing Involvement Within a Permanency Framework." In *Parents of Children in Placement* (see citation on p. 236), 461–475. The author describes the advantages of parent-child visiting in foster care. Citing evidence from her own research, as well as other studies, the author underscores the powerful role of visiting in achieving permanent plans for children in foster care.

C. Parent Groups

Carbino, Rosemarie. "Developing a Parent Organization: New Roles for Parents of Children in Substitute Care." In *The Challenge of Partnership* (see citation on p. 235), 165–186. The author describes the development of a parent organization as a means of creating new and more effective roles for parents of children in substitute care.

Hess, Peg, and Williams, Linda. "Group Orientation for Parents of Children in Foster Family Care." *Child Welfare* LXI (September/October 1982): 456–466. This article describes a structured 6-week foster care group orientation series for parents whose children have been placed in foster care. Preparation for the group, content areas, and parent and staff reactions to the program are discussed.

Murphy, Dorothy. "A Program for Parents of Children in Foster Family Care." *Children Today* 5 (November-December 1976): 37–40. [Reprinted in *Parents of Children in Placement: Perspectives and Programs* (see citation on p. 236), 433–439.] The author describes an educationally oriented program that involves parents in courses similar to those given for foster parents at a community college. The development and content of the curriculum are outlined.

"Natural Parent Newsletter." This monthly newsletter for parents is published by the Parent Encouragement Program, Victoria, British Columbia, Canada.

D. Parent Handbooks

Baum, Jan. "Foster Care Handbook for Natural Parents." Mimeo. Children's Service Society of Wisconsin, May 1, 1977. This handbook is given to all parents when their children enter care. It provides essential information about the agency's foster care program.

Hillside Children's Center. "Parent's Manual." Mimeo, n.d. 1183 Monroe Avenue, Rochester, New York 14620. This manual provides basic information to parents about the various programs at the Hillside Children's Center.

Jewish Child Care Association of New York. "Your Child in Foster Care." *Child Welfare* LV (February 1976): 125–131. A reprint of a brochure for parents of children in foster care. It treats parents as partners and stresses maintenance of family ties.

Rutter, Barbara. *A Way of Caring: The Parents' Guide to Foster Family Care.* New York, NY: Child Welfare League of America, 1978. This guide is written for parents of children in foster care and describes the foster care process and parental roles, as well as the rights and responsibilities of parents with children in care. The focus is primarily on parents of young children.

Special Services for Children. *Parents' Handbook: A Guide for Parents of Children in Foster Care.* The City of New York, Department of Social Services, March 1981. This handbook answers many of the questions asked by parents of children in foster care. It has been adapted by several state and local agencies throughout the country (see fig. 2.3 in chapter 2 for its table of contents).

III. Program Descriptions and Evaluations

Andrews, Mary, and Swanson, Jane. *An Evaluation of Parent Aide Programs.* East Lansing, MI: Michigan State University, Institute for Family and Child Study, December 1979. This is a report of a descriptive-comparative study designed to document the service delivery functions and impacts of three parent aide programs in Michigan. The evaluation includes a description of internal operations and processes, and a discussion of outcomes.

Boyd, Patty. "They Can Go Home Again!" *Child Welfare* LVIII (November 1979): 609–615. This article describes Temporary Foster Care (TFC), an 18-month pilot project of the Michigan Department of Social Services to plan and provide permanence for children in foster care. Major elements of the project in Muskegan County are described.

Callard, Esther, and Morin, Patricia, eds. *PACT—Parents and Children Together: An Alternative to Foster Care.* Detroit, MI: Department of Family and Consumer Resources, Wayne State University, 1979. The authors describe an intensive, home-based intervention program to low-income, inner-city families with children in foster care or at risk of placement. The thrust of the program is to bring about changes in the parents' child-rearing practices and home management skills so that the children may remain at home or be returned to their families. The volume includes a description of the program, a summary of statistics describing the population and the service, and an evaluation of the outcome. The appendix includes copies of the excellent recording forms used by project staff.

Case Record—A Bulletin About Permanency Planning. Published by the Regional Research Institute for Human Services, Portland State University, P.O. Box 751, Portland, Oregon 97207. (1) May 1979: North Carolina leadership development efforts; Texas focuses on local solutions. (2) November 1979: Case review team systems in North Dakota and Fort Worth, Texas. (3) February 1980: Prevention issue; voluntary placements. (4) August 1980: Update on major achievements in permanency planning nationwide. (5) October 1980: Resources for promoting permanency planning. (6) January 1981: Foster care teamwork in Kansas; foster parent education in Michigan. (7) Summer 1981: "Parental Involvement in Permanency Planning." (8) Fall 1981: "Advocacy." (9) Winter 1982: "Foster Care Review." (10) Spring 1982: "Foster Children and Permanency Planning."

Citizens' Committee for Children of New York, Inc. *The Parents' Rights Unit—Responding to Grievances of Parents with Children in Foster Care: An Evaluation Study,* October 1977. This report is an evaluation of the first months of operation of the Parents' Rights Unit (PRU), an ombudsman program for parents of children in foster care, run by New York City's Special Services for Children. Telephone interviews and/or written questionnaires were used with parents, agency directors, agency social workers, and PRU workers to solicit their reactions to the PRU. Findings and recommendations are reported.

Fein, Edith; Maluccio, Anthony; Hamilton, V. Jane; Ward, Darryl. "After Foster Care: Outcomes of Permanency Planning for Children." *Child Welfare* LXII (November/December 1983): 485–558. This report describes a study of the aftercare experiences of 187 children under age 14 who left the foster care system to go into placements that were considered permanent or stable. The study found that parent involvement made a difference in a child's adjustment to a permanent placement, whether placement was with the parent or another caretaker.

Gifford, Carla; Kaplan, Felisa; and Salus, Marsha. *Parent Aides in Child Abuse and Neglect Programs.* Washington, DC: National Center on Child Abuse and Neglect,

U.S. Department of Health, Education and Welfare, DHEW Publication No. (OHDS) 79-30200, August 1979. This manual provides the specific information needed to develop and implement a parent-aide program. It includes the goals and objectives of the program; the roles and responsibilities of professionals and paraprofessionals; and the recruitment, screening, and matching processes. It also provides guidelines for training, continuing supervision, and program evaluation.

Halper, Gertrude, and Jones, Mary Ann. *Serving Families at Risk of Dissolution: Public Preventive Services in New York City.* The City of New York, Human Resources Administration, Special Services for Children, February 1981. This is a two-part report of a preventive services demonstration project located in the Bronx, New York City. The first part provides a comprehensive description of the program—staff, clients, and operations. The second part is an evaluation of the program conducted by staff members of the Child Welfare League of America.

Jones, Mary Ann; Newman, Renee; and Shyne, Ann. *A Second Chance for Families: Evaluation of a Program to Reduce Foster Care.* New York, NY: Child Welfare League of America, 1976. Evaluation of a successful program to enhance parental competence and provide intensive family services to avert or reduce placement. Program description gives essential components necessary to successful implementation in other agency settings.

Lahti, Janet, and Dvorak, Jacquelyn. "Coming Home from Foster Care," in *The Challenge of Partnership* (see citation on p. 235), 52–66. The authors discuss the importance of continued social work services and adequate supports after a child is reunited with his or her family. Their discussion is based on findings from a demonstration project concerning planning, referred to as the "Oregon Project."

National Association of Social Workers. "Public Agency Offers Day Program for Mothers." *Practice Digest* 4 (September 1981): 25–26. The article describes a 16-week day treatment program for abusive and neglectful mothers, run by the public agency in Trenton, New Jersey.

National Association of Social Workers. "Getting Hard-to-Reach Families into Treatment." *Practice Digest* 2 (June 1979): 24–26. This article discusses techniques used by the staff at the Family Center, a demonstration project in Long Beach, New York, to involve "hard-to-reach" families in treatment programs.

Office for Families. *Promising Practices: Reaching Out to Families.* DHHS Publication No. (OHDS) 81-30324. Washington, DC: U.S. Department of Health and Human Services, May 1981. Selective efforts of various groups involved in identifying and dealing with concerns of families are described. These local programs demonstrate either unique approaches to reaching families or provide services to families in an exemplary manner. These programs are not specifically designed for parents of children in foster care.

Pike, Victor. "Permanent Planning for Foster Children: The Oregon Project." *Children Today* 5 (November-December 1976): 22–25. [Reprinted in *Parents of Children in Placement* (see citation on p. 236), 345–354.] The article describes the Oregon Project, which had as its goal permanent planning for children through reunion, relinquishment, or long-term foster care. Practice approaches emphasizing casework and legal skills are described.

Simmons, Gladys; Gumpert, Joanne; and Rothman, Beulah. "Natural Parents as Partner in Placement." *Social Casework* 54 (April 1973): 224–232. [Reprinted in *Parents of Children in Placement* (see citation on p. 236), 375–388.] This article describes the Family Residential Treatment Center set up by Brookwood Child Care in New York City in 1968, and shows how parents are involved in the residence.

Stein, Theodore; Gambrill, Eileen; and Wiltse, Kermit. *Children in Foster Homes—Achieving Continuity of Care.* New York, NY: Praeger, Publishers 1978. The methods and results of the "Alameda Project," an extensive demonstration program on working with parents of children in placement, are described. The authors also present a systematic approach to work with parents based on decision making, contracting, and behavior modification principles.

Watson, Kenneth. "A Bold, New Model for Foster Family Care." *Public Welfare* 40 (Spring 1982): 14-21. The author describes a new model for foster family care, in which the foster family is viewed as an extension of the child's family, rather than as a replacement for it.

IV. Administration

Boserup, Dan, and Gouge, George. *The Case Management Model: Concept, Implementation and Training.* Rev. ed. Regional Institute of Social Welfare Research, Inc., 455 North Milledge Avenue, P.O. Box 152, Athens, GA 30603, 1980. This manual addresses the reasoning and theoretical applications of the case management model. It can serve as a guide or "think-piece" for individuals responsible for designing, implementing, or evaluating case management processes at their agency.

Dormady, Joanne, and Gatons, Michele. *Case Management: Issues and Models.* New York, NY: Board of Social Welfare, 1980. This report examines case management as a generic entity and then focuses specifically on case management services for the developmentally disabled. It contains an excellent review of the literature, a discussion of selected case management models, and a comprehensive list of references.

Downs, Susan et al. *Foster Care Reform in the 70's: Final Report of the Permanency Planning Dissemination Project.* Portland, OR: Regional Research Institute for Human Services, 1981. The Regional Research Institute was responsible for disseminating the techniques and philosophy of permanency planning to the states. This report of that 4-year effort describes how states are carrying out critical components of permanency planning, such as case review, tracking and monitoring, training and manual and policy changes.

Dreyer, Linda. *Permanent Planning in Foster Care—A Guide for Program Planners.* Portland, OR: Regional Research Institute for Human Services, 1978. A manual useful to program planners and agency administrators interested in incorporating permanency planning into their programs for children in their agencies. The guide deals with organization of political support for the program, the key components of a good permanency planning program, and guidelines for implementation.

Lauffer, Armand. *Resources for Child Placement and Other Services.* Beverly Hills, CA: Sage Publications, 1979. A guide offering a concrete approach to the identification and development of resources for children and families involved in foster care and adoption. The guide is not specifically addressed to work with parents, but can be used by child welfare supervisors, administrators, and others for program development and training purposes. It includes guidelines for examining program resources, developing strategies for creating resources, and working with people as resources.

National Association of Social Workers. "Case Management." Special section. *Practice Digest* 4 (March 1982): 3-17. This special section includes several articles on case management in social services. "Definitions and Precursors" provides a good overview of issues. "System Prevents Clients' 'Falling Through Cracks' " includes a description of important case manager duties.

Regional Research Institute for Human Services. *Issues and Experiences in Permanent Planning: A Report on Seven Regional Work Sessions on Foster Care Reform.* Portland, OR: Regional Research Institute, n.d. This volume is a report on seven regional work sessions held during 1979 and 1980 to bring together child welfare professionals in each area of the country who were concerned with permanency planning for children in foster care. The first section of the report consists of five chapters concerning issues such as training and supervision, leadership, and the implementation of permanency planning from an administrative point of view. Participants at each of the work sessions are identified in the second part of the report.

Wells, Susan. "Case Management and Child Welfare." Mimeo. Region IX Child Welfare Training Center, UCLA School of Social Welfare, September 1980. This brief piece clearly explores several issues concerning case management in child welfare: elements of good case management, barriers to implementation, ways in which agencies can facilitate case management, and what case management can accomplish.

V. Permanency Planning

Finley, C. Anne, and Rothe, Deborah. *The Handbook for Service Plan Development.* Oklahoma Department of Institutions, Social and Rehabilitative Services, n.d. This "how to" handbook for caseworkers describes the critical components in the service planning process: assessment, formulation, evaluation, and recording.

Gambrill, Eileen, and Stein, Theodore. "Decision Making and Case Management: Achieving Continuity of Care for Children in Out-of-Home Placement." In *The Challenge of Partnership* (see citation on p. 235), 109–134. This chapter describes and illustrates a case management approach to achieving continuity of care for children that was tested and refined in the Alameda Project. A behavioral framework was used, with an emphasis on early decision making.

Jackson, Arlene, and Dunne, Michael. "Permanency Planning in Foster Care with the Ambivalent Parent." In *The Challenge of Partnership* (see citation on p. 235), 151–164. A discussion of techniques for working with parents who have difficulty making decisions concerning their childrens' futures.

Janchill, Sister Mary Paul. *Guidelines to Decision Making in Child Welfare: Case Assessment, Service Planning and Appropriateness of Service Selection.* New York, NY: Human Services Workshops, 1981. The author carefully describes what must be considered before decisions are made concerning children at risk of placement. Information needed to assess situations, plan for services, and choose appropriate services is identified.

Jones, Martha, and Biesecker, John. *Permanency Planning Guide for Children and Youth Services.* Training Resources in Permanent Planning Project, Millersville State College, Millersville, Pennsylvania, 1979. This basic guide outlines the various permanency planning options and details when to rule each out, and how to implement a plan for achieving the selected option.

Kuczkowski, Paul. *Permanent Planning in Maryland: A Manual for the Foster Care Worker.* Maryland Foster Care Impact Demonstration Project, August 1978. This handbook discusses how to select and implement a permanent plan. Since the project dealt with children who had been in care for many years, there are especially good chapters on case management and emancipation. Several sample forms are included. Although written for Maryland staff, this guide would be helpful to all foster care workers.

Marr, Pamela. "Foster Care Teamwork Comes to Kansas." *Case Record* 5 (January 1981): 1-2. This brief article contains an excellent description of the implementation of teamwork in Kansas. The process involved, as well as the advantages and disadvantages, are described.

McGowan, John, and Deyss, Christine. *Permanency Planning: A Casework Handbook.* Albany, NY: Welfare Research, Inc., March 1979. This handbook is designed for workers in New York State who are responsible for ensuring that children are provided with permanent homes. Based on the Pike et al. handbook (see citation below), it includes chapters on assessment, planning, structuring a service program, adoption, alternatives to return home or adoption, and caseload management.

Miniely, Janet, and Desgagne, Denise. "Success or Failure? A Case Study." *Child Welfare* LXII (March/April 1983): 129-139. The authors describe efforts to help a young couple learn more appropriate parenting techniques so as to maintain wardship of their children. Because the outcome of the case was opposite to what appeared to be the direction of progress, a number of compelling questions are raised.

National Association of Social Workers. "Placement Decided by Team." *Practice Digest* 4 (December 1981): 23-24. This brief article provides a detailed account of the use of teams in Louisiana child welfare services.

Pike, Victor et al. *Permanent Planning for Children in Foster Care: A Handbook for Social Workers.* DHEW Publication No. (OHDS) 78-30124. Washington, DC: U.S. Department of Health, Education and Welfare, 1977. This was the first handbook on permanent planning developed for social workers. It is a practical reference that can help workers to analyze available placement options, evaluate the factors pertinent in choosing an appropriate plan, and understand the casework and legal techniques for implementation. The handbook includes step-by-step procedures for achieving a chosen plan.

Rooney, Ronald. "Permanency Planning: Boon for All Children?" *Social Work* 27 (March 1982): 152-158. This article explores the implications of the movement to provide stable, continuous care to children, and raises the issue of whether all children in need of placement will invariably benefit.

―――. "A Task-Centered Reunification Model for Foster Care." In *The Challenge of Partnership* (see citation on p. 235), 135-150. The author describes a task-centered foster care reunification model, with clear guidelines for practice to assist workers providing services to parents. Development of the model was influenced by William Reid's description of task-centered casework.

Stein, Theodore; Gambrill, Eileen; and Wiltse, Kermit. "Dividing Case Management in Foster Family Cases." *Child Welfare* LI (May 1977): 321-331. During the Alameda Project, a demonstration program for working with parents of children in care, case management responsibilities were shared between workers responsible for services to parents and county child welfare workers who provided services to children in foster homes. The effectiveness of this approach is described.

Stein, Theodore; Gambrill, Eileen; and Wiltse, Kermit. "Foster Care: The Use of Contracts." *Public Welfare* 32 (Fall 1974): 20-25. [Reprinted in *Parents of Children in Placement* (see citation on p. 236), 363-373.] A step-by-step account of working with parents intensively in the early stages of placement, using contracts as a tool for encouraging parental participation in planning for their children, and early decision making. Using a typical contract, the authors present a roadmap for reaching the goal of family reunion.

Stein, Theodore, and Rzepnicki, Tina. *Decision Making at Child Welfare Intake: A Handbook for Practitioners.* New York, NY: Child Welfare League of America, 1983.

This manual describes procedures for decision making at child welfare intake for both protective services and voluntary child welfare services. The authors provide guidance concerning the critical decisions faced by the child welfare practitioner.

VI. Foster Parent-Parent Contact

Davies, Linda, and Bland, David. "The Use of Foster Parents as Role Models." *Child Welfare* LVII (June 1978): 380–386. [Reprinted in *Parents of Children in Placement* (see citation on p. 236), 415–421.] Identifying the components of a special program in a voluntary child welfare agency, the authors show how the use of foster parents as role models for parents is a powerful resource in enhancing the parents' child management skills and facilitating a child's return home.

Felker, Evelyn. "Maintaining Relationships With the Biological Family." In *Raising Other People's Kids: Successful Child Rearing in the Restructured Family*. Grand Rapids, MI: William B. Eerdmans, 1981. (See annotation on p. 236.)

Hess, Peg. *Working with Birth and Foster Parents: Trainer's Manual and Desk Reference*. Knoxville, TN: Office of Continuing Social Work Education, The University of Tennessee School of Social Work, 1838 Terrace Avenue, Knoxville, TN 37916, 1982. (See annotation on p. 236.)

Johnston, Edwin, and Gabor, Peter. "Parent Counselors: A Foster Care Program with New Roles for Major Participants." In *The Challenge of Partnership* (see citation on p. 235), 200–208. This chapter describes the concept behind, and use of, foster parents as parent counselors in a project conducted in Canada. In this program, selected children were placed in the homes of trained foster parents who participated in treatment planning and review.

Lee, Judith, and Park, Danielle. "Walk a Mile in My Shoes: A Manual on Biological Parents for Foster Parents." University of Connecticut School of Social Work, December 1979. This manual helps the foster parent to understand and empathize with parents who place children in foster care. Attitudes about and feelings toward parents are explored, and helping roles are described.

Loewe, Bessie, and Hanrahan, Thomas. "Five-Day Foster Care." *Child Welfare* LIV (January 1975): 7–18. [Reprinted in *Parents of Children in Placement* (see citation on p. 236), 389–400.] This article describes a program in which children are in foster care during the week and go home to parents on weekends, holidays, and vacations. It discusses the roles of the foster parent and social worker, and sees the parent as a partner and team member in the placement process.

McFadden, Emily Jean. *Working with Natural Families*, Instructor's Manual. Foster Parent Education Program, Eastern Michigan University, Ypsilanti, MI 48197, 1980. This manual is designed to be used in training families who provide service to foster children and their parents. Its underlying assumption is that foster parents are a part of the service team and therefore have a critical part to play in permanency planning. Emphasis is placed on the need to understand parents and techniques for working together.

Ryan, Patricia; McFadden, Emily Jean; and Warren, Bruce. "Foster Families: A Resource for Helping Biological Parents." In *The Challenge of Partnership* (see citation on p. 235), 189–199. This paper describes how foster parents can serve as a resource for parents of children in foster care.

Seaberg, James. "Foster Parents as Parent Aides to Biological Parents." In *The Challenge of Partnership* (see citation on p. 235), 209–220. This article explores the concept of foster parents as "parent aides" to parents and offers guidelines for redefining the roles of foster parents and effectively involving them as members of the team and resources for parents.

Watson, Kenneth. "A Bold, New Model for Foster Family Care." *Public Welfare* 40 (Spring 1982): 14-21. (See annotation on p. 240.)

VII. Residential Care and Parent Involvement

Finkelstein, Nadia. "Family-Centered Group Care—The Children's Institution, from a Living Center to a Center for Change." In *The Challenge of Partnership* (see citation on p. 235), 89-105. This article assesses the needs of children in institutional care, and examines and defines family-centered group care for the young, school-aged child and the immature early adolescent. The approach to residential care can be contrasted with the traditional child-centered group care.

Keith, Alan. "The Place of Families in Treatment." In *The Professional Child Care Worker: A Guide to Skills, Knowledge, Techniques and Attitudes*. New York, NY: Association Press, 1975. This chapter discusses why families must be involved in the therapeutic milieu of the residential center and how that effects the role of the child care worker.

Keith-Lucas, Alan, and Sanford, Clifford. *Group Child Care as a Family Service*. Chapel Hill, NC: University of North Carolina Press, 1977. In this volume, the authors discuss the basic theory and methods of the family-centered Children's Home. Special attention is given to the critical role to be played by parents while children are in residential settings.

Littauer, Celia. "Working with Families of Children in Residential Treatment. *Child Welfare* LIX (April 1980): 225-234. The author examines in detail, and illustrates, the many ways child care workers can work with families of children in residential centers to facilitate early return home—for example, by encouraging family involvement in cottage life, role modeling, providing direct help to the parents, and participating in aftercare services.

Magnus, Ralph. "Teaching Parents to Parent: Parent Involvement in Residential Treatment Programs." *Children Today* 3 (January-February 1974): 25-27. The author believes that treatment success is linked to parent involvement, and suggests concrete ways to increase the participation of parents in residential treatment programs.

Whittaker, James. "Family Involvement in Residential Treatment: A Support System for Biological Parents." In *The Challenge of Partnership* (see citation on p. 235), 67-88. This paper describes how parents can play an active role in residential treatment settings.

VIII. Training

Boothroyd, Roger, and Fitzpatrick, Jody. *An Assessment of Training Priorities: Implications of the Child Welfare Reform Act*. Albany, NY: Continuing Education Program, School of Social Welfare, State University of New York at Albany, July 1981. This report describes the development, implementation, and evaluation of training conducted in conjunction with the New York State Child Welfare Reform Act. Training priorities in five content areas—adoption, court processes, family rehabilitation, case management, and assessment—are identified.

Child Welfare League of America. *Introduction to Foster Parenting* (curriculum guides and audio-visual materials). New York, NY: Child Welfare League of America, 1976. This training curriculum for foster parents includes a session entitled, "Our Child's Natural Parents."

Craig, Heather et al. *Team Training—Manual II: A Foster Care Staff Development Curriculum.* Commonwealth of Virginia, Department of Welfare, n.d. This training curriculum, developed for public foster care staff in Virginia, identifies the foster care team—the social worker, foster parents, child and parents—and describes their roles and responsibilities.

Deighan, Mary Ellen. *Towards Collaboration in Foster Care: A Training Guide.* Albany, NY: Social Services Training Unit, Continuing Education Program, School of Social Welfare, State University of New York at Albany, 1980. This training guide for foster care workers includes a module entitled "Understanding Natural Families," which focuses on the significance of the parent-child relationship and the impact of separation on this relationship. It presents a general framework for understanding dysfunctional family patterns and intervention techniques.

Downs, Susan, and Taylor, Catherine, eds. *Permanent Planning in Foster Care: Resources for Training.* Regional Research Institute for Human Services, Portland State University, P.O. Box 751, Portland, OR 97207, 1978. Training materials are offered on a range of topics in direct service (e.g., decision making, assessment, service agreements, documentation) and legal aspects of foster care.

Gambrill, Eileen, and Stein, Theodore. *Supervision in Child Welfare: A Training Manual.* University Extension, University of California, 2223 Fulton Street, Berkeley, CA, June 1978. This manual identifies important administrative and educational components of supervision. A "how-to" guide for supervisors, it includes checklists, procedures, and guidelines.

Hess, Peg. *Working with Birth and Foster Parents: Trainer's Manual and Desk Reference.* Knoxville, TN: Office of Continuing Social Work Education, The University of Tennessee School of Social Work, 1838 Terrace Avenue, Knoxville, TN 37916, 1982. (See annotation on p. 236.)

Horejsi, Charles, and Schlinger, Jessie. "The Foster Care Game." Department of Social Work, University of Montana, Missoula, Montana, August 1980. This structured discussion tool is designed to promote communication and the exchange of ideas and viewpoints among social workers, foster parents, foster children, and their parents. It can be used in training sessions for social workers and foster parents.

Maluccio, Anthony, and Sinanoglu, Paula. "Working with Biological Parents of Children in Foster Care: Curriculum Guide." University of Connecticut School of Social Work, March 1980. This curriculum guide was used in the development of two graduate-level social work courses offered in Connecticut and Rhode Island. It includes a section on goals and objectives of working with parents, assessment, and intervention.

McFadden, Emily Jean. *Working with Natural Families*, Instructor's Manual. Foster Parent Education Program, Eastern Michigan University Ypsilanti, MI 48197, 1980. (See annotation on p. 243.)

McGowan, John, and Deyss, Christine. *Permanency Planning Training Resource: Parts 1 and 2.* Albany, NY: Welfare Research, Inc., n.d. Part 1 provides a description of the training program developed in conjunction with the project, "Foster Care Management: A Replication of the Oregon Project in New York State." Objectives, format, content, and resources for clinical and legal conferences are described. Part 2 contains reprinted articles from the permanency planning literature.

National Institute for Advanced Studies. *Child Welfare Training: Comprehensive Syllabus for a Child Welfare Training Program.* DHHS Publication No. (OHDS) 80-30276. Washington, DC: Children's Bureau, U.S. Department of Health and Human Services, October 1980. This syllabus can be used in the development of a curriculum to provide basic skills to child welfare staff. Two courses are described: "Foundations for Effective Child Welfare Services" and "Building Skills for Effective Service Delivery." Specific modules include family structures and lifestyles; skills at intake for assessing strengths/needs and developing service plans; skills for implementing service plans; and skills for the provision of intensive services to birth families.

—————. *Child Welfare Training: Catalogue of Training Materials for Child Welfare Services.* DHHS Publication No. (OHDS) 80-30277. Washington, DC: Children's Bureau, Department of Health and Human Services, May 1980. This catalogue references materials that have potential for the training of child welfare workers and supervisors in public agency settings (150 entries).

State University of New York at Stony Brook. "Child Welfare Reform Act Training Program." Stony Brook, NY: School of Social Welare, 1981. This training program was developed in conjunction with the Child Welfare Reform Act in New York State. It is divided into three parts—permanency planning, adoption, and legal aspects. Each module specifies objectives, key concepts, methods and activities, handouts, and resources.

Stein, Theodore, and Gambrill, Eileen. *Decision Making in Foster Care: A Training Manual.* University Extension, University of California, 2223 Fulton Street, Berkeley, CA 94720, 1976. This training manual for students and child welfare practitioners uses the behavioral approach to interpersonal helping. It covers the process of assessment, formulating contracts with clients, observation and recording, and intervention methods.

University of Georgia. "Biological Parents, Their Children and Foster Care: Issues of Rights and Responsibilities." Athens, GA: Office of Continuing Social Work Education. The University of Georgia has developed four training videotapes and accompanying discussion guides. The guides include training exercises and discussion regarding the rights and responsibilities of three parties to permanency planning activities—parents, foster parents, and workers—and the rights and entitlements of the children.

IX. State Manuals

During the exploratory research phase for this volume, program and policy manuals or statements were obtained from several states. Because the resources listed below contain excellent sections concerning parent involvement (some of which may be found in appendix A), they may be especially useful to administrators who are examining and modifying existing manual materials in their own states; extant policies may be adaptable to their needs. Other states, not identified below, may also have comprehensive program manuals.

Alaska

Alaska Division of Family and Youth Services Program Manual. (Contact: Alaska Division of Family and Youth Services, Pouch H-05, Juneau, AK 99811). This manual contains excellent sections concerning parent-child visiting and working with parents during placement (see pp. 179 and 184–186 for excerpts).

Kentucky

Bureau for Social Services Policies and Procedures Manual. (Contact: Bureau for Social Services, 275 E. Main Street, 6-W, Frankfort, KY 40621.) This manual contains excellent sections on planning conferences, parent-child visiting, and administrative review (see pp. 168–171 and 187 for excerpts).

New York

Uniform Case Record and Child Care Review Service (CCRS). (Contact: Division of Services, Department of Social Services, 40 N. Pearl Street, Albany, NY 12243. New York State has developed a uniform recording and monitoring system for use throughout the state. Many of its forms could be adapted for use in other locations.

Pennsylvania

Pennsylvania Department of Public Welfare Regulations, Foster Family Care Service for Children. (Contact: Pennsylvania Department of Public Welfare, Office of Children, Youth and Families, P.O. Box 2675, Harrisburg, PA 17105.) These regulations contain a detailed description of the service-planning process. In addition, the importance of a working relationship between parents and foster parents is implied in the list of qualifications for foster parenthood (see pp. 175–177 for excerpts.)

South Carolina

Permanency Planning Manual, South Carolina Department of Social Services. (Contact: Protective and Placement Services, South Carolina Department of Social Services, P.O. Box 1520, Columbia, SC 29202.) This excellent and complete manual contains detailed procedures for involving and/or working with parents in several areas: planning, visitation, review, monitoring, service provision. The forms used for recording purposes are also included (see pp. 172–174, 180–183, and 188–192 for excerpts.

Virginia

Permanent Planning Handbook: Case Management in Social Services, Foster Care. (Contact: Virginia Department of Welfare, 8007 Discovery Drive, Richmond, VA 23288.) This handbook is addressed in narrative form to the worker. It is especially supportive, informative, and easy to read. It contains an excellent overview on why working with parents is so important, as well as a complete section on formulating, evaluating, and modifying service plans (see pp. 166–167 and 178 for excerpts).

ABOUT THE EDITORS

Karen Blumenthal received her M.S. from the Columbia University School of Social Work. She was Special Assistant to the Assistant Commissioner of Special Services for Children (New York City), has held several part-time consulting positions in child welfare settings, and was Program Specialist for Resources for Permanence, Child Welfare League of America. Her publications include: *Why Punish the Children?: A Study of Children of Women Prisoners*; "Making Foster Family Care Responsive," in *Child Welfare: Current Dilemmas–Future Directions*; *The Parent's Handbook: A Guide for Parents of Children in Foster Care*; and "Issues Concerning Parental Visiting of Children in Foster Care," in *Foster Children in the Courts*.

Anita Weinberg graduated from the University of Michigan and Columbia University School of Social Work. She is the former Director of Resources for Permanence at the Child Welfare League of America. Ms. Weinberg's expertise is in foster care, adoption, and she also has worked in the area of juvenile delinquency. Co-author with Karen Blumenthal of an article for lawyers on parental visiting, published in *Foster Children in the Courts* by Butterworth Legal Publishers, Ms. Weinberg is attending law school in Chicago and serves on the board of Illinois Action for Foster Children. She is presently completing a book on foster care review to be published by the Child Welfare League of America.

CONTRIBUTORS

Peg Hess, M.A., ACSW
Assistant Professor
Indiana University
School of Social Work
Indianapolis, Indiana

Carla Overberger, M.S.W.
Human Factors Manager
Retail Branch Systems
Wells Fargo Bank
San Francisco, California

Victor Pike, M.S.W.
Consultant
John Day, Oregon

Karen Schimke, M.S.W.
Regional Director
New York State Department of Social Services
Buffalo, New York